THE EVERYTHING TOASTS BOOK

Find the right words for any occasion—
from weddings, to business functions,
holidays, gatherings, and more!

Dale Irvin

Adams Media Corporation
Holbrook, Massachusetts

Dedication

This book is dedicated to everyone who is celebrating an occasion that calls for a toast. If you have no occasion to celebrate, make one up.

Ackn

This book would not have been possib ance of all the friends and family with whom I have shared a cocktail a years. Special thanks to my wife Linda for her research, help, and s t. Here s looking at you, kid.

An Everything Series Book. The Everything Series is a trademark of Adams Media Corporation.

Published by Adams Media Corporation
260 Center Street, Holbrook, MA 02343

ISBN: 1-58062-189-9

Printed in the United States of America.

J I H G F E D C B

Library of Congress Cataloging-in-Publication Data
Irvin, Dale
The everything toasts book / by Dale Irvin.
p. cm.
ISBN 1-58062-189-9
1. Toasts. I. Title.
PN6341.178 1999
808.5'1 dc21 99-39946
CIP

Illustrations by Barry Littmann

This book is available at quantity discounts for bulk purchases.
For information, call 1-800-872-5627.

Visit our home page at http://www.adamsmedia.com

Contents

Chapter 3 Holiday Homage

How to use this book:

Each toast appears in its own set of quotation marks. Feel free to combine toasts or elements of any that appeal to you to create the perfectly personalized toast for your occasion.

CHAPTER 1

Here's to Ya

A History of Toasts

Toasts have been a part of history since the beginning of history, which happened a long, long time ago. In fact, Adam is said to have been the first person to deliver a toast when he first set eyes on Eve. As he cracked open a couple of coconuts and handed one to Eve with a straw, he toasted her with the words, "To Eve, the only woman on the planet for me."

The origin of the very first toast is not really known, but one theory is that the toast developed out of mutual mistrust. Back as early as the sixth century B.C., the practice became commonplace in Greece to drink to the health of a friend. After a toast such as "May health be with ye" was delivered, both parties would raise their goblets and drink. The reason for doing this was very simple. Back in the sixth century B.C., one of the most common ways of dealing with social problems like divorce, business competitors, or people who held different religious or political beliefs than you was to poison them. And the most common method of giving them the poison was in a goblet of wine. Therefore, if a toast was given to your health and the toaster drank from the same supply of wine as the toastee, chances are you will live to see another toast.

After awhile it became commonplace for a host to pour wine from a common pitcher, taste it to make sure it was OK to drink, and raise his glass to his friends in a toast. The Romans, not to be outdone by the Greeks, soon accepted this practice as well, and before you could say, "Cheers," the toast became as popular as the orgy.

> *"A toast to bread,*
> *as without bread,*
> *we'd have no toast."*

The actual term "toast" appears to have come from the Roman practice of dropping a piece of burnt bread into a glass of wine. Evidently, Roman wine was not of the best quality, and sometimes the charcoal formed by the burnt bread would purify the wine a bit and make it more palatable. It makes me wonder just how bad this wine was because if you have ever had a slice of burnt bread, you know that it is not the most savory taste you have ever experienced. If they were tossing this charred dough into their wine to improve the flavor, the wine must have originally tasted like old sandals. (Old Sandals was actually the brand name of an ancient Roman whiskey. It is believed to be one of the contributing factors of the fall of the Roman Empire.)

After years of putting burnt bread in their wine, the Romans accepted the word "tostus," meaning parched or roasted, to refer to the drink itself, and from there the practice of wishing good health to your drinking partners became referred to as a toast. It's a good thing the Romans didn't put a real piece of charcoal in their beverages or we would be giving "briquettes" at banquets instead of toasts.

By the 1800s, toasting was commonplace and drinkers began toasting everything from health and happiness to women and celebrities. In fact, it became a tradition at dinner parties for every glass to be dedicated to someone in the room. This was one of the ways you found out if you were in good favor with the hosts. If you did not receive a toast in your honor, you probably wouldn't be back for the next dinner party. Perhaps you should have brought a nicer gift for the host and not used your napkin to blow your nose.

Today toasts can be given for any occasion at any time. Formal toasts are presented at gatherings such as weddings and testimonial dinners while informal toasts can be given in bars, at ballgames, or in the sanctity of your own home.

The purpose of this book is threefold. First, it will provide you with some guidelines for giving a formal toast including proper etiquette and protocol. Second, it will teach you how to construct your own toast. Using the hundreds of samples provided here, you will discover how to take pieces of toasts along with quips and quotes to make your own toast for any occasion. It is fun to do and becomes, in and of itself, another reason to toast.

Finally, this book will hopefully make you laugh. Toasting is a fun experience and you should have fun while learning about it. I have included numerous pieces of fiction and fantasy within these pages to lighten your spirits and bring a smile to your face, because, after all, isn't that what toasting is all about?

One of the best toasts ever written, "to eat, and to drink, and to be merry," actually comes from the Bible (Ecclesiastes 8:15 to be exact). I think that other old toasts probably still exist from prehistoric times and distant cultures.

Record-Breaking Toasts

The greatest number of people ever involved in a toast was 50,304. On February 28, 1997 Guinness staged the Great Guinness Toast simultaneously in bars and restaurants in 31 U.S. metropolitan areas. At 11 P.M. EST a massive group toast was offered and the clinking of the glasses began. It is estimated that the last of the glasses will be clinked on June 22, 2001.

Toasts from the Bible

While the Bible never actually mentions the custom of toasting, many of these biblical quotes would make excellent toasts for just about any occasion.

A feast is made for laughter, and wine maketh merry.
(Ecclesiastes 10:19)

Wine maketh glad the heart of man.
(Psalms 104:15)

Forsake not an old friend, for the new is not comparable to him. A new friend is as new wine: when it is old, thou shalt drink it with pleasure.
(Ecclesiastes 9:10)

Let us eat and drink: for tomorrow we shall die.
(Isaiah 22:13)

The best wine . . . goeth down sweetly,
causing the lips of those that are asleep to speak.
(Song of Solomon 7:9)

Now that you know the real origin of the toast, let's explore some hypothetical possibilities. Let's assume that long before the Romans and Greeks there existed a society, which much like those to follow, reveled in the celebration of life's special occasions. One would assume that the normal action for such a celebration would be a toast. So travel back with me to the beginning of time and let's see how things might have happened.

Prehistoric Toasts

The first prehistoric toast was proposed in approximately 2,000,000 B.C. at the very first prehistoric cocktail party. Og and Ramone were neighbors who had just decided to bite the bullet and find themselves some wives. Og went for a lovely lass named Ook while Ramone decided that he wanted a good cook and clubbed a good homemaker named June. So Og and Ook and Ramone and June sat around the cave one night deciding how they could celebrate their nuptials.

June suggested a neighborhood cocktail party to which Og, Ook, and Ramone instantly replied, "A what?" for you see, the cocktail had yet to be invented. June explained that a cocktail party featured canapes, adult beverages, and mixed nuts. At this point, Ramone started to doubt the wisdom of his spousal selection.

June also informed the group that they should invent a toast to celebrate the upcoming gathering of friends and neighbors. The three put their sloping heads together and came up with the world's first toast.

> "*We like raw meat,*
> *And stuff from trees.*
> *We wear bear skins*
> *So we don't freeze.*
> *We're prehistoric*
> *Through and through*
> *But we invented*
> *This toast to you.*"

Unfortunately, the glasses Og and Ramone used for the toast were made of rocks and when they went to clink them together, they missed and bashed each other in the head. They died on the spot and Ook and June delivered this toast in their honor.

"*Here's to two men, one brain, and no sense.*"

This toast has been popular with women around the globe ever since.

A favorite occasion for a prehistoric toast was the hunt. Since good refrigeration methods were still years away, the prehistoric man had to hunt for fresh food every day. This, in fact, was his job. He would get up in the morning, meet the rest of the guys in his hunting pool, commute to the hunting grounds, and spend the day beating the bushes. And, just like guys with jobs have always done, they liked to stop off after work for some Happy Hour libations.

One of their favorite meeting places was the big rock, which functioned as the town center. After the hunt, the men would gather around the big rock and chew the fat, thus creating the world's first bar snacks.

As they sat around the rock, it was only natural to deliver a toast to the day's success.

Cro-Magnon Man #1: I'd like to propose a toast chaps.
Here's to my friends, and to my desire, that one of these guys, would discover some fire.
Cro-Magnon Man #2: I can't get anything out of my glass, it's frozen.
Cro-Magnon Man #1: See? My point exactly.

Other prehistoric toasts were simple wishes for things to make life longer, happier, and easier. Here are some examples deciphered from cave drawings found in Ohio.

"*To long lives*
Before we fossilize."

"*Here's to confused paleontologists.*"

Toasts from the Bible

Eat thy bread with joy, and drink thy wine with a merry heart.
(Ecclesiastes 9:7)

As we have therefore opportunity, let us do good unto all men.
(Galatians 6:10)

Wine maketh glad the hearts of man
(Psalms 104:15)

Drink no longer water, but use a little wine for thy stomach's sake.
(1 Timothy 5:23)

"Here we sit,
A cave man group,
Just crackers, in
The Primordial soup."

"To cross-eyed Tyrannosaurs."

"May you always have a warm animal hide, a sharp stick, and may you be sound asleep when the asteroid hits you."

Druid Toasts

Druids have been one of our more fun loving cultures. They love to wear hooded robes all day and worship rocks. Par-tee! But even though the Druids created great tourist attractions like Stonehenge, they still took time out to toast each other with their Druid liquor known as hooch. Since they participated in a lot of human sacrifices, I imagine they must have offered the condemned man a toast in his honor before they removed his vital organs and set him on fire. A typical Druid sacrificial toast may have been something like this.

Druid #1: May I have your attention please. I would like to propose a toast to our honored guest and main sacrifice of the evening. The man we have come to know and love as The Sacrifice Formerly Known As Prince is a man who will give his life to keep the bad wooja wooja (early Druidian for "mojo") away from the rest of us. I would like to offer three cheers for the Sacrifice, Hip Hip
Druids #2–36: Hooray
Druid #1: Hip Hip
Druids #2–35: Hooray
Druid #36: Hooray.
Druid #1: Try to keep up with the rest of the Druids #36. So, here's to The Sacrifice. We may pray to rocks but this guy . . . rocks out.!
Druids #2–36: Most excellent.

Eventually, the Druids caught on to the atmosphere of toasting and developed some rather intriguing toasts that we found spray painted on some big rocks in southern England.

> “*To all the food that will suffice,*
> *And to our human sacrifice.*”

> “*A plague on the Vikings.*”

> “*To mead and ale and wine with a bite,*
> *And a lucky draw in the fertility rite.*”

Medieval Toasts

Toasts flourished in medieval times. Knights toasted knights. Serfs toasted serfs. Robin Hood toasted the Merry Men, and everybody toasted the King. Imagine for a moment that you are attending a major royal party 400 years ago. You are one of about a hundred people seated at a long wooden table the size of a bowling alley. As you are snacking on sides of beef and quaffing the potent mead, a knight rises from his chair, raises his vessal, and says out loud, “Here's to good old whiskey, so amber and so clear, 'tis not so sweet as a woman's lips, but a damn sight more sincere.”

At this point, all of the diners would lift their vessals and say something medieval like, “Hooray.”

Knights were pretty tough guys in their day but they were still human and very susceptible to the charms and wiles of a fair damsel. I can imagine the following toast being given at a knight's bachelor party:

> “*Here's to women . . . would that we could fall into their arms, instead of their hands.*”

A variety of toasts were given to the King in medieval times. They ranged from the popular, “God save the King,” usually used at dinner and parties, to the seldom used, “Once a king always a king; but once a knight is enough,” which was generally heard at stag parties and golf outings.

Like the civilizations before them, the toasters of medieval times tended to toast to things that mattered most to them, their health, their fitness in battle, and, of course, all the fine maidens. The following toasts come from postcards King Arthur sent to his friend Sid.

> *“To ye who wear these suits of mail,*
> *A fervent hope ye zippers not fail.”*

> *“To spare keys and chastity belts.”*

> *“May your drawbridge always be open*
> *And may your turret always stand tall.”*

> *“Here's to the King*
> *We'll always be loyal.*
> *And we'll shower his foes*
> *With boiling oil.”*

> *“I toast you with wine, whiskey, and tonic;*
> *May the fleas of your rats be not bubonic.”*

And here is a toast that was favored by knights before a joust.

> *“To Rustproof Armor.”*

The Age of Toasts

Well they was a lot of people in the U.S. that was in flavor of Prohibition and finely congress passed a law making the country dry and the law went into effect about the 20 of Jan. 1920 and the night before it went into effect everybody had a big party on acct. of it being the last chance to get boiled. As these wds. Is written the party is just beginning to get good.

—Ring Lardner

The golden age of toasts existed from 1917 to 1933. This was the dark period in America's history known as Prohibition. During this time it was illegal to make, buy, drink, or bathe with intoxicating beverages. This law, of course, did not stop anyone from drinking but did create the new job category of bootlegger.

Drinking became a clandestine activity during Prohibition and those who wished to imbibe had to find their way to a hidden bar called a speakeasy. After giving the secret password ("Joe sent me") at the door, a citizen in search of a cocktail would enter an establishment selling homemade beer and bathtub gin, both of which tasted the same. And wherever you find drinking, you will find toasting. "Here's looking at you, unless this liquor makes me go blind."

Since the production and distribution of liquor was illegal, the government took great pains to try and keep people from drinking. They would raid speakeasies, destroy barrels of alcohol, and do battle with the likes of Al Capone and Bugs Moran. The main Prohibition law enforcement officers were a group known as the Untouchables. They were led by Elliot Ness and were called Untouchables because nobody wanted to touch them. Apparently they would go on stakeouts for weeks at a time without the benefit of showers, and when they re-entered society they were so rancid that nobody wanted to touch them. "To the Untouchables—may they always be downwind."

Here are some of the classic toasts that came from the era of Prohibition.

> "*A dry heaven, and a wet hell;*
> *So it is prohibitors tell;*
> *But who would to a desert go,*
> *When it's nice and soggy*
> *Down below?*"

> "*To my bootlegger: here's hoping he never has to drink any of his own.*"

> "*Thirsty days hath September,*
> *April, June, and November;*
> *All the rest are thirsty too*
> *Except for him who hath home brew.*"

An Arthurian Legend

Legend has it that King Arthur met with his knights around a table that was round so that there would be no head nor foot. The real reason he decided on a round table was to facilitate his favorite drinking game, Thumper. As the king and his knights sat around the table with their goblets of strong drink, they would pound on the table with the palms of their hands, flash hand signals at each other, and stop periodically to laugh and drink. The medieval rules of Thumper have been lost to the ages, but a similar game is popular today on college campuses. Now, like then, the object of the game was the same: to promote friendship and good cheer, and to drink until you threw up.

"Wise guys buy supplies,
Dry guys likewise."

"When men were free as a matter of course,
Millions of dollars in revenue came;
While now millions go, a law to enforce,
And all but the bootleggers lose at the game."

"God bless America and damn Prohibition."

Of all of the toasts condemning Prohibition, this one makes a valid point for its positive image.

"Here's to Prohibition:
May it continue to reduce the number of men who think they can sing."

"Ship me somewhere east of Suez,
where the best is like the worst,
Where there aren't no ten commandments an' a man
can raise a thirst."
(Rudyard Kipling)

"Mother makes brandy from cherries;
Pop distills whiskey and gin;
Sister sells wine from the grapes on our vine
Good grief how the money rolls in."

"Here's to Prohibition
The devil take it!
They've stolen our wine,
So now we make it."

"Here's to Carrie Nation
Of anti-drink renown
Who, though against libation,
Hit ev'ry bar in town."

While Prohibition ruled in America, the liquor flowed freely across the border in Canada. Here are some popular toasts that were given by our neighbors to the north.

> "*Four and twenty Yankees,*
> *Feeling very dry,*
> *Went across the border,*
> *To get a drink of rye.*
> *When the rye was opened,*
> *The Yanks began to sing*
> *God bless America,*
> *But God save the King!*"

> "*Forty miles from whiskey,*
> *And sixty miles from gin,*
> *I'm leaving this damn country,*
> *For to live a life of sin.*"

The best summary of Prohibition was written by Don Marquis,

> "*Prohibition makes you want to cry into your beer and denies you the beer to cry into.*"

Carrie Nation

Carrie (also spelled Carry) Nation (1846–1911) was a woman who really hated booze. Maybe it was something in her childhood, but the woman was very negative about cocktails. She thought God told her to smash every saloon she found so she embarked on a major act of vandalism. She was arrested thirty times for smashing saloons with an ax, but she focused public attention on the evils of liquor and helped to create a mood favorable to passage of the eighteenth constitutional amendment that created Prohibition.

When to Toast

While toasts are generally delivered in the atmosphere of a special occasion, a toast can also make any occasion special. It is customary to toast at a wedding, a birthday, or a retirement party, but toasts can celebrate matters as mundane as making the mortgage payment, finding your car keys, or locating a free parking spot right in front of your favorite restaurant. Any time is the right time for a toast.

If you bought this book because you are new to making toasts, good for you. You have made a very wise investment. If, however, you bought this book hoping for some never-before-seen toasts that have been handcrafted by the masters, well, good for you, too. Within these pages you will find some of the most unique toasts ever written along with plenty of old standards. There's a reason this book is called *The Everything Toasts Book*, it contains EVERYTHING.

Toasting is an art form. It is performance art. It is the ability to combine oratory skills with a poet's ability to arrange the language. A good toaster will learn many well-known and historic toasts but will also develop the skill to create a toast unique for the person or the occasion being honored. As with any other endeavor in life, the more you do it the better you will become. The more you give toasts, the better your toasts will become.

I urge you to celebrate as many occasions as possible with toasts. Toast before meals, toast the end of the day, toast the fact that your car didn't get repossessed today. If an occasion arises, the master toaster will be ready with a toast.

When you are asked to make a toast at a special occasion like a business entertaining event, be sure to work on your toast as far in advance as possible. Make sure that you have the proper pronunciation of the person you are toasting and/or the company he or she represents. Write your toast and rehearse it often. The best toasts are kept to one minute or less. Try to never give a toast over three minutes. Not only will you lose the attention of the audience, but the longer the toast, the better the odds that you will screw it up or forget it.

There are no hard and fast rules for when a toast should be delivered in a business entertaining situation, but most often they are delivered right after dessert is served. When you first see that dessert is coming out of the kitchen, rise to your feet and get the attention of the audience. A simple attention-getting device is to tap on the side of your water glass lightly with a spoon. Don't tap it too softly or no one will hear you and don't hit it too hard or you could break it. If everybody else in the room starts tapping their water glasses too, you will have to kiss the bride.

A more complex but equally effective method of getting attention is to stand up and start singing "Take Me Out To The Ballgame" at the top of your lungs. Trust me, everyone will stop what they are doing to either hear you sing or join you in the tune. Either way, you've got their attention.

Once you have everyone's attention, announce to the group that you would like to propose a toast. Ask them to raise their glasses and join you in toasting the person, event, or occasion that everyone has joined together to celebrate. Give them a few seconds to locate their glasses

Dormitory Sauvignon

I was not alive during Prohibition and therefore did not have the opportunity to learn to make my own gin in the bathtub. I did, however, go to college where I learned how to make wine in my dorm room. You may want to bookmark this page just in case Prohibition ever comes back.

Dormitory Sauvignon
Ingredients:
1 one-gallon glass jug
3 twelve-ounce cans of frozen grape juice
1 cup of sugar
3 packages of yeast
1 huge rubber balloon

Combine the grape juice, sugar, and yeast in the jug. Add water to within two inches of the top.

Put on protective goggles. Stir the mixture with anything that will fit in the neck of the jug. When all of the sugar and yeast have dissolved, cover the opening of the jug with the huge balloon. Don't skimp on quality here. I suggest a seventy-five-cent, fifteen-inch rubber balloon. Secure the balloon with a rubber band.

Place the jug in a closet or other dark place where it will not be disturbed. Don't mess with it for a full thirty days. At the start of the second week, you will notice the balloon is beginning to inflate. By the end of the second week, the balloon will be the size of a basketball. Don't mess with it. This balloon is collecting all of the fermentation gasses that are giving your wine its natural sparkle.

As your wine approaches the twenty-fifth day of fermentation, you will notice the balloon starting to deflate. This is a good sign. It indicates that the fumes of the wine, (or "bouquet" as we vintners like to say) have eaten through the latex of the balloon causing it to leak.

The thirtieth day has arrived. Put on your surgical mask and goggles. Also, rubber gloves are a handy accessory at this point. Carefully pour your wine into your filtering apparatus. If you don't have a filtering apparatus, an old (but clean) sweat sock stretched across the mouth of an empty mayonnaise jar and lined with coffee filters will do nicely. When all of the wine has been filtered, slowly pour it into the wine bottles you have saved over the past month and cork tightly. Slap on your own label and you have a vintage that would make any vintner green with envy. And it will make your friends and neighbors green with nausea.

and refill empty ones. This silence may seem uncomfortable at first but those few moments of saying nothing will focus the attention on you.

The toast you make should fit the occasion and should be of a light and festive tone. Make your toast complimentary of the guest of honor and appreciative of his or her achievements. Make it politically correct and unless the toast is given at a bachelor party or to celebrate a divorce, please try to make it tasteful.

Even if you are giving a toast in the Oval Office of the White House try to refrain from making references to any previous indiscretions that may have occurred in the room. I think even the most radical liberal would wince at a toast like . . .

> *"To the man from Hope who works in this room*
> *meeting leaders from England and France;*
> *Too bad that all we remember of him,*
> *Is how often he dropped his pants."*

If you are giving a toast in front of a large group of people, you will probably be a little nervous. It has been shown that the number one fear humans have is the fear of public speaking. This ranks higher than the fear of death. So if you are asked to give a toast at a funeral, you are in a worse situation than the guy in the box.

But even though you're nervous, refrain from excessive drinking before you give your toast. There is nothing worse than listening to a toast given by a person who is slurring their words. Here is a little test you can try at home which will prove my point. Recite this beautiful wedding toast taken from Shakespeare's Romeo and Juliet:

> *"May a flock of blessings light upon thy back."*

Now, have a few cocktails, a bottle of wine, or a six-pack—whatever you would normally consume to make you feel more at ease and try the toast again. When I tried to do this, the following toast came out.

> *"Maybe a funk of blisters lay upon your back . . . you horny devil."*

Just remember this—friends don't let friends toast drunk.

While toasts are intended to be light-hearted, they don't necessarily need to be funny. I enjoy giving funny toasts because I am a professional humorist.

But even if humor does not come easy to you, please do not feel compelled to deliver a funny toast. A toast is most effective if it is sincere; and if you can fake sincerity, you have a future in politics.

To help you sound as sincere as possible, make sure that you are looking the recipient of the toast right in the eye as you toast him or her. When you do this you will feel more sincere and your words will sound as if they come right from your heart.

At the end of your toast, raise your glass to eye level and nod to the recipient of your toast. As the other guests join you in the raising of the glass, drink your own glass dry and gargle with the contents. Ha, ha, ha, I got you on that one. A proper toaster will only take a small sip from his or her glass, preferring to drink the rest of the contents when everybody in the room isn't looking at them.

It is also a good idea to sip your drink because after you have given the elegant toast you are capable of, others may feel compelled to toast the guest of honor too. If there are twenty or thirty toasts going around and you are slugging back a tumbler full of wine each time, you will become very schnockered very quickly.

Of course, no one should feel compelled to toast only with an alcoholic beverage. A toast can be given and celebrated with a glass of water. It is not the liquid that makes the toast, but the words of the person giving it . . . not to put any pressure on you or anything.

Toasting Etiquette

The ritual of toasting a guest of honor is as old as the spirits chosen with which to make it. The host offers the first toast. If there is talking, he may quiet the room and gain attention by tapping carefully on the edge of a wine glass (don't try this on fine crystal!).

The host stands and raises his wine glass toward the honoree. Other guests merely raise their glasses. When the toast has been made, each guest takes a sip of wine.

Nondrinking guests may raise their empty wine glass, or a glass of whatever else they may be drinking. The recipient of the toast sits and does not drink to himself. He may respond with his own toast. In dining functions where there is a dais, only people on the dais may propose toasts.

How to Make Your Own Toast

While this book will present you with hundreds of useful toasts to use in a wide variety of situations, the best toasts are the ones that you will write yourself and are customized to the situation. All you need to do is to follow a few simple Toast Tips and you can be a toastmaster for any situation.

Toast Tip Number One

Toast number one is all about two. This is a quasi-clever play on words designed to emphasize the point that any toast you propose needs to be directed toward (or to) something. A toast can be a recognition or celebration of any person, event, location, concept, or abstract idea, but it must be aimed at a subject. You can toast to a birthday, a wedding, the government of Liechtenstein, the forty-second parallel, electricity, one's health or love, but it needs to have a subject. A toast without a subject is nothing more than just another sentence. Let me give you an example.

> A Toast: “*Here's to your new goatee, may it set your spirit free.*”

This is a good toast because it has a subject (your new goatee) and a good will wish (may it set your spirit free). The following is not a toast.

> Not a Toast: “*Your beard makes you look like a hippie.*”

Since this statement is not directed to anything it is not a toast. Also, it does not contain a wish for the recipient but only an editorial statement about his (or her) new beard.

Remember that your toast is a statement of jubilation, congratulation, or remembrance. What you are overjoyed about, celebratory of, or in remembrance of is completely up to you. Celebrate every aspect of life and toast often.

Toast Tip Number Two

Select the format of your toast. Toasts can be serious when used in a formal or business situation; they can be emotional when used at funerals; they can be sentimental when used for events like weddings and anniversaries; or they can be funny when used to toast friends, good times, and joyful events. They can also combine two or more of these elements if the situation warrants. The only rule of thumb in deciding which toast format is right for you is to use your common sense.

Common sense is the most important of our senses but it is also the most seldom used. We use our senses of sight, smell, touch, hearing, and taste on a daily basis but our common sense is too often overlooked. If you are toasting a serious situation such as the promotion of a fellow worker, your common sense would lead you to construct a toast like this:

> *"Congratulations to Bob,*
> *on a job well done,*
> *When it comes to great leaders,*
> *You are second to none."*

Without common sense. You may find yourself sitting around with your coworkers and making a toast to Bob like this:

> *"I can't believe you got the job,*
> *You stupid SOB*
> *If anybody deserved it,*
> *That somebody should be me."*

If the situation calls for humor, propose a humorous toast. If the situation calls for decorum, use a formal toast. If the situation calls for heartfelt sentiment, write a sensitive sentimental toast. If you use your common sense, will not find yourself making an inappropriate toast.

Toast Tip Number Three

Find your material everywhere and anywhere. Consider this book as merely a source book for your own toast research. You will find many toasts in these pages, some of which are hundreds of years old. And while some of the old toasts have become classics, you can create a new toast any time you like. All you have to do is to pick up an idea from this book or an idea from another source and combine them with your own imagination.

If you want to create a custom toast for a special occasion, don't let writer's block force you into nothing more than "Cheers." Although this book probably contains as many starter ideas as you will ever need, be sure to check other sources as well.

Quotations by famous people are always a good basis upon which you can build a toast. Your local library has countless quotation books covering any possible subject you wish to toast. Just to prove my point, I would like to make a toast right now about any subject you desire. We will use a simple game to help you choose a topic.

A Toast Test

If you are not sure if you are sober enough to propose a toast, try this simple little test. If you can pronounce the following tongue twisters three times in a row without sounding like a drooling idiot, feel free to propose a toast. If, however, you cannot get past the third word without slurring, sit down and keep silent.

If I fell on a felon feloniously,
Who's the felon—the felon I fell on, or me?

If you stick a stock of liquor in your locker,
It is slick to stick a lock upon your stock,
Or some joker who is slicker's going to trick you of your liquor,
If you fail to lock your liquor with a lock.

To Clink or Not to Clink

Large groups do not clink their glasses during toasts. Individuals (particularly lovers, but anybody toasting a special occasion) may touch their wine glasses together if they wish. Superstition suggests that the glasses be "clinked" at unequal height, never at the same level. If those raising their glasses in a toast are seated too far apart to touch them, the raising itself is sufficient.

First, think of any number between one and ten. Multiply that number by nine. Add the two digits together. Subtract five from the new number. Find the letter in the alphabet that matches this number, i.e. one equals A, seven equals G, and twenty-three means you have very poor math skills. Think of the first country that comes to mind that starts with that letter. Take the second letter of the name of that country and think of an animal that starts with that letter. So then, you want me to write a toast about elephants?

I looked in several quotation books and couldn't find a single quotation about elephants so I did the next best thing. Quick, what does an elephant have? No not a trunk, an elephant has a good memory. An elephant never forgets. Here, then, is my toast to a good memory.

> "*In the words of James Barrie, 'god gave us memory that we might have roses in December.' Here's to remembering all of the good things in life and forgetting the bad.*"

This may not be the most memorable toast ever written but it proves the point that a toast can be custom written for just about anything. If you can't find a quote that works for you, try looking up the subject of your toast in a poetry book. You can even borrow verse you find in a greeting card, which could make your toast special.

Don't rule out any source when you are writing a toast. Your possibilities are limitless.

Toasting Equipment

There are only two essential pieces of equipment needed for any toast. First, you need a liquid of some sort with which to offer the toast. Second, you need a vessel of some sort with which to hold the liquid. Without a liquid, you would be performing a "dry toast," which is as exciting as it sounds. Without a vessel to hold that liquid, you will wind up with very wet hands and possibly soiled clothing. Acceptable liquids for proper toasting include:

Wine	Milk
Beer	Juice
Spirits	Coffee
Water	Tea

Unacceptable liquids for proper toasting include:

Bleach
Gravy
Windshield washer fluid

It is important to remember that while a vast majority of the toasts given throughout the world are given using alcoholic beverages, alcohol is not a necessary ingredient. Toasts can be performed with soft drinks, juice, or water. They can be given by teetotalers and zealots whose religion bans alcohol. The spirit of the toast is one of friendship, congratulations, and celebration, which does not depend on alcohol for its bond. The choice is up to you.

If you are going to toast with an alcoholic beverage, you should probably know what you are drinking. Every alcoholic beverage is mostly water but the other ingredients are what make it fun. Here are some of the most popular alcoholic beverages and their core ingredients.

Bourbon whiskey—A grain mixture that is at least 51 percent corn. Interestingly, the word whiskey comes from the Irish Gaelic word "usquebaugh," which means "water of life." In this country, the word eventually became "whiskybae" and eventually whiskey. Whisky—without the "e"—is the British spelling and is applied to Scotch whisky and Canadian whisky.

Rye whiskey—A grain mixture that is at least 51 percent rye.

Scotch whisky— Malted barley, (single malt), which is nothing at all like malted milk.

Canadian whisky—A blend of corn, rye, and barley.

Irish whiskey—Barley and oats.

Gin—Gin gets its name from the French word "genievre," which came from the Dutch word "jenever," which means "juniper berries," the flavoring agent of

Glasses for Toasting

A well-stocked bar should be matched with carefully selected glassware. For the purist, a glass can be matched to every available drink. For the rest of us, if it doesn't leak it will work fine. Here are some different types of glasses you may want to keep behind your bar so as to be ready for any toasting occasion.

Old-fashioned glass—An all purpose glass with either straight, fluted, or barreled sides holding about seven ounces.

Highball or Collins glass—A tall thin glass holding from eight ounces to twelve ounces. Perfect for Tom Collins, gin and tonic, Bloody Mary, Screwdriver, etc.

Cordial glass—Also referred to as the pony glass, this one-ounce glass is elegantly designed for after dinner drinks.

Shot glass—1 ½ ounces in capacity and is used as a measurement glass as well as for shooters, or drinks consumed in one shot.

Brandy snifter—This glass has a large rounded bowl for savoring the rich volatile fragrance of fine brandy. They range in size from two-ounce capacity up to an eight ounce size. Very large snifters holding up to twenty-eight ounces are available but usually are used only to hold pennies or your collection of matchbooks.

Martini glass—The martini is a special cocktail and requires a special glass. The classic design is a funnel shape atop a stem. A new design looks like the funnel part with the stem broken off but it rests in a larger container filled with ice. This guarantees that your martini will maintain its chill to the last drop.

All-purpose wine glass—A tulip shaped glass holding eight to twelve ounces will work equally well for red or white wines. Any further wine glass specialization is a personal preference. Always remember, no matter how large or small the wine glass is, only fill it half full.

Champagne glass—Two basic shapes are available. The classic saucer shaped champagne glass that you see in movies and on TV is OK but it releases the bubbles in the champagne too quickly. The fluted, hollow stem glasses are much more aesthetically pleasing and the bubbles are more fun to look at.

Beer glass—The choice is yours from the slender pilsner glass to the heavy stein. When it comes to beer, use what you like best.

gin. Gin starts out as a clear grain spirit but then things like juniper berries, coriander, cardamon, and cassis bark are added to give gin its unique flavor.

Vodka—This term comes from the Russian word "voda," which means "little water." Originally made from potato mash (not mashed potatoes), vodka is now distilled primarily from corn, rye, or wheat. Vodka is known for its tastelessness but it still packs a punch.

Rum—The word rum comes from the English word "rumbullion" but nobody seems to know what this word means. My guess is that it is a word that was invented after drinking too much rum. Sugar cane is rum's main ingredient.

Tequila—The flesh of the maguey cactus plant.

Wine—Grapes.

Beer—Grain.

Glassware

The vessel that holds the toasting liquid can be something as simple as a glass, bottle, or can. In the movies you may have seen Ronald Coleman or one of those other famous dead leading men toasting a beautiful woman by drinking champagne out of her shoe. This is not recommended for several reasons.

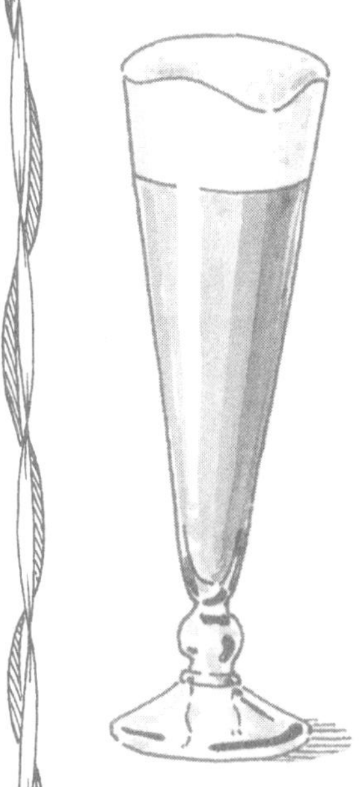

First, shoes, even those of the most beautiful woman on earth, contain their own "bouquet." This bouquet is usually nasty and will make even the finest champagne taste like socks. Also, women tend to maintain personal relationships with their shoes. Shoes are members of a woman's extended family and are treated with equal respect. Women have so many shoes not because they wear them out faster than men, but because a shoe purchase is a commitment and relationships are established. Therefore, if you pour champagne into a shoe with which a woman is in love, you will ruin both the shoe and your chances of advancing to more intimate procedures with said woman.

Another reason that footwear makes for a lousy toasting vessel is that it doesn't "clink." In order for a toast to convey the true meaning with which it is presented, the clinking sound is a must. Glasses clink, bottles clink, and even aluminum cans clink in their own way. They all produce a sound, which indicates that a toast has been performed. Shoes have little or no clinking value and

brandy snifter

collins glass

old fashioned glass

champagne glass

champagne flute

belong in the same category of poor toasting vessels as Styrofoam cups, plastic glasses, or wine-in-a-box.

If you are toasting at home, you have the privilege of selecting your favorite type of glassware. If you are toasting at a bar, restaurant, or banquet hall, you will have to propose your toast using whatever glassware you are provided. For this reason, I suggest that you use the type of glassware that makes you the happiest in your own home. If you like drinking fine wine from a crystal wine glass, good for you. But if you prefer to consume a fine Merlot from a former jelly jar decorated with cartoon characters, well, good for you too. You are a little weird, you know, but that is your own right. My only guess is that you don't get a lot of company over your house anyway so what the heck.

A typical inventory of glasses for toasting would include rocks glasses (the little ones), cocktail glasses (the bigger ones), wine glasses, chosen according to your preference, champagne glasses (fluted are the most interesting), a shot glass or two, and some beer mugs kept in the freezer. As your personal tastes change you find that you will start to break your old glasses. This is nature's way of purging your old stockpile.

Proper Toasting Attire

One of the nice things about making a toast is that you can do it in virtually any kind of dress, or undress for that matter. I venture to say that some of the best toasts ever given were delivered in a state of undress. These can take the form of private, intimate toasts or group hot tub toasts. Most of us will find ourselves as a participant in a naked toast at some time in our lives but that is best left for another book.

When addressing the topic of toasting attire, we must look at the toasts that are given in more formal environments. As we have said before, anyone can give a toast at any time, to any one. But on some occasions, if you are going to give a toast, you want to look like a toaster.

I love the old black and white movies where rich people like Rock Hudson and Ray Milland would toast their dates while attired in smoking jackets and ascots. Just for the record, they also had pants and shirts, but the jacket and ascot combination made the biggest impression on me. If you are going to have a formal dinner party in your home, you may want to request that the men come attired in smoking jackets and ascots and the women wear evening gowns and feather boas. Note: You probably won't get anybody to show up to your party with these rules but at least you made the effort.

At a wedding reception, the toast is generally given by the best man, who is most likely wearing some sort of formal garb. This is perfect, but if you are sitting in the audience wearing a less formal outfit, do not feel as though you could not give a toast also. In fact, the only people at a wedding who are not eligible to give a toast are the caterers, who may be dressed nicely enough but have no idea who the bride or groom is.

The bottom line is that it doesn't make the slightest difference what you are wearing, or not wearing, as long as the toast is presented with emotion, sincerity, and honesty—or as close to that as you can fake.

Details

A few details on the subject of toasting equipment: First if you are presenting a toast, make sure that everyone who wishes to participate has the equipment needed to do so.

For instance, if you are riding on a bus or subway and a lonely man named Ernie pulls out a bottle of bargain wine gaily decorated with a paper bag and wants to make a toast, do not feel compelled to join him. Unless Ernie brought enough bottles of wine wrapped in paper bags for the entire vehicle, he should not give a toast. If Ernie says that everybody can drink from his bottle, tell him you are allergic.

If no glassware is available for your toast you will have to improvise. Emergency cups can be folded out of paper. Bear in mind that while a properly constructed paper cup will hold liquid, it won't hold it for very long. If you are using paper toasting equipment, make sure that you give a fast toast with something other than piping hot soup.

Little Known Misinformation

The first time I heard someone say that you should never ASSUME because it makes an ASS out of U and ME I thought, "That's clever." And when I first heard someone explain the K.I.S.S. principle (Keep It Simple, Stupid.) I thought, "Wow." Well, I have come up with my own clever thought and it is to remind you how to deliver a toast. In fact, it is based on the letters in the word TOAST.

T—Take a glass in your hand.
O—Open your mouth
A—And
S—Say something.
T—Take a drink.

It may not be as clever as the ASSUME or K.I.S.S. examples but I guarantee that if you commit this concept to memory, you will very rarely forget how to spell the word TOAST.

CHAPTER 2

To Mark This Occasion

Wedding Rituals: Diamond Engagement Ring

In medieval Italy, precious stones were seen as part of the groom's payment for the bride. The groom would give a gift of such stones, which symbolized his intent to marry.

Toasts are almost always made to mark an occasion. At the very least they are made to life or to health or even to the next drink, but very rarely can the toaster not come up with a reasonable occasion to mark with his toast. Granted, I have been in college drinking situations where everyone around the table delivered a toast and consumed a drink and when it came time for the last person to propose a toast, he couldn't think of anything worth toasting. Usually I...I mean HE, would say something semi-coherent like "to blechhhh," which was not a word but rather more like a sound effect. After picking my head up from the slice of pizza into which it had dropped, the remaining revelers toasted the occasion of my inability to hold my liquor.

For practical purposes in this book, we shall assume that every toast is given to honor an occasion, no matter how minor it may seem. We will start with the most conspicuous of the toasting occasions: weddings.

Wedding Toasts

I think it is a safe assumption that sooner or later everyone in this country—and possibly the world—will attend a wedding as either a participant or as an innocent bystander. Having been both, I think there is much less pressure being a bystander. While a wedding participant will most assuredly receive gifts on his or her wedding day, an innocent bystander can party like it's going out of style. They probably won't go home with any presents other than a slice of wedding cake and a book of matches emblazoned with the name of the wedding couple. The benefit of being an innocent bystander as opposed to a wedding participant is that you can wear clothes you didn't have to rent and you don't have to get on a plane the next morning with a hangover.

Anyone attending a wedding has the right to deliver a toast to the nuptial couple. For the best man, the task is mandatory, but anyone else who feels the need can stand up and wish the couple well with their own choice of words.

If you don't already have a favorite wedding toast, you may find one in this collection that you can commit to memory and bring forth from the recesses of your mind on the appropriate occasion.

To make a wedding toast, first you have to get everyone's attention. This was covered in Chapter 1 but bears repeating here.

Earlier I mentioned that gently tapping on the side of a glass with your knife or spoon would alert the other partiers to the fact that you wanted the floor. Unfortunately, the sound of silverware clinking against glassware at a wedding sends a signal to the bridal couple that they are expected to kiss in front of the assembled multitudes. Therefore, you will most likely need to find a different method of gathering everyone's attention.

I would suggest approaching the band or the disc jockey, whichever is present at the wedding you are attending, and ask to use the microphone. Once you have control of the sound system, you have control of the party and can proceed with your toast.

First Weddings

Like most things in life, the first time is always the best. The term first wedding is a rather recent addition to English nomenclature replacing the previously used "wedding." Since 50 percent of marriages now end in divorce, half of the weddings you will attend in your life will merely be first attempts as opposed to the previously held concept of eternal bonds.

Since the bridal couple really have no idea what they are getting themselves into on their first go round, first wedding toasts have an air of celebration, good wishes, and above all, good luck. While the sample toasts shown below are categorized as wedding toasts, you may find one that will work equally well at an engagement announcement or a rehearsal dinner.

> *"A toast to love and laughter and happily ever after."*

For lovers who keep on keeping on with their love, there is never an end to the glories of marriage.

> *"The way to Happiness;*
> *Keep your heart free from hate,*
> *Your mind from worry,*
> *Live simply. Expect little. Give much."*

> *"The more that you love one another, the closer you will come to God."*

The Dry Toast

Weddings are not only happy events but they are also the site of one of the rarest of toast events: the dry toast.

In addition to the numerous champagne toasts that are proposed at a wedding, the ceremonial cutting of the cake provides the fuel for the dry toast. When the cake is presented to the guests, the bride and groom blow out all of the candles and start cutting the cake with a U.S. Cavalry saber. After hacking off a couple pieces of cake, the bride and groom each grab a chunk of cake and toast each other with it by gently jamming their cake into each other's mouths.

Invariably the happy couple will be a few inches off center and wind up smearing frosting on each others face. The photographer is ready when this happens and captures, on film, the wedding dry toast.

Wedding Rituals: The Ring Finger

The third finger on the left hand is considered the ring finger. All engagement and wedding rings are worn there because centuries ago that finger was believed to be connected by a vein directly to the heart.

"What is thine is mine, and all mine is thine."
(Plautus)

"What's mine is yours, and what is yours is mine."
(Shakespeare)

"What's yours is mine and what's mine is mine."
(My Uncle Lester who never really understood the concept of marriage.)

"Treasure the simplest of things. The grand events will come, and you will feel pride, but when you need comfort and direction, you will find it in the simple things."
(Bernice Smith)

"Marriage is that relation between man and woman in which the independence is equal, the dependence mutual, and the obligation reciprocal."
(Louis Kaufman Anspacher)

"Here's a toast to marriage, the greatest educational establishment in the world."

"In seeking a long lasting marriage, I think the words of Winston Churchill best summarize the feeling when he said, 'Never, never, never, never, give up.'"

"Here's to the Bride and the Groom!
May you have a happy honeymoon,
May you lead a happy life,
May you have a bunch of money soon,
And live without all strife."

"Here's to the groom with bride so fair,
And here's to the bride with groom so rare."

"Here's to the husband and here's to the wife,
May they be lovers for the rest of their life."

"Let us toast the health of the bride;
Let us toast the health of the groom,
Let us toast the person that tied the knot,
Let us toast every guest in this room."

Here's one you can use at the next Amish wedding you attend, but please make sure that the cider you are toasting with has not turned hard.

"Here's to thee and thy folks from me and my folks,
And if thee and thy folks love me and my folks
As much as me and my folks love thee and thy folks,
Then there never was folks since folks was folks
Loved me and my folks as much as thee and thy folks."

Here's one which seems to cover all of the legal bases.

"Here's to the bride and mother-in-law,
Here's to the groom and father-in-law,
Here's to the sister and brother-in-law,
Here's to friends and friends-in-law,
May none of them need an attorney-at-law."

The best toasts convey their point in only a few words. Shakespeare said that brevity is the soul of wit, well, it is also the soul of most toasts. Here are some short examples that still have a sentimental impact.

"May their joys be as bright as the morning,
and their sorrows but shadows that fade in the sunlight of love."

"May the two of you grow old on one pillow."

The Rehearsal Dinner

The night before the wedding, all interested parties, including the bride, groom, bridesmaids, ushers, officiant, parents, and readers gather at the ceremony site and do a quick run-through of the ceremony. After this, the whole gang leaves and goes to dinner.

Although no rule states that you *must* make toasts at the rehearsal dinner, traditionally the best man is the first to toast the couple. This toast is usually more lighthearted than the one he makes at the reception. Then the groom can toast his bride and future in-laws, and the bride can toast her groom and future in-laws. Sometimes the couple's parents like to get in a few words as well. Feel free to have as many toasts as you'd like; if everyone wants to make a toast and the mood calls for it, let them!

The High Cost Of Marriage

Rather than ask if the happy couple can afford marriage, consider the words of a wise anonymous sage who said:

The bride, white of hair,
stoops over her cane,
Her footsteps, uncertain,
needing guiding,
While down the church
aisle,
With a wan, toothless
smile,
The groom in a wheelchair
comes riding.
And who is this elderly
couple thus wed?
You'll find when you
closely explore it,
That here is the rare, most
conservative pair,
Who waited till they could
afford it!

"May your wedding days be few and your anniversaries many."

"Here's to the bride and here's to the groom,
And to the bride's father who paid for this room."

"To the newlyweds: May "for better or worse" be far better than worse."

"May your love be as endless as your wedding rings.
May their joys be as deep as the ocean,
And their misfortunes as light as the foam."

Irish toasts are covered in Chapter 4, but this wedding toast has Irish origins and makes sense to me.

"May you have many children
And may they grow as mature in taste and healthy in color,
And as sought after as the contents of this glass."

This toast is quite long and you may wish to read it rather than recite it from memory. Either way, it carries a great deal of touching sentiment.

"May you have enough happiness to keep you sweet,
Enough trials to keep you strong,
Enough sorrow to keep you human;
Enough hope to keep you happy;
Enough failure to keep you humble;
Enough success to keep you eager;
Enough friends to give you comfort;
Enough faith and courage in yourself, your business, and your country to banish depression;
Enough wealth to meet your needs;
Enough determination to make each day a better day than yesterday."

*"Two such as you with such a master speed
Cannot be parted nor be swept away
From one another once you are agreed
That life is only life forevermore
Together wing to wing and oar to oar."*
(Robert Frost)

*"May the two of you breakfast with Health,
Dine with Friendship,
Crack a bottle with Mirth,
And sup with the goddess of Contentment."*

"Here's to matrimony, the high sea for which no compass has yet been invented."
(Heinrich Heine)

"Nothing is worth more than this day."
(Goethe)

"Down the hatch to a wonderful match."

"May you always share your love and laughter."

"May your refrigerator always be full of beer, and may all of your ups and downs happen underneath the covers."

An excellent place to search for material for a custom written wedding toast is in the words of people who have been there. Here are some quotes from the famous and the not so famous that should be helpful.

"Marriage is not just spiritual communion and passionate embraces; marriage is also three meals a day and remembering to carry out the trash."
(Dr. Joyce Brothers)

Wedding Rituals: The Honeymoon

In ancient times, Teuton couples would marry beneath a full moon, then drink honey wine for thirty days after; hence the name.

Wedding Rituals: Throwing Rice

The tradition of throwing rice began in the Orient. Rice (which symbolizes fertility) was thrown at the couple in the hope that this would bring a marriage yielding many children.

"Marriage is three parts love and seven parts forgiveness."
(Langdon Mitchell)

"The sum which two married people owe to one another defies calculation. It is an infinite debt, which can only be discharged through all eternity."
(Goethe)

"A successful marriage requires falling in love many times, always with the same person."
(Mignon McLaughlin)

"Marriage is a fan club with only two fans."
(Adrian Henri)

"You will truly know you are married when the bills start to come and you learn to share the toothpaste."
(Bernice Smith)

"It is a lovely thing to have a husband and wife developing together. That is what marriage really means; helping one another to reach the full status of being persons, responsible and autonomous beings who do not run away from life."
(Paul Tournier)

"God, the best maker of all marriages,
Combine your hearts in one."
(Shakespeare)

"Happy marriages begin when we marry the one we love,
And they blossom when we love the one we married."
(Sam Levenson)

"Marriage is the alliance of two people, one of whom never remembers birthdays and the other who never forgets."
(Ogden Nash)

While most wedding toasts are thoughtful, introspective, and sentimental, every wedding will have at least one wise guy who will propose a humorous, cynical, or smart-ass toast. If you are that guy, these toasts are for you. A good friend offered these toasts, which would fit in perfectly if the wedding couple has a good sense of humor. If they don't have a good sense of humor, their marriage will probably not last.

Wedding Rituals: The Bridal Shower

This custom is believed to have started in Holland, where legend has it that a disapproving father would not provide his daughter with a dowry so that she might marry a less-than-wealthy miller. Her friends provided her with the then-essential dowry by "showering" her with gifts.

"To the bride and groom anew this day
The future full ahead.
To the time it takes to leave this place
And stagger off to bed."

"To a husband and wife who will last and last
Till death takes one of them.
Till the husband comes home too far past dark
And the wife makes that day then."

"A time to celebrate and think
Last chance to size up life.
'Cause soon the pants in the family shrink
Yet will oddly fit the wife."

"Two golden rings on two hands
Two lovers become so close
But experience and history often demands
That the ring hangs from one nose"

Another friend and toasting companion wrote this toast, as well as several others throughout this book. He and I have been known to sit around for hours making toasts to everything from the Chicago Bulls to last call.

"To tuna in cans and pork and beans,
'Cause now you'll know what poverty means."

Here are a few more toasts for the bridal couple who can love each other and laugh at themselves.

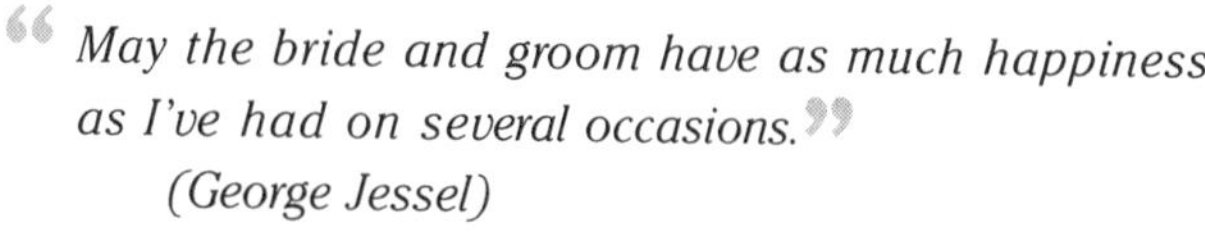

"May the bride and groom have as much happiness as I've had on several occasions."
(George Jessel)

"Marriage is a mistake
Every man should make"
(George Jessel)

"To your wedding;
May your love for each other grow as surely as your waistlines will."

"To your wedding;
Love not only makes the world go 'round,
But it also makes the trip worthwhile."

Specialty Wedding Toasts

While the wedding couple will be toasted by the other wedding attendees, it is also appropriate for the groom to propose a toast to his new bride and also to his new family. Likewise, in this age of equality it is equally appropriate for the bride to toast her new husband.

Again, if you are hung up on propriety, the first toast should be offered by the best man; this should be followed by a response from the groom. Next up to bat is the father of the bride, followed by the father of the groom. This is followed by toasts from the mother of the bride followed by the mother of the groom. Finally, the groom gets to toast his own bride and the bride can toast the groom. After that, it is pretty much open mike night.

Not to be left out of the specialty toast department, I have included a few toasts that the parents of the bride and/or groom can propose to the happy couple.

Toasts By The Best Man

Many times I have wondered exactly what a best man is. I have been a best man at a couple of weddings but I never really under-

Wedding Rituals: The Wedding Cake

Wedding cakes originated in ancient Rome, where a loaf of wheat bread was broken over the bride's head to symbolize hope for a fertile and fulfilling life. The guests ate the crumbs, which were believed to be good luck. The custom found its way to England in the Middle Ages. The guests would bring small cakes to a wedding; the cakes were put in a pile that the bride and groom later stood over and kissed. Apparently, someone came up with the idea of piling all the cakes together and frosting them, creating an early ancestor of the multi-tiered wedding cakes of today.

stood the role. Other than securing the location and entertainment for the bachelor party, the best man's biggest job is making sure that the groom shows up. Unfortunately, I did not know that the best man's role extends much further than that. Among the numerous duties of the best man you will find:

- Host the bachelor party for the groom.
- Arrange for ushers to be fitted for tuxedos.
- Help the groom get dressed for the wedding.
- Stay with the groom is a small room near the front of the church until the ceremony begins or until they can figure a way out of this mess.
- Make and/or confirm the couple's honeymoon arrangements.
- Drive the groom to the ceremony.
- Hold on to the marriage license and the wedding rings.
- Pay the clergyman, organist, soloist, and any other participants in the wedding.
- Give the first toast to the bride and groom at the wedding reception.
- Drive the couple to their hotel after the reception.
- Return to the reception and party down. You have had a big day.
- Return the groom's tux (and your own) to the rental store. Apologize for any rips, tears, or gravy stains.

Etiquette Tip: Wedding Liquor

Liquor can be served anytime, from mimosas at brunch to a full-scale open bar at a nighttime reception. For a luncheon reception, a fully stocked bar is unnecessary—mimosas, champagne, bloody marys, or other light drinks would be more appropriate.

Since the best man is in charge of the first toast given at the wedding, you had better plan out what you are going to say. If you are not accustomed to public speaking you should not only write out your toast but also rehearse it several times. The best toast is given from the heart. Say what you feel and your toast will have that much more meaning.

Here are some elements you can use to weave together your own eloquent toast.

> *"Here's to the bridal couple, may they always be in love. In the words of Jose Marti, "Love is born with the pleasure of looking at each other, it is fed with the necessity of seeing each other, it is concluded with the impossibility of separation."*

Wedding Season

June is the ideal time to get married. Not only is the weather probably going to be pleasant, but the NBA finals are over, the NFL is not even in summer camp, and baseball has not yet gotten exciting. In other words, other than fishing season and golf, there is very little to distract the groom.

"This wedding is more than a joining of two people in love. It is an occasion where more photos will be taken than were used to cover the entire Civil War."

"As we celebrate this wedding ceremony let us remember that a marriage is not just a ceremony, it is a creation. May this couple create a wonderful world together filled with love, laughter and life."

"Wise are they, who sense that the surest way to be fully loved is to love fully. Let us raise a toast to two wise people as they form their new life together."

"A toast to my friends who are each other's best friends. I recall the words of an ancient philosopher who said, "Friendship is love with understanding." May your friendship increase with your love, and may you remain together until the end of time."

Toasts by the Groom

"To my wife,
My bride and joy."

"Here's to my mother-in-law's daughter,
Here's to her father-in-law's son;
And here's to the vows we've just taken,
And the life we've just begun."

"In the words of the poet Robert Browning,
Grow old with me!
The best is yet to be,
The last of life,
For which the first is made."

"*My feelings for you reflect the words of Walter Winchell:*
Never above you.
Never below you.
Always beside you."

"*Fair is the white star of twilight*
And the sky clearer
At the day's end;
But she is fairer
And she is dearer,
She, my heart's friend.
Fair is the white star of twilight,
And the moon roving
To the sky's end;
But she is fairer,
Better worth loving,
She, my heart's friend.
(Shoshone Love Song)

"*O my luve's like a red, red rose*
That's newly sprung in June:
O my Luve's like the melodie
That's sweetly played in tune.
As fair art thou, my bonnie lass,
So deep in luve am I;
And I will luve thee still, my dear,
Till a' the seas gang dry."
(Robert Burns)

"*Plato once said that when man was created he had two heads, and four legs and four arms, and was very powerful. So man was cut in half and the halves were mixed up and to this day it is man's lifelong quest to find the missing halves. In finding each other, my love, we have accomplished that desire.*"

Etiquette Tip: Best Man

As the groom's legal witness, the best man should help the groom in any way possible. Where the bride has her entire family to support her, it is the best man who looks out for his friend, the groom.

Big brothers and close friends are usually chosen as best men, although this can vary depending on age and experience. The best man's foremost job is to get the groom to his wedding on time and, ahem, sober.

At the reception the best man mingles. He is not part of the receiving line.

Toasts by the Bride

"I drink to myself and one other,
And may that one other be he,
Who drinks to himself and one other,
And may that one other be me."

"You are my husband now,
And I am your wife.
I plan to be with you,
For the rest of my life.
I know I cannot change you,
And you know you won't change me.
Together let's go hand in hand,
Toward the best that life can be."

"If I could wrap love in a shiny silver box
With a big blue ribbon.
It would be my gift to you."

"I love you—
I love you for what you are, but I love you yet more for what you are going to be.
I love you not so much for your realities as for your ideals. I pray for your desires that they may be great, rather than for your satisfactions, which may be so hazardously little.
A satisfied flower is one whose petals are about to fall. The most beautiful rose is one hardly more than a bud wherein the pangs and ecstasies of desire are working for larger and finer growth.
Not always shall you be what you are now.
You are going forward toward something great. I am on the way with you and therefore I love you."
(Carl Sandburg)

Wedding Rituals: The Wedding Ring

The idea of the wedding ring itself dates back to ancient times, when a caveman husband would wrap circles of braided grass around his bride's wrists and ankles, believing it would keep her spirit from leaving her body. The bands evolved into leather, carved stone, metal, and later silver and gold. (Luckily, you only have to wear them on your finger nowadays—and the groom usually reciprocates.)

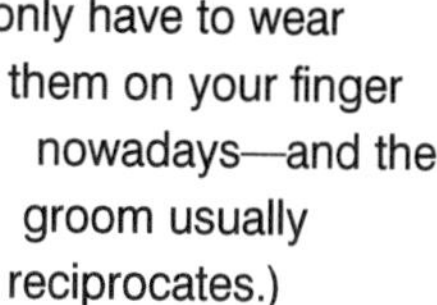

> “*Being loved by you makes me feel protected but*
> *not smothered,*
> *Challenged but not threatened,*
> *Directed but not controlled,*
> *Wanted but not possessed.*
> *You are the one with whom I am not afraid to become*
> *“we.”*”

> “*Drink to me only with thine eyes,*
> *And I will pledge with mine;*
> *Or leave a kiss but in the cup,*
> *And I'll not look for wine*”
> *(Ben Jonson)*

This toast was originally written by Jonson to a woman named Celia, but it is equally appropriate for delivery by a bride or the groom. After all, it's the thought that counts.

> “*It has been said that true love is like a ghost. Everyone talks about it but few have seen it. Here's a toast to my husband, we are among the lucky few.*”

> “*I have heard it said that people destined to meet will do so, apparently by chance, at precisely the right moment. We were destined to meet and destined to spend the rest of our lives together.*”

Toasts by the Parents

The parents of the wedding couple are invited to propose toasts at their children's wedding but not all of them take advantage of the opportunity. This is an excellent chance to tell your kids how much you love them and wish them well.

> “*May your home be filled with so much love that it rushes out of the door to greet your visitors. And may the two of you remain in love with each other until the end of time.*”

Best Man or Best Boy?

Contrary to what you might think, a best man is not a grown up best boy. A best man is the groom's chief attendant at a wedding, but a best boy is that job listed at the end of movie credits. If you're like me you probably saw that listing for best boy hundreds of times but never knew what it was. It is time you found out.

A best boy on a television or movie set, is the chief assistant to the gaffer. There, that should clear it up, unless you don't know what a gaffer is. A gaffer on a television or movie set is the electrician in charge of lighting. So, rather than have a gaffer's assistant called a "gaffer's assistant" or even a "gaffette" the entertainment industry has chosen to call this person a "best boy". I don't know if the job description of "best girl" exists but it should.

"*So much for the wedding, now let's get on with the grandchildren!*"

"*It has been written that when children find true love,*
parents find true joy.
Here's to your joy and ours from this day forward."

"*May we all live to be present at their golden wedding.*"

"*To the bride and groom;*
There are only two lasting bequests we can hope to give our children. One of these is roots, the other wings."
(Hodding Carter)

"*Much happiness to the newlyweds from the oldlyweds.*"

"*To the newlyweds;*
We will give you love, we will give you support, and we will give you help when needed. We ask only one thing in return...GRANDCHILDREN!"

Here's one from the bride's father to the groom.

"*I toast on behalf of myself,*
And I toast on behalf of my spouse.
We're glad you married our daughter.
And got her out of the house."

Anniversary Toasts

Next to your wedding, the most important day of your year is your wedding anniversary. In one way your anniversary is more important than your wedding. Nobody forgets the date of their wedding, but more than one person has forgotten their wedding anniversary—with serious repercussions I should add.

Wedding anniversaries are important to those involved but they are very important to women. You, as a guy, may forget a wedding anniversary, but the woman will never forget that you forgot and will dredge up that fact whenever she needs to for the rest of your life. Do not forget your anniversary. Better yet, make each anniversary special with a special anniversary toast.

One idea to remember your anniversary is to get married on a date you already have etched in your mind, like St. Valentine's Day. Other good choices for wedding dates would be Christmas, New Year's Eve, and the opening day of baseball season. You may even want to wait for leap year and get married on February 29 so that you only have to remember your anniversary once every four years.

Women are usually not to keen on getting married on an already existing holiday because it cuts down on their presents. It's kind of like being born on Christmas Day. You always get screwed out of presents. If you pick St. Valentine's Day as your nuptial date, the wife will be forever leery that the anniversary gift you gave her was something that she would have gotten anyhow because it is Valentine's Day. They want a separate day—aside from the special dates already printed on the calendar—to call their own.

For some peculiar reason, wedding anniversaries are the only holidays that have an official gift list. I'm sure you have seen a copy of this list printed in pocket calendars and yearly diaries. They show you what kind of present you should buy for an anniversary couple based upon the number of years they have been able to stay together. For instance, we all know that the twenty fifth anniversary is the silver anniversary and the fiftieth anniversary is the golden anniversary. This means that silver is the appropriate gift for a twenty-fifth anniversary and gold is appropriate for a fiftieth. But did you know that the appropriate gift for a first anniversary is paper? What kind of a crappy gift is this?

Anniversary Husband: Here's your gift dear. Happy first anniversary.
Anniversary Wife: Wow, a notebook. Here's yours.
Anniversary Husband: A family pack of toilet tissue. You're the best.

The official list of anniversary presents now consists of two lists, one designated as traditional and the other as modern. Paper is the first year gift on the traditional list while the modern list states that you should give the couple a clock. How did they get

Etiquette Tip: When Toasting Begins

After the receiving line has ended (finally!) and the wedding party and guests have been seated, everyone is served a glass of champagne or another sparkling beverage. The best man then stands up and toasts the newlyweds. The rest of the guests stand, too, but the bride and groom remain seated. Once the toasting is over, the dancing is started and dinner is served.

from paper to clocks? I have no idea, but the difference continues into the second year when the traditional list specifies a gift of cotton while the modern list indicates china. If you wanted to combine both lists, you could get the couple a set of plates and some dishtowels.

The traditional gift for the third anniversary is leather. Now we're getting somewhere. After three years the bedroom intimacy is starting to wane so why not pick it up with high leather boots or a pony harness? According to the modern list the gift should be of crystal or glass. These are deemed too fragile for use in the bedroom.

The most bizarre gift suggestions come on the seventh anniversary where the traditionalists recommend a gift of wool and/or copper. I guess the ideal gift to cover this base would be a sheep full of pennies. A modern seventh anniversary gift suggestion is a desk set. A desk set? Who would want a stupid desk set for an anniversary present? Do you have to get two desk sets, one for him and one for her? The only present with less romantic content would be a gift certificate for an exterminator. Quite honestly, I would rather have a sheep full of pennies.

Rather than try to conform to someone else's rules, I suggest that you prepare a special toast for the anniversary couple. It is much better than a desk set and it costs nothing. The guidelines for making an anniversary toast are the same making any kind of a toast. If you write it and say it with sincerity, it will be the most touching gift you could give.

Etiquette Tip: Toasting Order

After the best man, the groom can make a toast, then the bride, and then the parents, members of the wedding party, or other special guests can toast the newlyweds. After the toasting is completed, the best man can read any congratulatory telegrams that may have been received.

First Anniversary:

"*I can't believe it's been a year*
Since you two tied the knot
If your marriage were a thermostat,
The reading would be hot, hot, hot."

Second Anniversary:

"*Two years ago we gathered 'round*
To make your wedding day,
And now we celebrate your love,
Stronger in every way."

Third Anniversary:

"Three years have passed since both of you,
Pledged a life of love together,
We hope you both enjoy your gift,
It's a salad bowl made of leather."

Fourth Anniversary:

"Forty-eight months have come and gone,
Since you first said "I do."
So we give this toast to the bride and groom
They've made one out of two"

Fifth Anniversary:

"Your marriage passed another mark
You really are quite lucky.
The five year gift is forks and wood,
Here's a wood fork we got at Stuckey's."

Tenth Anniversary:

"For ten long years you've been a pair
You've gone a lot of places.
And everyone knows you're still in love,
By simply looking at your faces."

Twenty-Fifth Anniversary:

"It's your silver anniversary and we just want you to know
That you were in the perfect place when Cupid shot his bow.
For all these years you've been in love and that sure says a lot,
'Cause 25 years ago today, you were considered a very long shot."

"Love seems the swiftest, but it is the slowest of growths.
No man or woman really knows what perfect love is until they have been married a quarter of a century."
(Mark Twain)

Etiquette Tip: Reception Toasts

Reception toasts are usually a little more serious and sentimental than rehearsal dinner toasts. A toast from the best man could go something like, "To my best friend Jim, and his beautiful new wife Andrea. May we all experience the kind of love and happiness they share."

Etiquette Tip: Special Circumstances

Interim anniversaries celebrated by the two people involved—(one-month, six-month, anniversary of engagement, etc.) are not formal observances. Indeed, the best way to enjoy them most is probably alone.

If a divorced couple remarries, their anniversaries are counted from the date of their original marriage, as though they had never untied the knot.

Although a man or woman whose spouse has died is not, technically speaking, still married, the sense of loss and memory of the deceased will linger. It is a thoughtful gesture to remember the surviving spouse on the anniversary date by sending a brief, uplifting note, not mentioning death, but reminding her or him that you are "thinking of you."

Fiftieth Anniversary:

"*It's been a half a century*
Since you two pressed your lips,
And now you're standing here today
On artificial hips.
So raise your glass and give a toast
To a couple so in love,
That just one look into their eyes
Says this match was made in heaven."

"*With fifty years between you*
And your well-kept wedding vow,
The Golden Age, old friends of mine,
Is not a fable now."
(John Greenleaf Whittier)

On his fiftieth wedding anniversary, Albert Einstein was asked what attributed to the success of his marriage. Here is the response he offered.

"When we first got married, we made a pact. It was this: In our life together, it was decided I would make all of the big decisions and my wife would make all of the little decisions. For fifty years, we have held true to this agreement. I believe that is the reason for the success in our marriage. However, the strange thing is that in fifty years, there hasn't been one big decision."

Seventy-Fifth Anniversary:

"*The love we have in our youth is superficial compared to the love that an old man has for his old wife.*"
(Will Durant)

"*Your seventy-fifth anniversary is your diamond jubilee*
You must have gotten married when the bride was only three.
'Cause you don't look your ages; you look very youthful
and I mean it when I say that I am absolutely truthful."

Just for the record, the record for the longest marriage ever is shared by two couples, both of which survived eighty-six years of

wedded bliss. Sir Temulji Bhicaji Nariman and his wife Lady Nariman were married in 1853 and it lasted until 1940 when Temulji died. I don't know how old he was when he died but he had to be pushing 100...or pulling it.

The other couple tied for first place in the run for the roses are Lazarus Rowe and Molly Weber of New Hampshire who were married in 1743. The union lasted until Molly died in 1829.

I think that we will eventually see someone married for eighty-six years in modern society, but it will probably span fourteen or fifteen spouses. Here is my special toast for anyone married eighty-six years.

> "*Four score and six years ago*
> *You both said "I do."*
> *How anybody could last that long,*
> *I haven't got a clue.*"

In-Between Anniversaries

Not every anniversary is a milestone calling for a special customized toast, but every anniversary certainly deserves some type of toast. Here are some samples that can fit virtually any anniversary occasion. You can use these verses as the foundation for your toast, and, with a little bit of customizing, you can come up with a perfect salute to any anniversary.

> "*On your anniversary I toast you with the words of Sextus Propertius who wisely said, "Never change when love has found its home."*"

> "*Here's to the husband,*
> *And here's to the wife;*
> *May they remain*
> *Lovers for life.*"

> "*Here's to you both,*
> *A beautiful pair,*
> *On the birthday of*
> *Your love affair.*"

Most Married Ever

According to the *Guiness Book of World Records*, the greatest number of marriages ever entered in to by one person—in the monogamous world—is twenty-eight! Glynn "Scotty" Wolfe, a former Baptist minister from Blythe, California, was first married in 1927. He died in 1997. He was probably happy to go.

The record for most monogamous marriages by a woman belongs to Linda Lou Essex of Anderson, Indiana. Linda was married twenty-two times to fifteen different men. She divorced every one of them.

In the world of multiple marriages, Giovanni Vigliotto married 104 times in 27 states and 14 countries. In 1983 he was sentenced to twenty-eight years in prison on the charge of bigamy. He hasn't been married since.

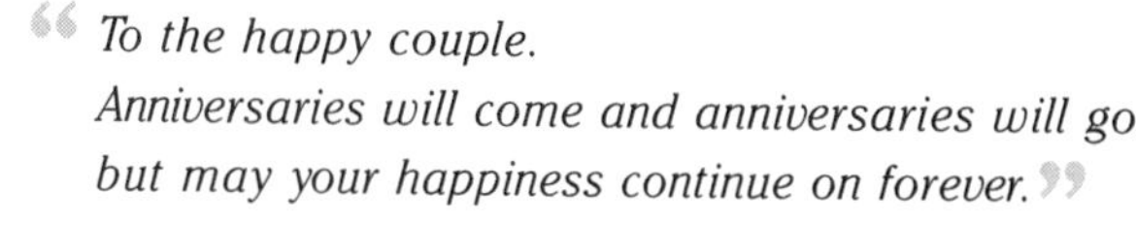

"To the happy couple.
Anniversaries will come and anniversaries will go,
but may your happiness continue on forever."

"May the warmth of your affections continue on forever."

"We've holidays and holy days,
And memory days galore;
And when we've toasted every one,
I offer just one more.
So let us lift our glasses high,
And drink a silent toast,
The day, deep buried in each heart,
That each one loves the most."

"A toast to your anniversary and the love
that has held you together these many years.
When the times are good, it's easy, brother.
When the times are tough is when you need one another."

"Here's to loving, to romance, to us.
May we travel together through time.
We alone count as none, but together we're one,
For our partnership puts love to rhyme."

"To the anniversary couple, the perfect illustration of the old adage:
A good husband makes a good wife;
A good wife makes a good husband."

"To your coming anniversaries—
may they be outnumbered only by your coming pleasures."

"Here's to a couple that stayed together for the kids...and the grandkids, and the great grandkids."

Etiquette Tip: Anniversary Parties

As if the joy of marriage isn't enough, there is the added occasion of the anniversary party. Invitations to an anniversary party are sent by the couple themselves for the first few years, and later (twenty-fifth onward) by their children.

If the gathering is planned as a small party, only family or intimate friends of the couple should be invited. These may be held at home or in a private dining room of a good restaurant. If a larger affair is desired (involving casual friends or business associates), then a restaurant, hotel ballroom, or club may be hired.

Unless age or infirmity precludes it, the honored couple should be stationed near the door to greet guests themselves. Musicians may also be appropriate, although not required (if they are used, be sure they know the tune the couple considers "our song").

"May the warmth of our affections survive the frosts of age."

"Let us love nobly, and live, and add again
Years and years unto years, till we attain
To write threescore: this is the second of our reign."
(John Donne)

"To keep you marriage brimming,
With love in the loving cup,
Whenever you're wrong, admit it;
Whenever you're right, shut up!"
(Ogden Nash)

"Here's a health to the future;
A sigh for the past;
We can love and remember;
And hope to the last,
And for all the base lies
That the almanacs hold
While there's love in the heart,
We can never grow old."

"As we toast this anniversary couple I am reminded of the story of old Hank who lived with his wife for 37 years and never spoke a single word. Then one winter morning at breakfast he looked at his wife and said, "Darlin', sometimes when I think about how much you mean to me it's almost more than I can do to keep from tellin' you.""

"In the words of Sam Levinson, "Love at first sight is easy to understand; it is when two people have been looking at each other for a lifetime that it becomes a miracle.""

"Sam is also credited with saying, "Happy marriages begin when we marry the one we love, and they blossom when we love the one we married.""

An Anniversary Joke

An elderly couple went to their attorney's office and told him that they wanted a divorce. The lawyer looked shocked and said, "How long have the two of you been married to each other?" The old man replied, "Fifty-seven years." "Then why on earth have you decided to get divorced now?" asked the lawyer. The old man looked at his wife, then turned to the lawyer and said, "We wanted to wait until the kids were all dead."

"My dear, we have been through much together, and although we are not as young as we once were, I recall the words of George Gershwin who wrote, The memory of all that—No, no! They can't take that away from me."

"You can tell that this couple have endured many years. (Woman's name) claims that (Man's name) is still only interested in one thing; except now he can't remember what it is."

Here's one from the husband—

"The secret to our success is that on the day we were married I let my wife know who was the boss. I looked her right in the eye and said, "You're the boss.""

"Over the years this couple has learned that it doesn't matter who wears the pants in the family, as long as there's money in the pockets."

"A toast to your anniversary and the devotion and love that has held you together for all these years:

When times are good, it's easy brother,
But when times are tough, that's when you need one another."

"As we toast this anniversary couple, let us remember great couples of the past.
Jack had his Jill and Sonny had Cher,
Till Cher had her fill and left in thin air.
Cleopatra had Tony; Bonnie had Clyde,
But as history taught us, they all up and died.
There was Popeye and Olive, Roy Rogers and Dale,
Jim Bakker had Tammy 'till he went off to jail.
But when our loving couple heard those church bells chime,
They vowed to be partners till the end of all time.
So we raise up our glasses and offer this cheer,
May you two be together for many more years."

"After _____ years together, I asked the bride (or use her name) if (man's name) was still the man she married and she said, "Are you kidding, he's almost twice that now.""

"When this couple married, (woman's name) said that she married (man's name) for better, for worse, for richer, for poorer, and she is bound and determined to stay with him until things start getting better and richer."

"Our anniversary couple has been married for quite a number of years now but we're not certain how many. Apparently it has been longer for her than it has been for him."

"As we toast the anniversary couple we need to remember that anniversaries are sometimes the hardest things for men to remember. Women, on the other hand always remember their anniversary. When I asked my wife if she had ever forgotten the day we were married she said "No, I've never forgotten the day we were married although heaven knows there have been times that I have tried.""

Some toasts are meant to be very sincere while others are meant to connote an air of levity. Here are some humorous lines and ideas you can use to construct a light-hearted anniversary toast.

"Here's a toast to the many good times you've enjoyed together...
And to the one or two that you just tolerated."

"A toast to your anniversary. You've had many good years together, either that or one heck of a prenuptial agreement."

"Many years ago, our guests of honor set sail on the sea of matrimony. And tonight, despite a few barnacles, they're still afloat."

Anniversary Commemoratives

Theater critic Alexander Woollcott once wrote the following message to his friends George and Beatrice Kaufman on the occasion of their fifth wedding anniversary: "I've been looking around for an appropriate wooden gift and am pleased to present you with Elsie Ferguson's performance in her new play." Woollcott was correct in noting that the fifth anniversary is the "wooden" one that may be honored with an item crafted from wood.

Wedding Anniversary Gifts

	Traditional	Modern	Stone Age
First	Paper	Clocks	Rock
Second	Cotton	China	Rock
Third	Leather	Crystal/Glass	Rock
Fourth	Fruit/Flowers	Appliances	Big Rock
Fifth	Wood	Silverware	Rock on a stick
Sixth	Candy/Iron	Wood	Dirt
Seventh	Wool/Copper	Desk Sets	Pointy Stick
Eighth	Bronze/Pottery	Linens/Lace	Poke in the Eye
Ninth	Pottery/Willow	Leather	Dead Animal
Tenth	Tin/Aluminum	Diamond Jewelry	Dead Animal on a Stick
Eleventh	Steel	Fashion Jewelry	Sea Shell
Twelfth	Silk/Linen	Pearls	Anything Edible
Thirteenth	Lace	Textiles/Furs	Stuff from Tar Pit
Fourteenth	Ivory	Gold Jewelry	Bone
Fifteenth	Crystal	Watches	Animal hide
Twentieth	China	Platinum	New Cave
Twenty-Fifth	Silver	Silver	Seeds
Thirtieth	Pearl	Diamond	Something Shiny
Thirty-Fifth	Coral	Jade	Egg
Fortieth	Ruby	Ruby	Back Scratcher
Forty-Fifth	Sapphire	Sapphire	Bugs
Fiftieth	Gold	Gold	Fur
Fifty-Fifth	Emerald	Emerald	Something Green
Sixtieth	Diamond	Diamond	Coal
Seventieth	Platinum	Platinum	Anything

“To two people who were made for each other. Think about it, who else would have them?”

“For their anniversary he bought something for the house...a round of drinks.”

“The loving couple has already exchanged their anniversary gifts. He gave her a piece of cheap jewelry and she gave him a piece of her mind.”

“Henny Youngman said that for his anniversary his wife wanted to go someplace that she had never been before. So he took her to the kitchen.”

“For this anniversary, he decided to get his wife something that she has been wanting since 1981; a Cadillac automobile. So this year he bought her...a 1981 Cadillac.”

“For her anniversary she told a friend that she wanted to get something that's useful around the house. He overheard her and got worried. He thought she was going to get another husband.”

“She had a terrible time trying to pick out an anniversary gift for her husband. It's hard to find something for the man who has everything but she said it's even harder to get something for the man who understands nothing.”

“Marriage is for a lifetime...with no opportunity for parole.”

“He said that he threw away their marriage license and she asked him why. He said, if marriage is a lifetime commitment, there's no need to save the receipt.”

> *I am so happy to see this couple married for ___ years. Myself, I've been married for 27 years...but it took me three wives to get up to that number.*

> *Let us toast the anniversary couple who have been together longer than any of us ever thought they would be.*

> *Raise your glasses and offer a toast,*
> *To this loving couple of whom we can boast.*
> *They've been together for so many years,*
> *Through laughter and good times; sadness and tears.*
> *She still thinks he's handsome, he still makes her swoon.*
> *To their years together—One long honeymoon.*

Of course, not all marriages are of the fairy tale variety. Some more closely resemble a Steven King novel. If you are toasting a couple who has remained together despite the odds, you may wish to consider a toast similar to the following:

> *To a couple who fits together like oil and water, like apples and oranges, like cats and dogs. We don't know how you stayed together all these years, but we're happy you did. Otherwise we wouldn't be having this party tonight.*

Christening Toasts

In the Christian religion, the baptism of a newborn represents the soul of the child being committed to the Lord. It is a solemn yet happy occasion that is usually followed by a big party that the baby misses because he is taking a nap. Nonetheless, christening toasts are delivered to the parents of the baby and can be delivered by the godparents, the grandparents, or the real parents. In fact, they can be delivered by anybody. The baby, on the other hand, should only be delivered by a licensed medical professional.

If you are a stickler for propriety, etiquette states that the first toast offered to the newly christened child is given by the godparents. This is then followed by a toast given by the parents. After the parents have toasted their new baby, the brothers and sisters of the child are welcome to propose a toast. If they are very young, however, the toast may not be the most eloquent selection you have ever heard.

> *"Here's to my baby brother.*
> *If I catch him breaking any of my toys he's history."*

Finally, in this atmosphere of formality, the guests are invited to propose a toast. Here are some samples.

> *"A baby will make love stronger, days shorter, nights longer, bankroll smaller, home happier, clothes shabbier, the past forgotten, and the future worth living for."*

> *"A new life begun,*
> *Like father like son."*

> *"Here's to the baby—man to be,*
> *May he be as fine as thee."*

> *"Like one, like the other,*
> *Like daughter, like mother."*

> *"Here's to baby—woman to be,*
> *May she be as sweet as thee."*

> *"May this be the last bath at which your baby cries."*

> *"In Nicholas Nickleby, Charles Dickens wrote,*
> *"Every baby born into the world is a finer one than the last.*

> *"Father of fathers, make me one,*
> *A fit example for a son."*
> *(Douglas Malloch)*

> *"Here's a toast to your new baby...*
> *because nobody wants to give birth to an old baby."*

Baptismal Notice

Notice in a church bulletin: We now have baptismal fonts in the north and south ends of the church. Babies will now be baptized on both ends.

If you, as the toaster, are a little older than the proud new parents, you may want to use this toast, which is direct and funny.

> *"A toast to your blessed event. For people your age, that means you've had a baby. For people my age, blessed event means you've won the lottery."*

> *"Here's to the stork, a most valuable bird,*
> *That inhabits the residence districts.*
> *He doesn't sing tunes, nor yield any plumes,*
> *But he helps with the vital statistics."*

> *"The stork has brought a little peach!"*
> *The nurse said with an air.*
> *"I'm mighty glad" the father said,*
> *"He didn't bring a pair."*

> *"To quiet nights and dry diapers."*

> *"Mark Twain put forth this toast most elegantly when he said, "We haven't all the good fortune to be ladies; we have not all been generals, or poets or statesmen; but when the toast works down to babies we stand on common ground. We've all been babies."*

> *"A generation of children on the children of your children."*

Confirmation Toasts

Confirmation is another rite of passage followed in the Christian religion. It represents the acceptance of young people as members of the church body. It is bestowed upon them after they have successfully completed a course of study about their religion. Catholic denominations generally celebrate confirmation in the form of First Communion. When a child is approximately eight years old, he or she is instructed in the catechism to prepare them for First Communion. At the ceremony, they experience the sacrament of communion, or the sharing of the body and blood of Christ for the first time.

Protestant denominations usually practice confirmation when the child is about thirteen and has undergone similar religious studies. At this point they too are welcomed to partake of communion with the other church members. Of course, variations in these broad guidelines exist among the different Christian factions, but the general theory remains the same.

In either case—First Communion or Confirmation—the religious ceremony is followed by a celebration in the form of a party, most likely held at the home of the newly confirmed child. It is at this party that the child experiences the real reason he or she studied so diligently for this day: envelopes filled with money.

Most of the toasts given at a confirmation party will take the form of generic prose wishing the child a long life, happiness, and many blessings. Here, however, are some specialized ones that you may wish to add to your repertoire.

A Quote for Toasts

"The man or woman you really love will never grow old to you. Through the wrinkles of time, through the bowed frame of years, you will always see the dear face and feel the warm heart union of your eternal love."

—Alfred A. Montpert

“In the words of Ralph Waldo Emerson, “God enters by a private door into each individual.” May this young person's door always be open to the lord.”

“The truth shall make you free.”
(John 8:32)

“As this child enters the membership of the church, let us remember Paul's words to the Galatians, “As we have therefore opportunity, let us do good unto all men.””
(Galatians 6:10)

“No longer a child
You're a soldier of God
So pray right now
That he finds you a job.”

Bar Mitzvah Toasts

As confirmation is to the Christian faith, Bar Mitzvah (or Bat Mitzvah, for girls) is to the Jewish faith. The celebration represents the uniting of a young person with the membership of the congregation, and the passage into adulthood. Bar Mitzvahs occur around the time the child turns thirteen and usually involves a religious ceremony, and a party. It is inappropriate to make a toast during the religious ceremony, but definitely expected of either the parents or grandparents at the reception. And if you have a particularly theatrical child, he or she can make a toast as well.

At the reception or party, there are traditional prayers recited before the meal begins. These prayers are not considered toasts. There are almost always at least two prayers recited: a prayer over the traditional bread (challah), and a prayer over the wine. Although many of the celebrants are not of legal drinking age, the prayer over the wine can be made over any type of fruit beverage—grape, kiwi, apple, whatever. Whoever is making these prayers simply asks all guest to raise their glasses in honor of the Bar Mitzvah celebrant.

The moments following this prayer might be a good time for the toast. Another alternative would be when the dessert is served. The general Jewish toast of "Mazel Tov" is quite acceptable at Bar Mitzvahs or any Jewish gathering where the word "congratulations" is meant to be applied.

Generally, a child would toast his/her parents, and thank teachers, friends, and family for attending, making special note of people who are particularly close, or those who have traveled from very far away.

Parents or grandparents might share a story from their own experience of Bar Mitzvah. Even nicer would be a personal story about the child: one that demonstrates their qualities of adulthood. These stories should not be embarrassing to the child, as this celebration honors the child, and not the parents. Keep in mind that teens can be particularly sensitive to having so much attention drawn to them, so that even a good-humored jab could be taken the wrong way. So make your toast thoughtful, and brief, and go back to enjoying the party.

Graduation Toasts

Just about all of us graduate from one level to another at some time in our lives. The most common milestones of graduation are high school, college, law school, medical school, and graduate school. Each of these occasions calls for a party, and as we know by now, every party calls for a toast.

High School Graduation

America's high school graduation rate is over 80 percent. This means that you have a real good shot at attending a high school graduation party at least once in your lifetime. Accepting this fact, you should prepare yourself immediately.

High school graduation is the first major accomplishment of many young people. They have completed the required level of education and now hold their futures in their own hands. For the first time in their life, high school graduates are free to pursue their own path. In other words, it's a big deal.

One thing to remember in proposing a high school graduation toast is that the person you are toasting is not yet old enough to drink, unless they have been in high school for a very long time. Because of this you should avoid any references to beer, wine, hooch, moonshine, or likker when making your toast. For instance, this would be considered a high school graduation toast of poor taste:

> *"Congratulations graduate*
> *I think it's plain to see,*
> *That you've been drinking lots of beer*
> *That you bought with a fake I.D."*

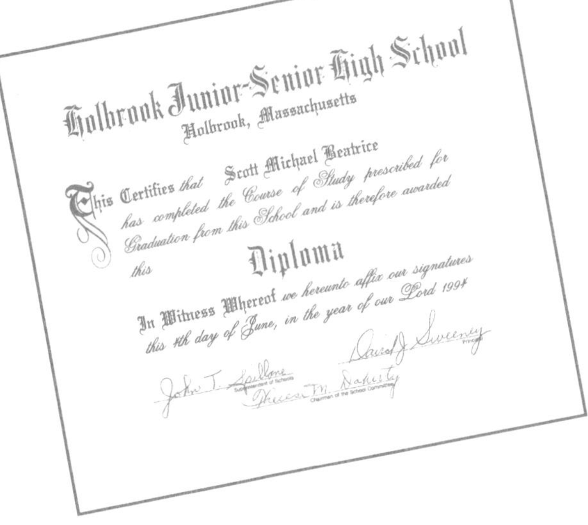

Holbrook Junior-Senior High School
Holbrook, Massachusetts

This Certifies that Scott Michael Beatrice has completed the Course of Study prescribed for Graduation from this School and is therefore awarded this

Diploma

In Witness Whereof we hereunto affix our signatures this 4th day of June, in the year of our Lord 1994

Once again, use your common sense along with a little research and you can put together a high school graduation toast that will be long remembered.

> *"A toast to the graduate—in a class by himself (or herself, as the situation warrants)"*

"To our fine educations, may they go to our heads."

*"Let him be kept from paper, pen, and ink.
That he may cease to write and learn to think."*

*"Calculus and English Lit.
American History,
You have finally made it through
With a grade point of a C."*

"As you depart from the odyssey of high school, may you take the things you have learned and use them to your advantage on the rest of life's adventures."

"You may not have been the brightest student, the most gifted athlete, or the homecoming queen, but we're proud of you son."

"As phase one of your education fades away and phase two comes into view, we wish you the brightest future filled with hopes, dreams, and promises of a wonderful life."

When we think about high school graduation, we can't help but think about how much the educational process has changed over the years. I remember the old song that had lyrics like this:

*"School days, school days,
Good old golden rule days.
Reading and writing and 'rithmetic,
Taught to the tune of a hickory stick."*

Not only do kids today not know what a hickory stick is but any teacher who even thought of brandishing one would be brought to court on charges of student abuse. If that song were to be rewritten for today, the lyrics might go more like this:

> *"School days, school days,*
> *Let's break all the rule days.*
> *Piercings and brandings and big tattoos,*
> *We'll do to our bodies whatever we choose."*

Mark Twain had much to say about education and his words can form the foundation for many graduation toasts. Here are some of my favorites:

> *"Training is everything. The peach was once a bitter almond; cauliflower is nothing but cabbage with a college education."*
>
> Pudd'nhead Wilson

> *"Soap and education are not as sudden as a massacre, but they are more deadly in the long run."*
>
> The Facts Concerning The Recent Resignation

> *"In the first place God made idiots. This was for practice. Then He made School Boards."*
>
> Following The Equator

> *"I am thankful that the good God created us all ignorant. I am glad that when we change His plans in this regard we have to do it at our own risk."*
>
> *In a letter to the San Francisco Alta California*

If a teacher or two are invited to your graduation party, it would be a nice idea to offer a toast to him or her as a salute to their contribution to your education.

> *"A toast to the teachers. In the words of Margret Mead, 'The most extraordinary thing about a really good teacher is that he or she transcends accepted educational methods. Such methods are designed to help average teachers approximate the performance of good teachers.' We toast your extraordinary methods and their wonderful results."*

If you are the graduate, you may wish to propose a toast to your parents for their support throughout the years. Here's one of my favorites.

> *"To Mom and Dad*
> *Who have helped me so far,*
> *May I ask one small favor?*
> *The keys to the car."*

College Graduation

After four (or more) long years, the college graduate is finally ready to enter the workforce and become a significant member of society. Gone are the days of dorm life, all-night parties, and wild weekends. When graduates receive their sheepskin, they say good-bye to their youth and hello to the responsibilities of adulthood.

Because of this awesome obligation, a college graduation toast should wish the graduate a bright future and much success. It should not point out the fact that they just finished the best days of their lives and don't even realize it yet.

> *"To the future, and the leaders of tomorrow."*

> *"To the graduate:*
> *You have fought a good fight. You have finished the course. You have kept the faith. Congratulations on your accomplishment and all the best in your future."*

> *"Congratulations on your achievement. Over the last four years you have spent 1,725 hours attending fraternity parties; 2,334 hours sitting in the student union doing nothing; and almost 4.5 hours actually studying. We don't know how you did it but we're glad you did."*

> *"Today is the biggest day of your life;*
> *It's yours and yours alone.*
> *Now go out and tackle the world my friend,*
> *And pay back your student loan."*

"Now that you are a college graduate remember that a college degree does not guarantee you success, happiness, or intellectual fulfillment. All it guarantees you is that you will get regular correspondence from your alma mater asking for donations."

"You've earned a Bachelor of Science,
By passing all of the tests.
But remember what your degree really means,
You're a specialist with B.S."

"Now that you have graduated, you have climbed a rung on the ladder of maturity. As you go through your life remember that maturity means:
Sticking with a job until it is finished;
Bearing an injustice without wanting to get even;
Being able to carry money without spending it;
And doing one's duty without being supervised."

"As you leave the world of academia and enter the world of reality, remember that the best way to change the world is to set an example for others to follow."

"As a college graduate I'm sure you can remember the words of Epictetus, the stoic Greek philosopher who said, 'We are not to give credit to the many, who say that none ought to be educated but the free; but rather to the philosophers, who say that the well educated alone are free.'"

"As Benjamin Disraeli once said, 'A University should be a place of light, of liberty, and of learning.' Today we toast your enlightenment, your liberation, and your knowledge."

"We have always believed in you, through and through;
Even though just last year, your grade point was 2.
But we knew that you'd graduate because you are scrappy,
Now go get a job and make us all happy."

A Lawyer Joke

A man and his wife were worried about their son and what he would become when he grew up. The man said to his wife, "Let's give him a little test. We will put a $10 bill on the table along with a Bible and a bottle of whiskey. If he goes for the money he will become a banker; if he goes for the Bible, he will be a minister; and if he goes for the whiskey, he will become a bum."

They set the items on the table and hid behind a door just as the young lad walked into the room. As they watched him he picked up the $10 bill and put it in his pocket, he picked up the Bible and hid it under his coat, and he picked up the whiskey and chugged the contents in one motion. Then he walked out of the room whistling.

The man turned to his wife and said, "Well I'll be darned, he's going to be a lawyer."

"Always remember that your education is important. It's what you have left over after you have forgotten everything you have learned."

"As we toast the graduate, we hope for only one thing—that he has not been educated above his intelligence."

"As you pass from the experience of college to the experience of life, remember the words of Horace Mann, a teacher who said, 'Education alone can conduct us to that enjoyment which is, at once, best in quality and infinite in quantity.'"

"This day you will toss up the caps in bliss
You will start up your plans for career
Graduating from this day I hope you won't miss
All the days you tossed up all those beers."

"Now that you have a college degree, may you go out into the world and become educated."

"A toast to the graduate who has put in hard work,
endured long hours,
and studied diligently; my only advice to you
is to go out and make the world better by making
a difference."

It is not unusual for the graduate to offer a toast to all of the family and friends that join together to help him celebrate. Here are some examples of toasts by the graduate.

"To my parents. Thank you for your support, your help, and most of all, your money. I fully intend to pay back the support and help."

"A toast to my family and my friends who join me in celebrating this graduation day. The more schooling that I receive and the more knowledge I attain only reinforces what

I have known all along, that you are the greatest gifts with which I have ever been blessed."

"*It's hard to believe that four years ago I couldn't even spell education, and now I done got myself one.*"

Law School Graduation

At last count, we had approximately 946,499 lawyers in this country. That works out to about one lawyer for every 276 people. At this point in time we probably have more lawyers than we really need. In the words of Shakespeare, from *Henry VI*, "The first thing we do, let's kill all the lawyers." We have all had occasion to use a lawyer from time to time and may even have attorneys as friends, but there is something about the noble profession of jurisprudence that causes people to react the same way they do when they see a large rodent, i.e., "Quick, hit it with a shovel."

But attorneys have invested many years of education in learning their art and deserve to be toasted upon the completion of their studies as much as anybody else. So to law school graduates everywhere, "Quick, get a shovel."

"*A good lawyer knows the law.*
A great lawyer knows the judge."

"*A bumper of good liquor*
Will end a contest quicker
Than justice, judge or vicar;
So fill a cheerful glass,
And let good humor pass."
(Richard Brinsley Sheridan)

Here's a toast to a person of great trials and many convictions. (Note: this is not a good toast for someone about to become a defense lawyer)

"*Here's to the lawyer, a bright man who rescues your estate from your enemies, and keeps it himself.*"

"And whether you're an honest man,
Or whether you're a thief,
Depends on whose solicitor
Has given me my brief."
(W.S. Gilbert)

"A countryman between two lawyers is like a fish between two cats."
(Benjamin Franklin)

"A lean award is better than a fat judgment."
(Benjamin Franklin)

"Justice while she winks at crimes,
Stumbles on innocence sometimes."
(Samuel Butler)

"Let us drink to the law school graduate and remember the words of Joseph Choate, who once said, 'You cannot live without lawyers, and certainly you cannot die without them.'"

"May we always lie upon our left sides, since the law will not permit us to sleep on our rights."

"The law: It has honored us; may we honor it."
(Daniel Webster)

"'Virtue in the middle' said the devil, as he seated himself between two lawyers."

"The illegal we do immediately. The unconstitutional takes a little longer."
(Henry Kissinger)

"Lawyers are the only persons in whom ignorance of the law is not punished."
(Jeremy Bentham)

"As you enter the noble legal profession, let us remember the words of Mae West who once said, 'it ain't no sin if you crack a few laws now and then, just so long as you don't break any.'"

"When a festive occasion our spirit unbends,
We should never forget the profession's best friends.
So we'll pass 'round the wine
And a light bumper fill
To the jolly testator who makes his own will."

"Some people think about sex all the time, some people think of sex some of the time, and some people never think about sex; they become lawyers."
(Woody Allen)

"If it does not fit, you must acquit."
(Johnny Cochran)

"If law school is so hard to get through, how come there are so many lawyers?"
(Calvin Trillin)

"The laws of God, the laws of man,
He may keep that will and can;
Not I; let God and man decree
Laws for themselves and not for me."
(E. Houseman)

Know Your Laws

It is an attorney's job to know the law but it doesn't hurt for the common layman to be familiar with it as well. Here are some laws you should know.

Law of Gravity—What goes up, must come down. This law does not apply to blood pressure.

Law of the Jungle—Anything Tarzan does is all right. Any other humans are to be killed and eaten.

Law of Supply and Demand—If you have something that somebody wants, you can charge as much as you can get. If you have something that nobody wants, put it on sale.

The Speed of Light—This is established at 186,000 miles per second. If you break the speed of light you could be sent to federal prism.

"He saw a lawyer killing a viper
On a dunghill hard by his own stable;
And the devil smiled, for it put him in mind
Of Cain and his brother Abel."
(Samuel Taylor Coleridge)

"I learned law so well, the day I graduated I sued the college, won the case, and got my tuition back."
(Fred Allen)

Medical School Graduation

The time and effort that some invest in education in order to be called doctor often amazes me. There is, of course, four years of undergraduate work, followed by four more years of medical school, followed by internship, followed by residency, all to get hired by an HMO. Graduation from medical school is indeed a big event in a doctor's life. Celebrate this event with a toast Hippocrates would be proud of.

"You've sewn up flesh,
You've cast out germs,
You've even reset bones.
Now your last challenge
Before you rest,
Is paying your student loans."

"We toast the new doctor with a special drink. It is a daiquiri made with the essence of the hickory tree, said to impart divine knowledge. So raise your glasses to the new physician, it's a Hickory Daiquiri, Doc."

"Congratulations doctor
I've imagined for a long time
Your name with this degree
So raise your glasses high my friends,
To (name here) M.D."

"Unto our doctors let us drink,
Who cure our chills and ills,
No matter what we really think
About their pills and bills."
(Philip McAllister)

"Let us raise our glasses to the new doctor, a person whom we will trust with our lives and our fortunes."

"Here's to the new doctor—may the rest of us never need your services."

"To mankind we drink; 'tis a pleasant task;
Heaven bless it and multiply its wealth.
But it is a little too much to ask,
That we should drink to its health."

"God heals, and the doctor takes the fees."
(Benjamin Franklin)

For Dentists

Dentists are among the least liked people on earth. It is not that folks hate the *people* who are dentists, they just hate the idea of having to go visit someone who uses an electric drill to put holes in their head and makes them spit into a tiny toilet bowl. The problem I have always had with dentists is that when they examine your teeth they tell you that the X-rays are perfectly safe. Then, they go and hide in another room while millions of roentgens (dangerous invisible death rays) penetrate your body. If the X-rays are so safe, why don't they stay in the same room with us rather than skulking off to their bunker. How are you supposed to trust someone like this?

I once had a friend who was graduating from dental school approach me and ask me to help him with his final exam. Now I don't know a lot about dentistry, but I figured if I could provide this guy with a couple of answers I would be more than happy to help

Making the Perfect Daiquiri

The daiquiri is named after the village of Daiquiri in eastern Cuba. I think it is located between the towns of Bacardi and Mai Tai. The daiquiri is a rum-based drink and the perfect libation for summer afternoons. The basic cocktail is made with 2 ounces of light rum, ½ ounce of lime juice, and ½ teaspoon of sugar. Simply combine these ingredients with a lot of ice in a cocktail shaker and shake vigorously. Serve in an old-fashioned glass . . . or a new fangled one if you don't have old fashioned ones lying around. You can also flavor your daiquiri to suit your particular taste by adding ingredients such as bananas, strawberries, guava, passion fruit, orange juice, or any other flavor you desire. Hickory is not a good flavor to add unless you are going for a woody flavor.

out. Unfortunately, he didn't want me for my knowledge, he wanted me for my cavities.

A dentist's final exam consists of working on a real live patient in front of a real live doctor who has the power to pass or fail the student. Oh, no pressure here! Let me just say that you never want to have your teeth worked on by a nervous dental student who is faced with the choice of either passing the exam and becoming a dentist or failing the exam and having to get a real job. To impress the examiner, my "friend" drilled holes in several of my teeth, some of which did not previously have holes in them. I guess he was going for quantity rather than quality. The most amazing thing to me was that he actually passed the exam and today is a practicing dentist. I just won't ever let him practice on me again.

Graduation toasts for those graduating from dental school are different than toasts for those graduating from medical school. For one thing, when the toast is given, the drink is held in the mouth until the new dentist gives the word to "rinse and spit."

“*To the man (or woman) who deals with the tooth, the whole tooth, and nothing but the tooth.*”

“*To the new dentist who will make his living hand to mouth.*”

“*Congrats, you are a dentist now,*
We're filled with lots of pride.
'Cause now we have some place to go,
To get nitrous oxide.”

“*To the new dentist, the top of his class,*
The best we have ever seen.
When you open your practice, all that we ask,
Is get some new magazines.”

“*'Open wide' my dentist said,*
'Let's have a look around.'
Then he picked up his drilling tool
Which made that awful sound.

So I reached out and grabbed him hard,
And he started to turn blue.
I said, 'Hey doc I got a deal,
Don't hurt me and I won't hurt you.'"

Other Advanced Degrees

In addition to doctors and lawyers, there are many other advanced degrees offered every year. So many in fact, that it would be impossible to list all of them here. Here is a sampling of toasts for other graduates from fields of higher learning.

"You've studied hard, you've studied long,
You've studied ever faster.
But now, at last, it's all paid off,
Today you got your masters."

We all know what B.S. is and M.S. means more of the same. But today you have a Ph.D. which simply stands for a Pile Higher and Deeper. Here's a toast to somebody who really knows his . . . stuff.

"It's been _____ long years but you got every education tool. The biggest news to all of us is that you're finally out of school."

"Education is an ornament in prosperity and a refuge in adversity."
(Aristotle)

"Plato once said that 'Knowledge which is acquired under compulsion obtains no hold on the mind.'"

"Here's to your advanced degree and to your yearning and desire."

Birthday Toasts

Birthdays are the one characteristic all humans have in common—well, that and belly buttons—and celebrating those birthdays is at the very least one holiday that we will have every year. With this is mind, birthday toasts should be among the most universal toasts of all. We will start off with some generic birthday toasts and move to some special toasts for those special birthday milestones.

While it may not be thought of as a toast per se, the song "Happy Birthday" contains all of the necessary ingredients found in a toast. The only difference is that instead of hoisting a glass at the end of the toast, the person being toasted extinguishes the fire on his or her birthday cake. Just in case you have been living in a cave all of your life and this is the first book you have ever read, the traditional birthday singing toast goes like this.

> "*Happy Birthday to you,*
> *Happy Birthday to you,*
> *Happy Birthday dear (your name here),*
> *Happy Birthday to you.*"

Like other toasts, this song also has its variations. For instance my wife's family likes to display their Catholic background by adding a second verse to the toast:

> "*Happy Birthday to you*
> *In all that you do,*
> *May Mary and Joseph,*
> *Smile down upon you.*"

My family, on the other hand, enjoyed adding a note of levity to the second verse of the toast by changing the words to:

> "*Happy Birthday to you,*
> *Happy Birthday to you,*
> *You look like a monkey,*
> *And you smell like one too.*"

Here are some other non-singing toasts for the next birthday you celebrate.

*"Another candle on your cake?
Well, that's no cause to pout.
Be glad that you have strength enough
To blow the damn thing out."*

*"Another year older?
Think this way;
Just one day older
Than yesterday."*

*"To your birthday, glasses held high,
Glad it's you that's older—not I."*

*"To wish you joy on your birthday
And all the whole year through,
For all the best that life can hold
Is none too good for you."*

*"Happy birthday to you
And many to be,
With friends that are true
As you are to me."*

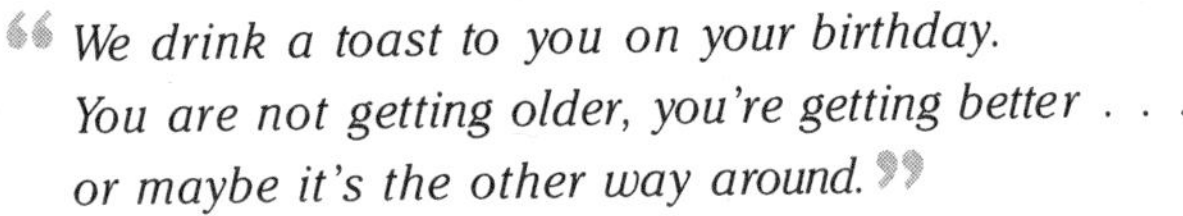

*"We drink a toast to you on your birthday.
You are not getting older, you're getting better . . .
or maybe it's the other way around."*

*"Remember, you're not getting older, you're getting better . . .
You are also getting wider, balder, crankier, and more
forgetful."*

*"We drink a toast to your birthday.
It was either that or chip in some money and buy you a
present."*

"You know you are getting older when you stoop down to tie your shoes and wonder what else you can do while you're down there."

(George Burns)

"Many happy returns on the day of your birth;
Many blessings to brighten your pathway on earth;
Many friendships to cheer and provoke you to mirth;
Many feastings and frolics to add to your girth."

(Robert H. Lord)

"Here's to you! No matter how old you are, you don't look it."

The Irish have always had a way with the words of a toast, and this simple birthday message is no different.

"May you live to be a hundred years with one extra year to repent."

"God grant you many and happy years,
Till, when the last has crowned you,
The dawn of endless days appears,
And heaven is shining round you!"

(Oliver Wendell Holmes)

"A health, and many of them. Birthdays were never like this when I had 'em."

"May you have been born on you lucky star and may that star never lose its twinkle."

"May you live all the years of your life."

(Jonathan Swift)

> *May you live as long as you want*
> *And may you never want as long as you live.*

Twenty-First Birthday—Now You Can Drink Toasts

Twenty-one is the age of majority in this country. When you reach twenty-one years of age you can participate in any legal activity that this land has to offer. You can drink alcohol in any of the fifty states. You can own land, get married, get divorced, gamble, and hold political office. In other words, you are your own dog when you reach twenty-one.

The most common way to celebrate this introduction to adulthood is to consume your own body weight in alcohol. At least this is what my friends and I did when we turned twenty-one. I only hope that my daughter has more common sense than I did when she reaches this chronological milestone.

> *You don't look like twenty-one*
> *I think that's plain to see.*
> *But now at least you will not need*
> *That counterfeit I.D.*

> *When I was one and twenty*
> *I heard a wise man say,*
> *'Give crowns and pounds and guineas*
> *But not your heart away;*
> *Give pearls away and rubies,*
> *But keep your fancy free.'*
> *But I was one and twenty*
> *No use to talk to me.*
> (A.E. Housman)

> *Today you have turned twenty-one,*
> *You'll watch your dreams unfurl,*
> *I just suggest you watch your drinks,*
> *So that you do not hurl.*

Fortieth Birthday—Welcome To Midlife Crisis Toasts

Forty is one of the roughest birthdays to weather. When you reach this age you realize that you are not going to be a millionaire before forty; you realize that the Chicago Cubs are not going to call you to play second base; and you realize that women you lust for are now calling you "sir."

It is also a time when your waist gets thicker while your hair gets thinner. For women, forty represents the end of the child-bearing years and the beginning of those years when it takes longer and longer to try to look younger and younger.

Since the average life span for men in this country is about seventy-three and for women it is seventy-eight, turning forty means that you are most definitely on the downside of the life cycle. You have passed the midpoint and are closer to the nursing home than you are to high school. Before you know it you will be entering your second childhood. By this I mean that you will once again be wearing diapers, using a walker to get around, and waking up in the middle of the night to go to the bathroom. Life is on the downward slide and you are going to fight it all the way.

So how do we fight the fact that for the first time in our lives we worry that Social Security will be available for us? It's easy, we act like idiots. Women will have face lifts, tummy tucks, and constant hair color changes, while men will opt for sports cars, trophy wives, and season tickets to sporting events where they can watch men half their age earn more money in one night than they will earn in the next five years.

It's tough being forty, but in the words of the old philosopher, it beats the alternative. If you or your friends are preparing to take the journey "over the hill", here are some toasts to use for their bon voyage party.

"So now you're really over the hill
Like a barrel falling over Niagara.
Hey, don't you despair,
You've still got some hair
And for the rest there's a pill called Viagra."

"It's amazing just to ponder
That forty years ago
A little baby first cried out
And then began to grow.
Then fell and took some stitches
Then talked out loud in class.
For forty years
You've been a prince (queen)
And a royal pain in the ass."

"Lordy, lordy, look who's forty."

"Life begins at forty."
(A popular adage)

"Happy fortieth birthday and remember, when your parents were your age, they were OLD."

"Be wise with speed;
A fool at forty is a fool indeed."
(Edward Young)

"One time we were the same age,
But now I am behind.
'Cause though you're turning forty,
I'm remaining thirty-nine."

"To our favorite old hippie. I want to remind you that this is a real celebration and not an acid flashback."

"To middle age, which Don Marquis once described as 'the time when a man is always thinking that in a week or two he will feel as good as ever.'"

"To Europe, where they believe that women get more attractive after thirty five, of course, we all believe that too."

Etiquette Tip: The Big Four-O

Years ago the caution was, "Never trust anybody over thirty." Now that baby boomers are getting older, the battle cry has become "Never trust anybody under thirty." Somewhere in the middle of that skirmish is the fortieth birthday and, with it, the fortieth birthday party.

Self-help babble aside, you're as old as younger people make you feel. Hitting "the big four-o" can be a devastating event for some people, and a party calling attention to it can be worse. Before throwing a fortieth birthday party for a friend, make sure he or she wants one.

In general, cards that call attention to a person's age—or are otherwise vulgar or cruel—demean the giver as well as the getter. In the end, the nicest card is the one you write yourself, not just sign.

An Old Joke

Three clergymen were trying to decide when life actually begins. The Protestant minister stood up and said, "We believe that life begins at the moment of birth." The Catholic priest then stood and said, "We believe that life begins at the moment of conception." Finally the old rabbi stood up and said, "No, you're both wrong. When the kids move away and the dog dies, *this* is when life begins."

> *"To middle age, when we begin to exchange our emotions for symptoms."*

> *"Here's to a man who has discovered what really separates the men from the boys—many years."*

Fifty-Fifth Birthday—Time To Join The AARP Toasts

Congratulations! You have achieved the milestone of fifty-five, or is it millstone? You are beginning to discover that your bodily functions have a mind of their own. You think that it is normal when going for a ride in the car with another couple for the men to sit in the front seat while the women sit in the back. And you start to take car rides strictly for the sake of taking car rides. You have no destination in mind but just head out to "the country" and look for yard sales.

Good restaurants are no longer defined by their cuisine or the training of their sous chef, but by whether or not they accept coupons and offer an "early bird" special. You will start going to dinner at 4 P.M. and going to bed at 9 P.M.

When you get together with your friends you no longer talk about your dreams and aspirations but rather about your medical problems and your mutual fund performance. Terms like "those damn kids nowadays" and "pot luck supper" start to creep into your vocabulary. Your biggest financial commitment is no longer your house but your kid's college tuition, or even worse, your kid's house.

You are starting to pay more attention to those commercials for hearing aids and hemorrhoid ointments, and the only thing you notice about the "kid's music" is that it is LOUD. Here, then, are some toast for those of you who have turned the corner on youth.

> *"You're not as young as you used to be*
> *but you're not as old as you're going to be, so watch it!"*

> *"To you and wine which both improve with age.*
> *I like you both more the older I get."*

"Here's to absent friends—both the long-lost friends
of our youth
and our long lost youth."

"To age. In the words of Frank Lloyd Wright, 'The longer I live, the more beautiful life becomes.'"

"To the most closely guarded secret in this country—your real age."

"To a man who is aging wonderfully. Nothing about you is getting old except a few of your jokes.
Or, put another way;
May you live to be as old as your jokes."

"Only the good die young. You, my friend, have a good shot at living forever."

"May you live to be 100—and decide the rest for yourself."

"May we keep a little of the fuel of youth to warm our body in old age."

"To the old, long life and treasure;
To the young, all health and pleasure."
(Ben Jonson)

Sixty-fifth Birthday—Crack Open The IRA Toasts

Welcome to the golden years. By now you have retired from your career and can look forward to spending your days watching TV, going for walks in the mall, and puttering in the back yard. You are in the home stretch of life and your only remaining responsibility is to enjoy yourself.

You will start to spend more time with your kids than you did when they were children, and if they have moved out of town you will plan all of your travels to visit them. You have grandchildren now and you will take pictures of them about every four minutes to show your friends.

If you are a man, your hair has either left the planet or turned completely grey. If you are a woman, your hair has turned blue. Florida seems like the perfect destination every winter and you find yourself talking a lot about the "good old days." Automobiles are no longer chosen for their speed but for their comfortable ride and, most importantly, their gas mileage, which you measure every day. Senior citizen discounts affect every purchase you make now that you are on a fixed income, and sex is nothing more than a fond memory.

Your proudest possessions are your camera, your fly rod, and your remote control for the TV. You wear a baseball cap wherever you go and the word "fashion" has left your personal dictionary. One of your favorite activities is watching the noon news because that weather girl "sure is a cute one." Your entire family will gather around for your sixty-fifth birthday because they all want to make sure that you know who they are in case you need to make any changes to your will. Happy sixty-fifth birthday but take it easy on the cake, it's hard on the digestive system.

"I wish that everyone you know could be here for this day,
But truth is some just had to go they really could not stay.
They loved the food, they love the drink, they loved the birthday games,
But when they lit the candles, several burned up in the flames."

"Old wood to burn,
Old wine to drink,
Old friends to trust,
And old authors to read."
(Francis Bacon)

"Or to put it in the words of Oliver Goldsmith;
'I love everything that's old—old friends, old times, old manners, old books, old wine.'"

“May the clouds in your life be only a background for a lovely sunset.”

“Do not resist growing old—many are denied the privilege.”

“Youth is for freedom and reform, maturity for judicious compromise,
and old age for stability and repose.”
(Winston Churchill)

“Here's health to the future;
A sigh for the past;
We can love and remember,
And hope to the last,
And for all the base lies
That the almanacs hold
While there's love in the heart,
We can never grow old.”

“To the metallic age,
gold in our teeth, silver in our hair, and lead in our pants.”

“To age. In the words of William Allen White, 'I am not afraid of tomorrow, for I have seen yesterday and I love today.'”

“To old age—it's not how old you are, but how you are old.”

“Here's that we may live to eat the hen
That scratches on our grave.”

“May we keep a little of the fuel of youth to warm our body in old age.”

The Ten Best Things About Being Sixty-five

1. You can collect Social Security, if it has not gone bankrupt by then.
2. Senior citizen discounts everywhere!
3. You can wear tennis shoes anywhere.
4. Stripes with plaids? No problem.
5. You can clean your teeth while you sleep.
6. People expect you to forget their names and birthdays.
7. Nap time lasts all day long.
8. White belt and white shoes.
9. No more pesky life insurance salesmen coming to the house.
10. You can leave your turn signal on forever.

"To my cronies—may we never be too old to be young."

"To old age; may it always be ten years older than I am."

"May virtue and truth
Guide you in youth
Catnip and sage
Cheer your old age."

"There may be snow on the roof,
But there's a fire in the furnace."

"You're never too old to become younger."
(Mae West)

"Age is not a handicap. Age is nothing but a number. It is how you use it."
(Ethyl Payne)

"To the Old Guard, the older we grow,
The more we take and the less we know.
At least the young men tell us so,
But the day will come, when they shall know
Exactly how far a glass can go,
To win the battle, 'gainst age, the foe.
Here's youth . . . in a glass of wine."
(James Monroe McLean)

One Hundredth Birthday—You've Outlived Social Security Toasts

Not many of us will have the opportunity to attend someone's one hundredth birthday party, and even if we did, how good of a party could it be? I imagine there would be a lot of other one hundred-year-olds sitting around wearing party hats and complaining that the music is too loud and the room is too cold. When it came time to blow out the candles on the cake, the birthday boy would probably need the help of an air compressor to get up enough wind. And you can just forget about any excitement when it comes time to open the presents, "Oh, look, another pair of socks."

Since you may never get to use any of these toasts at a one hundredth birthday party, feel free to use them for the birthday of any old person you know.

"*May our lives, like the leaves of the maple, grow*
More beautiful as they fade.
May we say our farewells, when it's time to go,
All smiling and unafraid."
(Larry E. Johnson)

"*Beautiful young people are accidents of nature. But beautiful old people are works of art.*"
(Marjorie Barstow Breenbie)

Oliver Wendell Holmes wrote this toast for a friend:

"*Let him live to be a hundred! We want him on earth.*"

"*He's so old that when he orders a three-minute egg, they ask for the money up front.*"
(Milton Berle)

Zodiac Toasts

Birthdays can be defined by the number of years the celebrant has been on this planet, but they can also be classified by the time of the year when the birthday boy or girl was born. Astrology has been around since the beginning of time and helps to categorize us by similar traits possessed by people born under the same sign. Here are some toasts designed for each of the zodiac signs.

AQUARIUS (January 20 to February 18)
An Aquarian is a water bearer
A friend through thick and thin.
Perhaps the most famous of all,
Was that guy named Gunga Din.

PISCES (February 19 to March 20)

On this birthday of Pisces the Fish
We all get together to grant you this wish.
Here's to long life and always good health,
And just for good measure, a large dose of wealth.

ARIES (March 21 to April 20)

To Aries, it's a mighty sign,
Symbolized by the Ram.
We wish you happy birthday,
And hope you're happy as a clam.

TAURUS (April 21 to May 20)

As we make this toast, let us join like a chorus,
And wish happy birthday, to our friend the Taurus.

GEMINI (May 21 to June 21)

Here's to Gemini, represented by the twins.
With you as our friend, we can't help but win.

CANCER (June 22 to July 22)

Hey, Crabby, here's a toast to you,
'Cause you're a Cancer through and through.
You are sensitive and very loyal,
But when you get mad it's a big crab boil.

LEO (July 23 to August 22)

Leo the Lion has the characteristics of generosity, courage and strength. Here's a toast to our friend who becomes more lion-like every day.

VIRGO (August 23 to September 22)

This toast does not rhyme, ergo;
It's perfect for our friend, Virgo.

LIBRA (September 23 to October 22)

Born under the sign of Libra the Scales, our friend was given a great sense of spotting beauty, so it must please him greatly to be able to look out at the rest of us this evening.

There's More Than One Way To Chart A Birthday

In addition to signs of the zodiac with which we are most accustomed, personality traits can be charted via the Chinese horoscope. The Chinese horoscope is based on the year in which you were born as opposed to the time of the year. For instance, If you were born any time from January 28, 1960 and February 14, 1961, you were born during the Chinese year of the Rat. From February 15, 1861 to February 4, 1962, you would have been born in the year of the Ox.

To find out the exact time of the Chinese calendar in which your birthday falls, you will have to either consult a chart of Chinese horoscope lunar years, or you can visit a Chinese restaurant and read it off of the placemat. Once you have determined your sign, you can find the traits attributed to it.

Year of the Rat—You have a proclivity towards fortune and wealth.

Year of the Ox—You espouse patience, responsibility, and industriousness.

Year of the Tiger—You are powerful, aggressive, and impulsive.

Year of the Rabbit—You like carrots. Also, you will be bestowed with good fortune, and sensitivity.

Year of the Dragon—You have energy and enthusiasm but you do have a tendency towards having an inflated ego.

Year of the Snake—You are shrewd and mysterious.

Year of the Horse—You like carrots too. You also show signs of determination, optimism and occasional fickleness.

Year of the Goat—You are gentle, compassionate, and sensitive.

Year of the Monkey—You are intelligent, versatile and humorous.

Year of the Rooster—You wake up early in the morning, you're proud, and you are independent.

Year of the Dog—You are loyal, fair, and you don't mind fetching things.

Year of the Pig—You have been bestowed with a good sense of humor, as well as traits of honesty and sensuality.

SCORPIO (October 23 to November 21)

While Scorpions are considered creatures of the desert, our friendship with our Scorpio friend will always prosper and bloom.

SAGITTARIUS (November 22 to December 21)

A toast to our friend the Saggitarius; we know that the arrows you fire have all gone straight to our hearts. We love you, man.

CAPRICORN (December 22 to January 19)

As I propose this birthday toast I mean it in the best possible way. Happy birthday to a Capricorn . . . you old goat.

Retirement Toasts

There comes a time in most people's lives when they no longer want to work for a living. For me, this time came on the second day of the first job I ever had. But the good old American work ethic dictates that we work until big business deems that we are no longer useful to the U.S. workforce. At this point we retire and spend the rest of our days on a fixed income.

Retirement is a time of rest and leisure. Current U.S. law specifies that when you retire, you are required to spend at least twelve hours a day talking about the good old days, and the other twelve hours of the day napping in your recliner chair. Many states also require their retired citizens to spend the winter months in Florida.

Retirement parties are usually great fun because the person of honor can basically say anything they want about their former employer. What are they going to do, get fired? If you are planning to help a retiree celebrate his or her new found freedom, you may want to take one of these toasts with you.

"*To a man who now has the freedom to do all the things he spent the last forty years dreaming of doing.*"

"*Retirement is nature's way of telling you you're not getting any more paychecks.*"

“*Here's to the holidays—all 365 of them.*”

“*When you're sitting at home with nothing to do,*
Think of us still at work. We're doing that too.”

“*To my boss—or former boss,*
Whatever the case may be,
If I spelled your job backwards
You'd be a double S.O.B.”

“*To your retirement. A well deserved reward for a job well done.*”

“*In the words of British historian Arnold Toynbee, 'To be able to fill leisure intelligently is the last product of civilization,' Here's to one of the most civilized people we know.*”

“*Learn to live well, or fairly make your will*
You've played, and loved, and eat, and drunk your fill;
Walk sober off; before a sprightlier age
Comes tittering on, and shoves you from the stage;
Leave such to trifle with more grace and ease,
Whom Folly pleases, and whose follies please.”
(Alexander Pope)

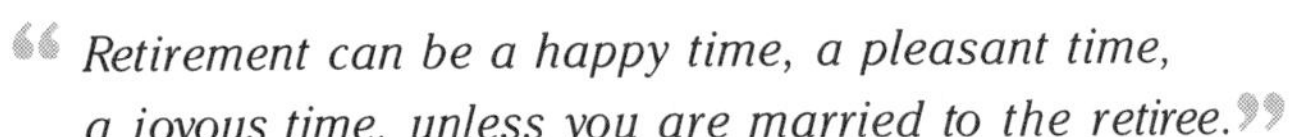

“*Retirement can be a happy time, a pleasant time, a joyous time, unless you are married to the retiree.*”

“*The Roman dramatist Seneca once wrote, 'The gradually declining years are among the sweetest in a man's life.' May yours be a confection of honeys.*”

“*To our former coworker. We don't know what we are going to do without you, but we're sure ready to find out.*”

On the lighter side, retirement toasts can be a time for levity and laughter. If you want to add a few laughs to your toast, consider some of these samples.

"*To your retirement:*
Remember when you have nothing to do,
That no one does that better than you."

"*Gardening, reading, golf, and fishing,*
May you lead the life for which we've all been wishing.
Here's to doing nothing at all.
Relax, enjoy, and just have a ball."

"*Retirement does not mean that the employee is no longer wanted or needed by the company. In this case, it happens to be true.*"

"*A toast to you as you move onward and upward to bigger and better endeavors. We hated to lose you to retirement but it was the only way we could get rid of you.*"

"*I think (name)'s boss best summed up his long career with us. When I asked him if he wanted to say a few words at (name)'s retirement party he said, 'Retirement party, I thought I fired that jerk years ago!'*"

"*Congratulations on your retirement. It could not have happened to a nicer person. More deserving maybe but none nicer.*"

"*Our guest of honor tonight started with this company as a nobody. And look at him today, a nobody with a better parking place.*"

"A toast to our retiring friend. We know that you will not let your elevation to a better lifestyle go to your head. Many of us have known you for years and know that very little never goes to your head."

"We offer this toast tonight to (name) because he has decided to stop working here. That was years ago but now he has decided to retire. Now he's going to start not working at home."

"In proposing this toast to (name) I am reminded of the words of Henny Youngman who said, 'I went to the doctor last week. He told me to take a hot bath before retiring. That's ridiculous. It'll be years before I retire.' Well, (name) it's bath time."

"Our guest of honor is retiring. No longer will we see his (or her) smiling face around the office. No more will we hear his silly laugh or have him around to help us with our problems. On the other hand, I think this is a great time to buy stock in the company."

"You're concerned about retiring,
But we say, 'What the heck.'
Everything will remain the same,
Except for the monthly check."

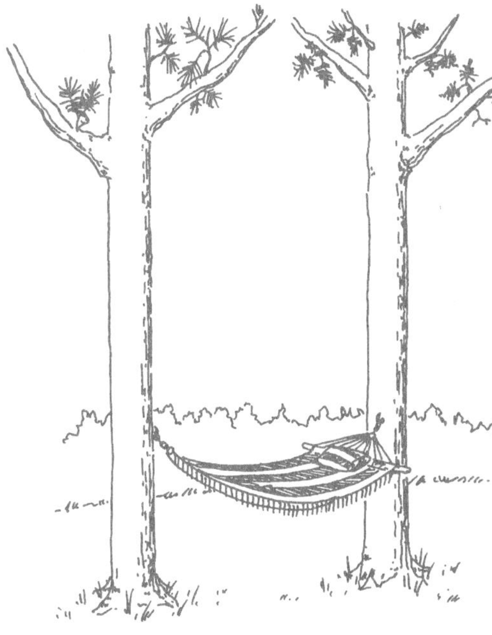

"Here's to (name) who doesn't know the meaning of the word 'retirement.' He doesn't know the meaning of a lot of words which is why we're glad to see him go."

"Here's to retirement; that time in your life when you go home from work and never have to go back. Sort of like when you take a box of kittens out to the country."

"Retirement can be a time of happiness, joy, and relaxation. Unless you have the bad fortune of being (name)'s wife."

"I think we need to offer this toast to (name)'s wife who said that she will be glad to have him at home. She said, 'For years he has been coming home from work and asking me what I did all day. Now he can stay at home and watch me do it.'"

"Unlike many people, (name) should have no trouble adjusting to sitting around the house and doing nothing all day. That's what he did here at the company for years."

"As we toast our elder statesman here this evening, let me just say that it was a pleasure working with you. I'm sorry about all those jokes I made about your age but how many times in your life does a guy have a chance to meet somebody whose Social Security number is 3?"

"Not to say you are old but when you were a kid the Dead Sea was only slightly ill."

"(name) has planned out his retirement just like he planned out each business day. Show up. Have a donut. See what happens next."

"I can see (name) patterning his retirement after the words of Groucho Marx who said, 'I'm an ordinary sort of fellow: 42 around the chest, 42 around the waist, 96 around the golf course, and a nuisance around the house.'"

"As a retirement gift we are happy to present (name) with subscriptions to National Geographic *and* Playboy *magazine. They both contain full color pictures of places he's never going to visit."*

"As we toast our guest of honor we know that he is going to miss all of us just as much as we will miss him. So If he starts to long for the good old days I want him to remember the words of Oscar Wilde who said, 'Work is the refuge of people who have nothing better to do.'"

"As you retire from this company, remember the words of James Barrie, 'Nothing is really work unless you would rather be doing something else.'"

"As we toast your retirement we could look upon the increased free time you will have, the freedom to travel, or the bargains you can get by going out to dinner at 4 P.M. Instead, I think we need to toast something you will never need again. Here's to no more alarm clocks."

"We salute you as you retire. Now you will be able to dedicate more time to your favorite hobbies instead of just 9 to 5 every business day."

"The good news is that you are retiring. The bad news is that somebody invested the entire 401K account in something called 'Soap On A Stick.'"

"If the retiree is leaving a career in the banking industry, consider using the words of John Kenneth Galbraith: 'Banking may well be a career from which no man really recovers.'"

"Author Joseph Heller once said, 'I think that maybe in every company today there is always at least one person who is going crazy slowly.' Congratulations on leaving before it's too late."

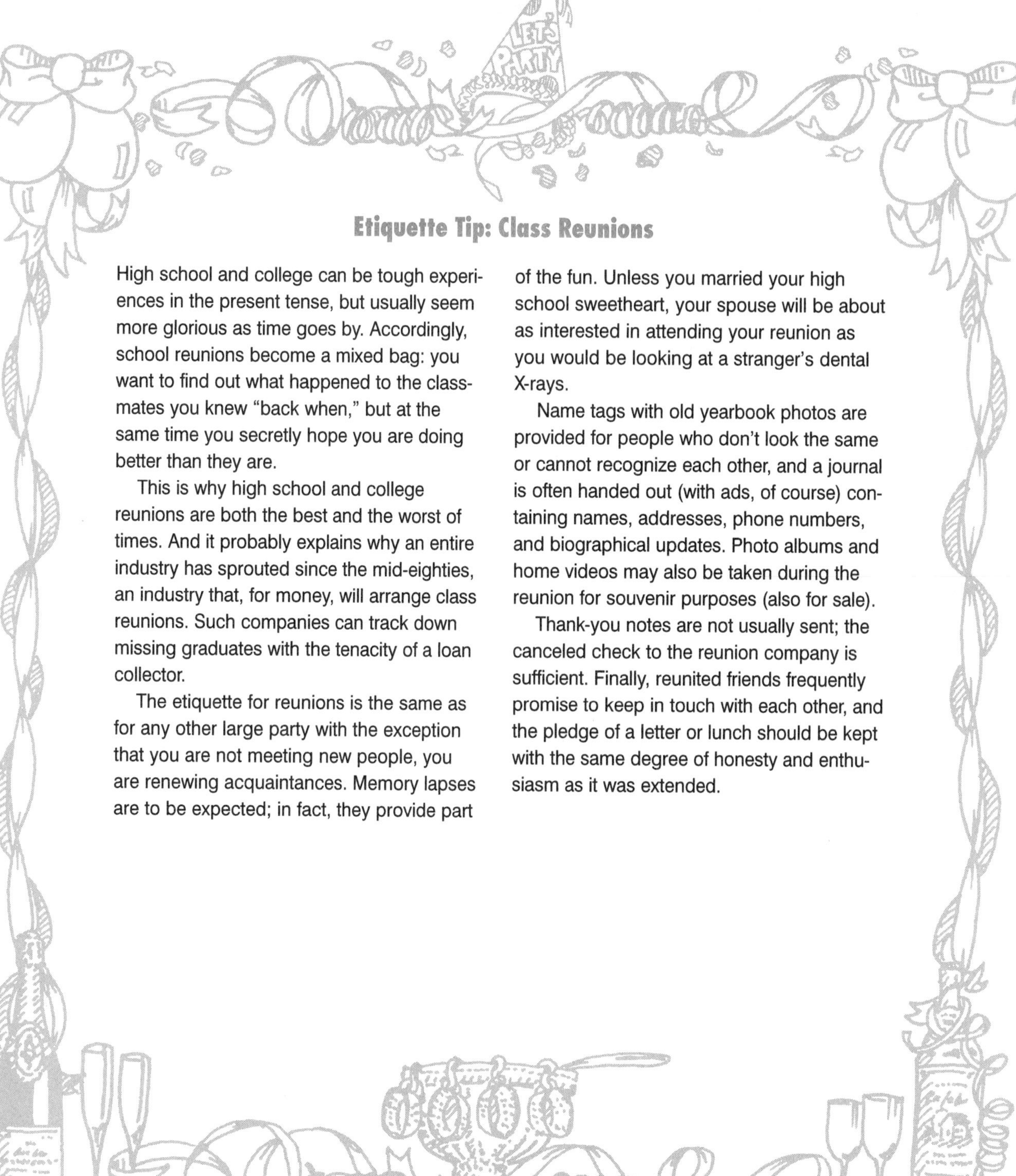

Etiquette Tip: Class Reunions

High school and college can be tough experiences in the present tense, but usually seem more glorious as time goes by. Accordingly, school reunions become a mixed bag: you want to find out what happened to the classmates you knew "back when," but at the same time you secretly hope you are doing better than they are.

This is why high school and college reunions are both the best and the worst of times. And it probably explains why an entire industry has sprouted since the mid-eighties, an industry that, for money, will arrange class reunions. Such companies can track down missing graduates with the tenacity of a loan collector.

The etiquette for reunions is the same as for any other large party with the exception that you are not meeting new people, you are renewing acquaintances. Memory lapses are to be expected; in fact, they provide part of the fun. Unless you married your high school sweetheart, your spouse will be about as interested in attending your reunion as you would be looking at a stranger's dental X-rays.

Name tags with old yearbook photos are provided for people who don't look the same or cannot recognize each other, and a journal is often handed out (with ads, of course) containing names, addresses, phone numbers, and biographical updates. Photo albums and home videos may also be taken during the reunion for souvenir purposes (also for sale).

Thank-you notes are not usually sent; the canceled check to the reunion company is sufficient. Finally, reunited friends frequently promise to keep in touch with each other, and the pledge of a letter or lunch should be kept with the same degree of honesty and enthusiasm as it was extended.

"We wanted to get you something that we knew you could use in your retirement. So we got you lessons to do something you don't know how to do . . . make coffee."

If the guest of honor is known as a rather 'frugal' individual, you can offer this toast.

"We toast one of the most generous men I have ever known. I remember when I first started working here and he treated the entire office to donuts and orange juice. It really shocked me. I hadn't planned on donating blood that day."

Class Reunion Toasts

One of the most uncomfortable times in an adult's life is when he or she has to attend a class reunion. Class reunions are very scary times because while we have kept our bodies in pristine condition, we are afraid to see what the rest of our poor classmates have done to theirs.

Class reunions are when the people who would never talk to you in high school now try to sell you plumbing supplies. Class reunions are when you see homecoming queens who have become fat and the captain of the football team who has gone bald. Class reunions are a time to measure your successes against those of your peers. They are a time when you can actually tell your teachers what you thought of them in high school. They are times to find out who has moved the farthest away, who has been married the most times, and who has the most kids. In other words, class reunions are a time of comparison, reflection, and reunion.

Here are some class reunion toasts and some ideas for making your own.

"Here's a health in homely rhyme
To our oldest classmate, Father Time;
May our last survivor live to be
As bold and wise and as thorough as he!"
(Oliver Wendell Holmes)

The Reunion Rap

At your reunion, you want a with-it, happening toast that reflects your lifestyle.

So here's your toast done in the popular rap format of today. First of all, you must get the attention of your classmates, but you do not want to resort to the hackneyed method talked about earlier of tapping your water glass with a spoon. Here is the first part of the toast—a guaranteed attention getter.

Yo, Yo, Yo, Check it out over here.

When you have their attention, proceed with your rap-toast:

I wanna give you all a very cool toast,
'Cause of all of my homies, I dig you guys the most.
So raise your glass high over your head,
And party like an animal, that's what I said.
Word.

Make an Impression

The main thing anybody wants to do at a class reunion is to impress all of the losers with whom you went to school. Here are some sure-fire methods of creating that impression.

1. Hire a male (or female) model (or body builder) to attend the reunion in your place. Brief them on what they need to know and turn them loose in the sea of overweight balding classmates.
2. Arrive at the reunion in a limousine or rent a Ferrari Testarossa for the day. Either way, your friends should be impressed.
3. Drop names like Bobby De Niro, Billy Gates, and the Popemeister. Believe it or not, some people will actually think that you know them.

(continued)

"*Here's a toast to all who are here,*
No matter where you're from;
May the best day you have ever seen
Be worse than the worst to come."

"*Here's to all of us!*
For there's so much good in the worst of us
And so much bad in the best of us,
That it hardly behooves any of us,
To talk about the rest of us."

"*To friends: As long as we are able*
To lift our glasses from the table"

"*To the good old days . . . we weren't*
So good, 'cause we weren't so old!"

"*Here's to us that are here, to you that are there, and the rest of us everywhere.*"

"*I drink it as the Fates ordain it,*
Come, fill it, and have done with rhymes;
Fill up the lonely glass, and drain it
In memory of dear old times."
(William Makepeace Thackeray)

"*To the good old days—which are taking place right now.*"

"*Here's to our friends, here's to our school,*
Here's to the class of seventy-two,
I hope you will achieve in life,
All the dreams you may pursue."

This toast will work equally well for the classes of '52, '62, '82, and '92. If you graduated in a year ending in another number, you may replace the second and forth lines of the toast with the following substitutes.

> *"Here's to our friends, here's to our school,*
> *Here's to the class of seventy-one,*
> *I hope you will achieve in life,*
> *Love, success, and fun."*

> *"Here's to our friends, here's to our school,*
> *Here's to the class of seventy-three,*
> *I hope you will achieve in life,*
> *All the dreams that make you free."*

> *"Here's to our friends, here's to our school,*
> *Here's to the class of seventy-four,*
> *I hope you will appreciate,*
> *The beauty life holds in store."*

> *"Here's to our friends, here's to our school,*
> *Here's to the class of seventy-five,*
> *I'm glad that we're all gathered here,*
> *And I'm glad we're still alive."*

> *"Here's to our friends, here's to our school,*
> *Here's to the class of seventy-six,*
> *Here's to everything we learned,*
> *The education and the tricks."*

> *"Here's to our friends, here's to our school,*
> *Here's to the class of seventy-seven,*
> *And for those who went to law school,*
> *Here's to the legal word 'replevin.'"*

(According to my good friend and attorney—and the dictionary—replevin is the action to regain possession of personal property unlawfully retained. It doesn't come up much in daily conversation, but it is a killer word to sue in Scrabble.)

Make an Impression

4. Carry a cellular phone with you at all times and have someone call you at regular intervals (every fifteen minutes). Whenever the phone rings, just answer it and say things like, "Geeze Greenspan, how many times are you going to ask me what to do about the interest rate? Can't you make your own decisions for a change?"
5. Rent a date. Nothing says success more than a beautiful man or woman on your arm. When it comes time to tip the coat check person, ask loudly if anybody has change for a Kruggerand.

"Here's to our friends, here's to our school,
Here's to the class of seventy-eight,
I hope success in every form,
Is the destiny of your fate."

"Here's to our friends, here's to our school,
Here's to the class of seventy-nine,
Here's to old friends, and memories,
That improve like vintage wine."

If you graduated in a decade starting year like 1950, 1960, 1970, 1980, 1990, or the upcoming 2000, you are on your own to construct your class reunion toast. To help you out, here are some words that rhyme with each of the aforementioned years.

1950—drifty, nifty, rifty, shifty, thrifty.
1960—orange
1970—heavenly
1980—lady, matie
1990—month
2000—silver

As you know, there are no rhyming words for orange, month, or silver. There are also no rhyming words for sixty, ninety, or thousand.

Finally, we must not forget the best known class reunion toast, which is actually a song with the following lyrics:

"Hail, hail, the gang's all here,
So what the hell do we care?
What the hell do we care?
Hail, hail the gang's all here,
So what the hell do we care now?"

Family Reunion Toasts

Family reunions are becoming more and more popular since an ever increasing number of families are scattering themselves all over the country. It is not unusual to find mom and dad in New York City, Bud working in Colorado, and Sissy living in L.A. The nuclear family has experienced fallout, and it is making the demand for family reunions even greater.

Don't get me wrong, we used to have family reunions when I was a kid but we called them weddings and funerals. We never got together just to get together because, ah, well, we weren't really all that close. We didn't hug, we shook hands, which is a pretty distant way to greet your mom.

The other fact contributing to the increase in family reunions is the fact that the typical Leave-It-To-Beaver family no longer exists. Today, families come with mom, dad, step-mom, step-dad, siblings, step-siblings, and even step-step-siblings. You can't tell the players without a scorecard, or at least a greeting card.

If you are headed for a gathering of the clans, you may wish to arm yourself with one or more of the following family reunion toasts.

> *"To my family: those who know me best and, for some reason, still love me."*

> *"May we be loved by those we love."*

> *"To our house and home;*
> *Where there's a world of strife shut out,*
> *And a world of love shut in."*

> *"Here's to family, the people who treat us the best*
> *and the ones about whom we grumble the most."*

If your family reunion has a guest who has never been with you before, i.e., a new spouse or significant other of a family member, this toast is a good way to welcome them.

> *"To the newcomer—welcome aboard.*
> *To the parents—congratulations.*
> *To the grandparents—bask in the sunshine of your happiness."*

> *"To my brothers and sister, my uncles and aunts,*

Beaver's Legacy

Leave It To Beaver, that popular TV show from the 1960s, raised the bar for expectations. In this series, parents expected every child to behave properly at all times, and kids came to expect their mom to wear pearls every day and their dad to wear a tie around the house. Neither of these expectations could be realized, of course, which led to an entire generation left in the wake of shattered hopes. It's no wonder we went nuts in the '70s—our hearts were broken. We didn't have moms that wore stockings and heels to make breakfast and we didn't have dads that didn't swear. And as far as naming the kid Beaver, didn't anybody on that show ever question this wisdom?

To the ones who wear dresses and the ones who wear pants,
I am glad that we've gathered together right here,
And I'm even more glad that it's just once a year."

If your family has a good sense of humor, you may wish to toast with the words of Oscar Wilde, who once said, "Relations are simply a tedious pack of people, who haven't got the remotest knowledge of how to live, nor the smallest instinct about when to die."

Housewarming Toasts

The average American moves fourteen times in their lifetime. This means they have the potential for fourteen housewarming parties. This seems like a lot until we do the math. If the average person moves fourteen times, you have to figure that at least half of those moves took place when they were kids. This leaves seven adult moves. Of these, half again are probably to apartments, which really don't call for housewarming parties. It is not a house, it is an apartment. If they wanted to have a housewarming party at an apartment don't you think they'd call it an apartment warming party?

This leave us with three and one-half housewarming parties for the average adult. If you are invited to any of those parties you will be required to bring a gift. An affordable, yet appreciated gift is a nice bottle of wine, and if you come to the party armed not only with a bottle of wine but a lovely toast as well, you leave the hosts with no recourse but to open your bottle of wine to enjoy your toast. So you not only get credit for giving a nice gift, but you get to enjoy some if it as well.

Here are a few housewarming toasts that are guaranteed bottle openers.

"*May your fire be as warm as the weather is cold.*"

"*May your well never run dry.*"

"To the pleasures of home: a good book, a bright light, and an easy chair."

"To your new home—the father's kingdom, the child's paradise, the mother's world."

"May blessings be upon your house,
Your roof and hearth and walls;
May there be lights to welcome you
When evening's shadow falls;
The love that like a guiding star
Still signals when you roam;
A book, a friend—these be the things
That make a house a home."
(Myrtle Reed)

If you are the recipient of a housewarming party, in other words, the people with the new house, you may wish to propose a toast to your guests who not only came to your party but also brought you that nice bottle of wine you are already drinking.

"Here's to our guest—
Don't let him rest.
But keep his elbow bending.
'Tis time to drink—
Full time to think
Tomorrow—when you're mending."

"The ornament of a house is the guests who frequent it. That you for making our house the most brilliantly decorated one of all."

"In the words of Myrtle Reed, 'May our house always be too small to hold all our friends.'"

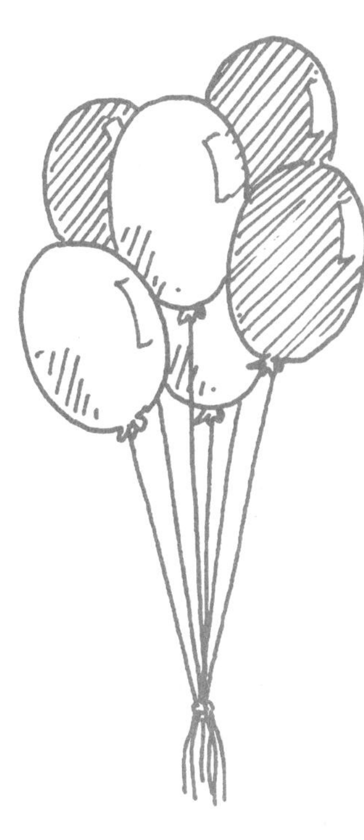

"Come in the evening, or come in the morning—
Come when you're looked for, or come without warning;
A thousand welcomes you'll find here before you,
The oftener you come here the more I'll adore you."
(Thomas Davis)

"In the words of history's most gracious host, Count Dracula, 'Welcome to my house. Come freely. Go safely. And leave something of the happiness you bring.'"

Here are some good toasts to you as either the housewarming guest or the housewarming host.

"A health to you,
A wealth to you,
And the best that life can give to you.
May fortune still be kind to you,
And happiness be true to you,
And life be long and good to you,
Is the toast of all your friends to you."

"May thy life be long and happy,
Thy cares and sorrows few;
And the many friends around thee
Prove faithful, fond and true."

"He who clinks his cup with mine
Adds a glory to the wine."

Funeral Toasts

Funerals are times of grieving, sadness, and personal reflection. But funerals are also a time to celebrate the life of the departed. The good times they brought and the memories they recall are the things to which a glass should be raised in remembrance.

"To live in hearts we leave behind is not to die."

"Oh, here's to other meetings,
And merry greetings then;
And here's to those we've drunk with,
But never can again."
(Stephen Decatur)

"When you come to the end of your journey
And enter your eternal home,
May God be looking for you from an upstairs window,
And arm in arm you watch the dawn."

"Yea, though I walk through the valley of the shadow of death, I will fear no evil; for thou art with me; thy rod and thy staff they comfort me."
(Psalms 23:4)

"When one man dies, one chapter is not torn out of the book, but translated into a better language."
(John Donne)

"In the words of Samuel Johnson, 'It matters not how a man dies, but how he lives. The act of dying is not of importance, it last so short a time.' Here's to our dear departed friend who lived life to its fullest."

"Here's to the tears of affection,
May they crystallize as they fall,
And become pearls, that in the after years
We'll wear in memory of those whom we have loved."

"To our loved one who has passed away, may the winds of heaven whisper hourly benedictions over his/her hallowed grave."

"May every hair on your head turn into a candle to light your way to heaven, and may God and his Holy Mother take the harm of the years away from you."

Bon Voyage Toasts

A bon voyage toast is different than a funeral toast. While they both deal with people who are going away for awhile, the recipient of a bon voyage toast has a much better shot at coming back within the next few weeks.

Bon voyage toasts are given to people who are going on vacation, usually on board a ship. Back in the early eighteenth century the term "bon voyage" first came into general usage and translates to "have a nice cruise and enjoy the midnight buffet." Today, a bon voyage toast can be given to anyone going on vacation whether it be on board a ship, a train, or a plane. Bon voyage toasts are generally not given to people who are going on vacation via mobile home, Greyhound bus, or by hitchhiking.

"*May the road rise to meet you.*
May the wind be always at your back,
The sun shine warm upon your face,
The rain fall soft upon your fields,
And until we meet again
May God hold you in the hollow of his hand."

"*Bon voyage to you and may you incur no seasickness on your journey. Seasickness is traveling over the water by rail.*"

"*I've traveled many a highway*
I've walked for many a mile
Here's to the people who made my day
To the people who waved and smiled."
(Tom T. Hall)

"*We'll leave a light on for you.*"
(Tom Bodett)

"*In the words of the philosopher Kermit the Frog, 'Wherever you go, there you are.'*"

"Here's to a sophisticated traveler . . .
even though you choose your airline for their in flight meals."

"Here's to you and here's to me,
Wherever we may roam;
And here's to the health and happiness
Of the ones who are left at home."

Toasts for Showers

Bridal Showers

Modern bridal showers are usually thrown by the mother, the sisters, the bride of honor, or anybody who really wants to host a shower. A bride to be can have as many showers as she has friends, but if the same people are invited to every shower, they tend to start bringing cheaper presents to the last ones.

Nowadays, wedding showers are no longer restricted to the bride. It is not uncommon for a groom to have a shower thrown in his honor also. The wedding shower for the groom differs from the wedding shower for the bride in several respects. First, all of the gifts tend to be power tools. Second, tea and finger sandwiches are replaced by beer and nacho chips. And third, somebody usually gets a stripper. Other than that, they are exactly alike.

As far as toasts for wedding showers is concerned, many suitable choices can be found throughout this book. Check the toasts for brides, girls, friends, and weddings. If you don't find anything appropriate there, try one of these.

"Showers are our time
To wish you every happiness.
To wish you love, and wish you joy,
And wish you great success."

"Here's to the happy couple—may you survive your wedding and still be in love."

Etiquette Tip: Bridal Showers

Two to three weeks before the wedding, the bride's friends hold a party in her honor at which they "shower" her with gifts. This is a party for those close to the bride, but is not typically hosted by her immediate family (although they will attend). Showers also may be jointly hosted. They are usually held at midday lunch or on a weekend day in a private home or separate dining room of a restaurant.

An invitation to a shower implies that a gift is expected. (Shower gifts are separate from wedding gifts.) As such, the honoree is asked to make up a guest list. Showers are generally small affairs and should not overshadow the wedding reception. Should the marriage later be called off, shower gifts must be returned.

> *To the bride to be;*
> *We've been friends through thick and thin,*
> *Through every type of weather,*
> *So we don't care if you wear white to your wedding,*
> *Even though you've been living together.*

Etiquette Tip: Baby Showers

A baby shower is scheduled anywhere from four to six weeks before the due date, usually in the afternoon. It is hosted by a close friend at the friend's home or the function room of a club or restaurant. More and more, men are also being invited to showers.

Only one baby shower need be held, and then only for the first child, as subsequent children will have the benefit of hand-me-downs. In the case of a couple who adopt a child, shower invitations should include the child's gender and clothing sizes. The shower hostess may coordinate gift giving among the guests; this allows several guests to pool their resources to buy more expensive gifts such as strollers or cribs. Some department and baby specialty stores now offer registry services.

Baby Showers

Baby showers differ from bridal showers in several aspects. First of all, it is normal protocol for a baby shower to be held after a bridal shower. Granted, this is not always the case, but it does cut down on the questions.

Secondly, while the gifts at a bridal shower are for the bride, who is present at the party, gifts at a baby shower are for the baby who is not actually present at his or her own party. The baby at a baby shower is still sequestered inside of the mother-to-be and has no intention of showing his face, or any other part of himself at the party. If, by chance, the baby does make an appearance at the shower, it tells you that whoever planned the event had their timing all screwed up.

Another point of etiquette at a baby shower is that each time the Mom-to-be opens a gift, all of the other ladies in attendance should look at the gift and remark, "Isn't that adorable?" or "Oh, this is cute." Or even, "You can always use more of those."

As with the bridal shower toasts, baby shower toasts can be adapted from toasts listed in this book for christenings but you may wish to set your toast apart from everybody else's toast. If that is the case, you may find the perfect selection right here.

> *We meet today to celebrate,*
> *Your baby's pending birth,*
> *You'll be so happy when he (or she) is born,*
> *And you can lose that big 'ol girth.*

> *A baby is an inestimable blessing and bother.*
> *(Mark Twain)*

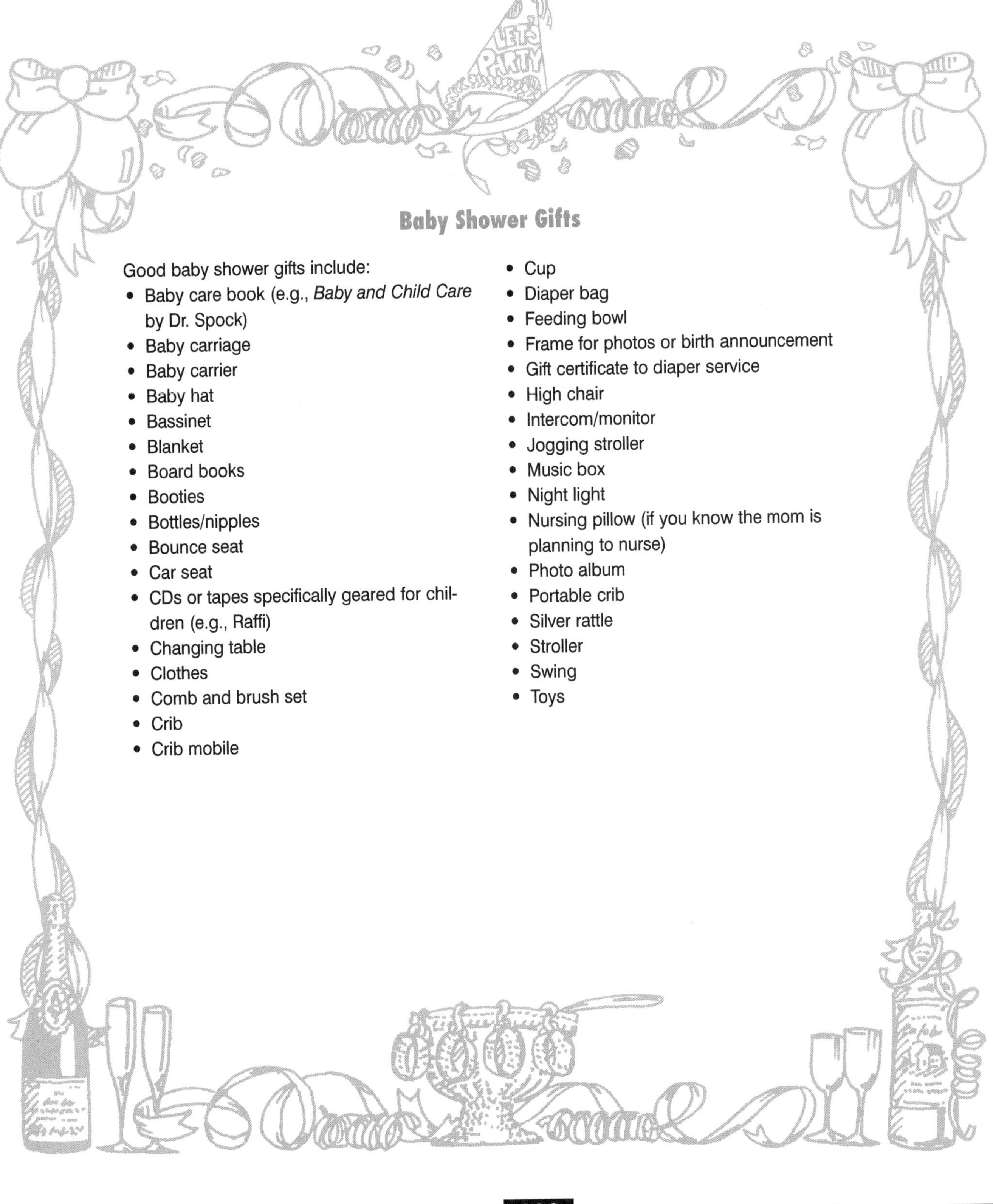

Baby Shower Gifts

Good baby shower gifts include:

- Baby care book (e.g., *Baby and Child Care* by Dr. Spock)
- Baby carriage
- Baby carrier
- Baby hat
- Bassinet
- Blanket
- Board books
- Booties
- Bottles/nipples
- Bounce seat
- Car seat
- CDs or tapes specifically geared for children (e.g., Raffi)
- Changing table
- Clothes
- Comb and brush set
- Crib
- Crib mobile
- Cup
- Diaper bag
- Feeding bowl
- Frame for photos or birth announcement
- Gift certificate to diaper service
- High chair
- Intercom/monitor
- Jogging stroller
- Music box
- Night light
- Nursing pillow (if you know the mom is planning to nurse)
- Photo album
- Portable crib
- Silver rattle
- Stroller
- Swing
- Toys

Etiquette Tip: Baby Showers for Unwed Mothers

Unwed mothers are just as much in need of baby items as married mothers are. It would be considered rude to exclude them from any prebirth rituals.

"Parents were invented to make children happy
by giving them something to ignore."
(Ogden Nash)

"Here's to life;
The first half is ruined by our parents,
And the last half by our children."

"Your mom and dad have waited,
For this day when you are grown,
Now you'll see what they went through,
With children of your own."

"In toasting the mother to be, I recall the words of Winston Churchill who said, 'There is no finer investment for any community than putting milk into babies.'"

"Our birth is but a sleep and a forgetting;
The soul that rises with us, our life's star,
Hath had elsewhere its setting,
And cometh from afar;
Not in entire forgetfulness,
And not in utter nakedness,
But trailing clouds of glory do we come
From God, who is our home."
(William Wordsworth)

CHAPTER 3

Holiday Homage

Holidays are a source of great joy, coupled with the angst of having to spend time with one's own family. They are times for celebrating, and parties, and, of course, toasts. And since every holiday celebrates a different occasion, everyone should have its own toast. Here, then, is an explanation of some of our holidays accompanied by holiday toasts.

New Year's Toasts

New Year's is the first official holiday on the calendar. It celebrates the renewal and the beginning of a brand new year. It is a time of hope, optimism, and rededication. It is also a time when many people make New Year's resolutions. New Year's resolutions are promises you make to yourself to change a selected pattern of your behavior that needs changing. For instance, your New Year's resolution may be to quit smoking, lose weight, or finally throw out those leisure suits from the seventies. The bad thing about New Year's resolutions is that virtually all of them are broken before it is time to eat the New Year's Day dinner. Breaking our resolutions makes us feel guilty that we have failed. I say that when you break a New Year's resolution you didn't fail, you just gained a reason for another toast.

> "*Whatever you resolve to do,*
> *On any New Year's Day.*
> *Resolve to yourself to be true*
> *And live—the same old way.*"

> "*I resolve this year to shed some pounds,*
> *I'm going to lose some weight,*
> *But the dinner sure looks good today,*
> *I guess the weight can wait.*"

In order to fully grasp the importance of the New Year, I thought it would be a good idea to tell you the story of the first New Year ever celebrated. From the archives of the Crenshaw Institute for Historical Studies I am pleased to present "The First New Year."

The day after the first Christmas was very hectic, especially in England and Canada where there was fighting in the streets. That is why they call it Boxing Day. In the greater Bethlehem metroplex, everyone was abuzz about the live nativity show at the Sands Hotel and Stable. But after the excitement died down, one of the elders brought up an interesting point. The birth of Jesus marked a definite change in the calendar system. Up until December 24th, the time was known as "B.C.," which stood for "Before Christ," but now that Christ was here, all of the calendars would have to be changed over to "A.D." which stands for "Ages, Dark." This unforeseen dilemma set the calendar makers in a tizzy. They had less than six days to reprint all of their calendars with the new year 1 A.D.

Note: It has always amazed me that nobody saw this coming. You would think that after years of watching the year numbers decline (50 B.C., 49 B.C., 48 B.C., Hike) that they would realize 1 B.C. would be the last of the B.C. series.

Word soon spread throughout the village that a big New Year's event was about to happen. It was going to be the start of the first millennium. There was a lot of work to do but everybody pitched in to help. The event organizers came up with the idea of a parade featuring floats made of flower petals until someone pointed out that since they lived in a desert that there would not be a lot of flowers available. Huge helium balloons were chosen instead.

Dickus Clarkus was contracted to do the New Year's Eve countdown and Guy Lombardo and the Royal Corinthians were booked for the big dance. By New Year's Eve all there was to do was to blow up the balloons, hang the streamers, and put the Korbel on ice.

As the sun set on December 31, everyone gathered at Town Square to party down. After much merry making and wine guzzling, someone asked the question, "When's midnight?" This prompted the person standing next to him to ask, "What's midnight?" You see, since the watch had yet to be invented and sundials couldn't be read at night, no one could comprehend the concept of "midnight." Eventually, everyone agreed that midnight would occur in one hour since the only working time piece was an hourglass.

As the sands drifted from the top of the glass to the bottom, people started to make "resolutions." These resolutions were promises that were meant to be broken as soon as after midnight as possible. The folks attending from Sodom and Gomorrah won this event hands down.

Spirited Holidays

Holidays only come once a year—every year. We look forward to their rituals and traditions and recognize their importance in our lives. But they should be fun. To keep them fresh and lively, entertaining and interesting, requires some inventiveness . . . and spirits. This chapter contains a few suggestions to make your holidays much more spirited.

New Year's Eve Drinks

New Year's Eve can be terribly elegant or downright silly with crazy hats and creaky noisemakers. Why not combine the two? Let your guests decide. Let them choose the sophistication of "Bubbly Mint" in champagne flutes and "Coffee Nut," with Frangelico and Amaretto, in fine china cups. Or let them say good-bye to the old year with paper horns and "Snakebite" in a shot glass. Either way, the new year is coming!

Champagne Punch

1 bottle dry white wine
16 oz. grapefruit juice
1 pineapple, diced and crushed in a blender, or one large can of crushed-pineapple
1 bottle champagne, chilled

Combine all ingredients except the champagne in a punch bowl. Add ice and chilled champagne just before serving. Makes about 15 servings.

With just a few grains of sand remaining, Dickus Clarkus led the crowd in a chant as a big ball started to descend from atop the Tower of Babel. Dickus had the entire crowd chanting, "X, IX, VIII, VII, VI, V, IV, III, II, I, Happy New Year!!!" At the stroke of midnight there was much merriment. People were kissing and hugging, horns were blowing, and the band began playing Auld Lang Syne, which everyone sang but no one understood. The party continued until the wee hours of the morning at which time designated camel drivers were called.

The first New Year's Day featured massive hangovers and the annual football game between the Pharisees and the Saducces known as the Manna Bowl. This was followed by the January White Sale.

Four weeks later, news of the calendar change reached China. That's why their New Year is a month after ours.

(Note: there is not a speck of truth in this story.)

Here are some samples to help you on your way to making your first toast of the New Year.

> *"Happy New Year!"*

(Yes, I know this is rather simplistic, but it is also the most universally recognized of the New Year's toasts)

> *"Welcome be ye that are here,*
> *Welcome all, and make good cheer,*
> *Welcome all, another year."*

> *"Here's wishing you the kind of troubles*
> *That will last as long as*
> *Your New Year's resolutions!"*

> *"Let's drink to our noble purpose,*
> *Then forget it—like always."*

> *"Another year is dawning. Let it be true*
> *For better or for worse, another year with you."*

"*Here's to a bright New Year*
And a fond farewell to the old;
Here's to the things that are yet to come
And to the memories we hold."

"*One swallow doesn't make a summer . . . but it breaks a New Year's resolution.*"

"*I hereby resolve to keep my resolutions*
And start them at the stroke of twelve.
For who knows better than this assembled group
That procrastination is the thief of time."

"*Here's to the bright New Year*
And a fond farewell to the old;
Here's to the things that are yet to come
And to the memories that we hold.
A song for the old, while its knell is tolled,
And its parting moments fly!
But a song and a cheer for the glad New Year,
While we watch the old year die!"
(George Cooper)

"*Stir the eggnog, lift the toddy,*
Happy New Year, everybody."
(Phyllis McGinley)

"*The New Year is ringing in,*
May he be bringing in
The Good Times we've waited for so long in vain!
Without the demanding
All rise and drink standing,
And so say we all of us again and again."

"*The Old Man's dead. He was okay, maybe*
But here's a health to the brand new baby.
Happy (year)!"

More New Year's Eve Drinks

Non Egg Nog
(Non-alcoholic)
1 egg
1/4 tsp. almond extract
1/4 tsp. vanilla extract
1 Tbs. fine sugar
6 oz. Milk
nutmeg

Combine ingredients in a shaker half filled with ice. Shake well. Strain into a highball glass without ice. Sprinkle with nutmeg.

Night Cap
2 oz. light rum
1 tsp. fine sugar
warm milk
nutmeg

Pour ingredients into a mug. Stir. Sprinkle with nutmeg.

Coffee Nut
1 oz. Amaretto
1 oz. Frangelico
hot black coffee
2 oz. cream or whipped cream

Pour ingredients except cream into a mug. Top with whipped cream or cream poured over the back of a spoon to float on top.

"Let us resolve to do the best we can with what we've got.
(William Feather)

"May this sweetest old-time greeting
Heavily laden with good cheers
Bring content, and peace and plenty
Enough to last through all the year."

"In the year ahead,
May we treat our friends with kindness
And our enemies with generosity."

"Be at war with your voices, at peace with your neighbors,
and let every new year find you a better man."
(Benjamin Franklin)

"May we have a few real friends rather than a thousand acquaintances."

The Irish always seem to have the best toasts, and why should New Year's be any different. Here are the best of the Irish New Year's toasts.

"In the New Year,
May your right hand always be stretched out in friendship,
But never in want."

"As we start the New Year,
Let's get down on our knees
To thank God we're on our feet."

"May the New Year grant you
The eye of a blacksmith on a nail
The good humor of a girl at a dance
The strong hand of a priest on his parish."

"May the New Year bring summer in its wake."

"May the Lord keep you in his hand
And never close his fist too tight on you.
And may the face of every good news
And the back of every bad news be toward us
In the New Year."

"May you have an average year:
Better than last year but not as good as next."

"May your nets be always full—
Your pockets never empty.
May your horse not cast a shoe
Nor the devil look at you
In the coming year."

"To a firm hand for a flighty beast
An old dog for the long road
A kettle of fish for Friday
And a welcome for the New Year."

"May the New Year grant you
A clean shirt
A clear conscience
And a ticket to California in your pocket."
(Nineteenth century)

Of course, the most frequently quoted New Year's toast (after Happy New Year!) comes from the words of Scottish poet Robert Burns. "Auld Lang Syne" has been sung on New Year's Eve for hundreds of years even though we do not know what it means. Unfortunately, it is the only New Year's Eve song we have. So until somebody like Michael Jackson or Randy Newman writes another one, we are stuck with it. Here it is in its entirety, all three verses.

Even More New Year's Eve Drinks

Champagne Cooler
1 oz. Brandy
1/2 oz. Triple Sec
1 tsp. fine sugar
champagne, chilled

Combine brandy, Triple Sec, and sugar in a large wine glass. Add champagne and garnish with a sprig of mint.

Bubbly Mint
1/2 oz. white crème de menthe
champagne, chilled

Pour crème de menthe into champagne glass and add champagne to fill.

Happy Youth
1 oz. cherry brandy
2 oz. orange juice
1 tsp. fine sugar
champagne, chilled

Dissolve sugar in brandy and orange juice in a champagne glass. Fill with champagne.

Still More New Year's Eve Drinks

Spirited Raspberry Punch
(Non-alcoholic)
1 (12 oz.) can frozen raspberry juice
1 (12 oz.) can frozen lemonade
1 quart ginger ale, chilled
1 pint raspberry sherbet

Dilute the juices two to one with water. Before serving, add ginger ale. Spoon sherbet into punch.

Single Egg Nog
1 egg
1 1/2 oz. rum (or liquor of choice)
6 oz. Milk
nutmeg

Combine ingredients in a shaker half filled with ice. Shake well. Strain into a highball glass without ice. Sprinkle with nutmeg.

Kamikaze Shooter
1/2 oz. Vodka
1/2 oz. Triple Sec
1/2 oz. lime juice

Combine ingredients in a shaker half filled with ice. Shake well. Strain into a shot glass.

"*Should auld acquaintance be forgot,*
And never brought to min',
Should auld acquaintance be forgot
And days of auld lang syne.
For auld lang syne, my dear,
For auld lang syne,
We'll tak' a cup o' kindness yet,
For auld lang syne
(second verse)
And here's a hand, my trusty fierce,
And gie's a hand o' thine
And we'll tak' a right guid willie-waught,
For auld lang syne.
For auld lang syne, my dear,
For auld lang syne.
We'll tak' a cup o' kindness yet,
For auld lang syne
(third verse)
And surely ye'll be your pint stowpt,
And surely I'll be mine,
And we'll tak' a cup o' kindness yet,
For auld lang syne.
For auld lang syne, my dear,
For auld lang syne,
We'll tak' a cup o' kindness yet,
For auld lang syne."

Valentine's Day Toasts

Valentine's Day is a day for lovers—or people who want to be lovers, or people who are looking to be lovers for only one day. It is a day of romance, greeting cards, flowers, candy, and gifts. Only the romance is available at little or no cost. Part of the romance is, of course, a very romantic toast. As for the rest of the gifts, I have always depended on homemade cards, cemetery flowers, leftover Halloween candy, and gifts available at the airport. So you can see, a romantic Valentine's Day toast is extremely important to me.

"*Here's to love and its day of dedication.*
May its spirit be with us for all our years to come."

"Hearts were made to give away
On Valentine's dear day."
(Annette Wynne)

"To my Valentine,
'I love you
Not only for what you are,
But what I am
When I am with you.'"
(Roy Croft)

"Were't the last drop in the well,
As I gasped upon the brink,
Ere my fainting spirit fell,
'Tis to thee I would drink."
(Lord Byron)

Note to guys: ATTENTION, the toast above is a sure-fire winner. In order for it to have its full effect, however, make sure you memorize it and practice it over and over until you have it down perfectly. Then look directly into your companion's eyes as you clink glasses to your perfectly polished toast. It will not have nearly the same romantic effect if you pull out a three-by-five card and stumble through the recitation. You only have one shot at making a beautiful romantic toast. If you do it correctly, the rest of the evening will proceed smoothly. If, however, you screw it up, well, you're on your own . . . literally.

"Because I love you truly,
Because you love me, too,
My very greatest happiness
Is sharing life with you."

"Roses are red,
Violets are blue,
I hope that you know,
How much I love you."

Valentine's Day Drinks

The perfect Valentine's Day party may be just for two. Even three can be a crowd. But if more is merrier, be ready with drinks for all your guests' romantic or unromantic circumstances. For the determinedly single, there's the "Confirmed Bachelor." For the amorous, try a "Cherry Kiss." And for the jilted, the lonely, the searching, and the jealous, the drink of the day is definitely "Stupid Cupid."

Stupid Cupid

1 1/2 oz. vodka
1/2 oz. sloe gin
1 oz. lemon juice or juice of 1/2 lemon

Pour ingredients into a mixing glass nearly filled with ice. Stir. Strain into a cocktail glass. Garnish with a cherry.

"*Come live with me, and be my love,*
And we will all the pleasures prove,
That valleys, groves, or hills, or fields,
Or woods and steepy mountains yield."
(Christopher Marlowe)

"*Here's to the prettiest, here's to the wittiest,*
Here's to the truest of all who are true,
Here's to the neatest one, here's to the sweetest one,
Here's to them all in one—here's to you."

Here's a Valentine's Day toast you can use with only a glass of water with which to toast.

"*Here's to this water,*
Wishing it were wine,
Here's to you my darling,
Wishing you were mine."

"*I drink to your charm, your beauty and your brains—which gives you a rough idea of how hard up I am for a drink.*"
(Groucho Marx)

Another note to guys: The Groucho Marx toast is for your reading amusement only. Under no circumstances should you actually use this toast with anyone other than an ex-spouse or ex-girlfriend.

"*I love you more than yesterday, less than tomorrow.*"

"*Let's drink to love,*
Which is nothing—
Unless it's divided by two."

Here's a toast you can propose if you find yourself dateless on Valentine's Day and sitting at the bar with a bunch of other dateless people.

"Here's to Dan Cupid, the little squirt,
He's lost his pants, he's lost his shirt,
He's lost most everything but his aim,
Which shows that love is a losing game."

"If I'm asleep when you want to, wake me,
And if I don't want to, make me."

"Here's to love, a thing so divine,
Description makes it but the less.
'Tis what we feel, but cannot define,
'Tis what we know but cannot express."

"Here's to the love that I hold for thee;
May it day by day grow stronger;
May it last as long as your love for me—
And not a second longer!"

"To the wings of love—
May they never lose a feather,
But soar up to the sky above,
And last and last forever."

"Thou hast no faults, or no faults I can spy;
Thou art all beauty, or all blindness I."

Here is one I like to call 'Ode To The Trophy Wife'

"Here's to the red and sparkling wine,
I'll be your sweetheart, if you'll be mine,
I'll be constant, I'll be true,
I'll leave my happy home for you."

More Valentine's Day Drinks

Pink Valentine Punch

1 bottle champagne, chilled
1 bottle rosé wine
10 oz. frozen strawberries, thawed
1/4 cup fine sugar

Place sugar and strawberries (with their juice) in punch bowl. Stir to dissolve sugar. Add wine and champagne.
Approximately 15 servings.

Confirmed Bachelor

1 1/2 oz. gin
1 tsp. Rose's lime juice
1 tsp. grenadine
1 egg white

Combine ingredients in a shaker half filled with ice. Shake well. Strain into a cocktail glass.

Seething Jealousy

1 oz. sweet vermouth
1 oz. scotch
1/2 oz. cherry brandy
1/2 oz. orange juice

Combine ingredients in a shaker half filled with ice. Shake well. Strain into a cocktail glass.

Even More Valentine's Day Drinks

Pink Lady
2 oz. gin
1 tsp. cherry brandy
1 tsp. grenadine
1 tsp. light cream
1 egg white

Combine ingredients in a shaker half filled with ice. Shake well. Strain into a cocktail glass.

Cherry Kiss
1 oz. Irish cream liqueur
1 oz. Chambord

Use a pousse-café or cordial glass. Pour Irish cream liqueur first. Then add Chambord by pouring it over the back of a spoon so that it floats on top.

Frozen Pink Valentine (Non-alcoholic)
4 oz. cranberry juice
1/4 cup raspberries, fresh or frozen
1 scoop vanilla ice cream

Put all ingredients in a blender and blend. Pour into a collins or parfait glass. Serve with a straw.

"We'll drink to love, love, the one irresistible force that annihilates distance, caste, prejudice and principles.
Love, the pastime of the Occident, the passion of the East.
Love, that stealeth upon us like a thief in the night, robbing us of rest, but bestowing in its place a gift more precious than the sweetest sleep.
Love is the burden of my toast—Here's looking at you."

"Amor vincit omnia (love conquers everything)."
(Virgil)

"All you need is love."
(John Lennon)

St. Patrick's Day Toasts

On March 17, everybody is Irish. St. Patrick's Day has become one of this country's biggest drinking events. In Ireland, it is ranked with the top four drinking events, the other three being weekdays, Saturday, and Sunday.

St. Patrick is the patron saint of Ireland and is responsible for driving all of the snakes out of the country. Not much is known about the real St. Patrick so I fabricated the following true story.

The Real Story of St. Patrick

St. Patrick was born Patrick Horowitz on March 17, 389 in a small village in England. This makes him English. I wonder if the Irish know about that? Anyhow, When Pat was eighteen years old, he left England to look for work in Ireland. He was a singer, a juggler, and a darn good mechanic. Unfortunately, there weren't a lot of cars to fix in 389 and cabaret had not yet been invented. So Patrick had to find a different form of employment.

While swatting at some flies in his apartment, Patrick came upon the idea that would make him famous. With a cash investment of about twelve cents, Patrick opened up Exterminating By Pat and soon had a thriving business getting rid of mice, leprechauns, and bubonic plague germs. He was known throughout the land as "Patrick, The Guy Who Kills Things."

The word of Patrick's expertise reached the chamber of commerce, which was struggling with a nasty snake problem. It seems that Ireland was plagued with millions of snakes and they were really taking a bite out of the tourism business. People didn't want to visit a land inhabited by both snakes and lawyers. So they called on Patrick to rid the island of snakes.

Patrick called up his old friend, the Pied Piper of Hamlin, and subcontracted his services. The Piper, who specialized in the elimination of rats and children, soon had all of the snakes gathered together, boxed them in a big crate, and sent them to Patrick. Since he sent them via air freight, the crate got lost and all of the snakes disappeared. When Patrick put in a lost cargo claim, he was recognized as the hero who rid the island of snakes. Patrick soon parlayed his notoriety and branched out into other businesses. He opened Patrick's Travel and Tours, a successful travel agency, and The Golden Shillelagh, a gentlemen's club featuring the two-dollar lap dance. Before he knew what was happening, Patrick was the richest man in Ireland.

Patrick may have been rich but he was also very generous and bestowed gifts upon his countrymen who, in turn, promised their allegiance. This paid off in 404 A.D. when Patrick ran for Patron Saint and won! His first act of sainthood was to declare his birthday a national holiday and to declare green his favorite color. Before you could say "Kiss Me, I'm Irish," the public embraced the new holiday with a celebration of political parades and public intoxication.

Now you know the real story, and to be ready to celebrate you need some real toasts. Erin Go Bragh!

"*Success attend St. Patrick's fist,*
For he's a saint so clever;
Oh! He give the snakes and toads a twist,
He banished them forever."

"*To St. Patrick on his day. May the shamrock be green forever.*"

"*On St. Patrick's Day you should spend time with saints and scholars, so you know I have two more stops to make.*"
(Jim Wright)

Saint Patrick's Day Drinks

There'll be the wearing of the green today and the drinking of it, too—with "Green Machine" punch and the "Saint Pat." Irish eyes will be smiling in song as well as in person as everyone raises a toast to St. Patrick who gives us this chance to celebrate.

Green Machine Punch

2 liters vodka
1 (12 oz.) can frozen limeade concentrate
1/2 pint lemon sherbet
1/2 pint lime sherbet

Defrost limeade and dissolve in vodka. Add sherbets. About 35 servings.

Everybody's Irish or Saint Pat

2 oz. Irish whiskey
1 oz. green crème de menthe
1 oz. green Chartreuse

Pour ingredients into a mixing glass nearly filled with ice. Stir. Strain into a cocktail glass.

This comes from a St. Patrick's Day toast delivered by Congressman Jim Wright to his colleagues in Congress in 1988.

"May the Irish hills caress you.
May her lakes and rivers bless you.
May the luck of the Irish enfold you.
May the blessings of St. Patrick behold you."

"Today's the day to wear the green,
And take a nip of whiskey.
To drink and sing and kiss the girls,
And get a little frisky."

"On St. Patrick's Day I give a toast
And make a little wish,
That every day was Paddy's Day,
And everyone I-rish."

One of the odder traditions of St. Patrick's Day is to dye everything you can get your hands on green. People dye their hair green on St. Patrick's Day and paint their fingernails to match. In Chicago they dye the Chicago River kelly green for a day. The rest of the year it is a lovely kelly brown. The thing that bothers me though is when taverns feel compelled to dye their draft beer green for a day. I wish they wouldn't do this. Even though it doesn't change the taste of the beer, it just doesn't look good.

"Lift your glasses and show no fear,
It may be green but it's still good beer."

"May the Leprechauns be near you to spread luck along your way.
And may all the Irish angels smile upon you on St. Pat's Day."

"Saint Patrick was a gentleman,
Who, through strategy and stealth,
Drove all the snakes from Ireland—

Here's a bumper to his health,
But not too many bumpers,
Lest we lose ourselves, and then
Forget the good Saint Patrick,
And see the snakes again."

"We'll toast Old Ireland!
Dear Old Ireland!
Ireland, boys, hurrah!"
(Timothy Daniel Sullivan)

"Here's to health, peace, and prosperity;
May the flower of love ne'er be nipped by the chill of disappointment;
Nor the shadow of grief fall upon us.
But like the green shamrock of Saint Patrick,
May peace and joy spring from the seeds of contentment."

April Fools' Day Toasts

April Fools' Day is my favorite holiday of the year. Even though nobody gets to take a day off and there are no presents, parades, or fireworks involved, I love April Fools' Day. On this day you can pull pranks and play practical jokes and nobody can get mad at you for doing it like they do at a funeral. April Fools' Day is the perfect day for the joker and the wise guy. It's a day for joy buzzers, Whoopie cushions, and squirting flowers. It is time for a party, and that calls for a toast.

"Let us toast the fools; but for them, the rest of us could not succeed."
(Mark Twain)

"May the jokes we fall for today, be the only ones we fall for all year."

"Lord, what fools these mortals be."
(Shakespeare, A Midsummer Night's Dream*)*

The Easter Parade

I have celebrated Easter all my life but I have never experienced the Easter event that has been lauded in song. I speak of the oft-mentioned Easter Parade. Unlike the Macy's Thanksgiving Day Parade and the Rose Bowl Parade, the Easter Parade is not televised. It is also not very organized. It never has any news coverage and is rarely mentioned in the newspapers. In fact, the only place you ever hear about the Easter Parade is in that dang song. Maybe I am just paranoid, but I think that the Easter Parade is a secret clandestine event attended only by people who are invited to participate. Apparently I am not on the A list because I have never been invited to the parade. I'll keep waiting, but I'm not going to hold my breath.

"May the skepticism you develop on April Fools' Day protect you for the rest of the year."

"To April 1st, the birth date of politicians and lawyers."

Easter and Passover Toasts

Easter and Passover are the holiest of holidays as celebrated by the Christian and Jewish religions. But just as the celebration of Christmas has crossed the secular border, Easter also represents a return to spring and a renewal of life for virtually everyone.

Today, Easter and Passover are celebrated both as the sacred days that they are and also as a time of family get togethers and a celebration that, year after year, life goes on. Because religious days require their own religious toasts—which vary from person to person, family to family, and religion to religion—we shall concentrate on Easter and Passover toasts more as toasts of life, renewal, and the burgeoning springtime.

Easter Toasts

"Easter Day, glad Easter Day,
Winter snows have gone away."

"Here's to finding all of your eggs and putting them in one basket."

"Christ the Lord is risen today! Alleluia."

"I cannot write like Shakespeare,
I cannot write a sonnet.
But I wish you Happy Easter
And a Happy Easter bonnet."

Passover Toasts

Passover is a holy day as is Easter, but it has not also become a secular holiday. Hence, there really are no general toasts for

Passover. According to Rabbi Mark Diamond, the closest thing to a toast occurs during the Seder dinner.

There are four cups of wine during the Seder, and each is preceded by the traditional blessing: "Praised are You, Adonai our God, Ruler of the universe, who creates the fruit of the vine."

Additionally, there are traditional greetings and blessings that can be used to toast family and friends.

> "*Hag samayah! (traditional greeting meaning Happy Holiday)*"

> "*Hag kasher v'samayah! (meaning A happy and kosher holiday)*"

Summertime Toasts—From Memorial Day to Labor Day

Summertime is party time and party time is toast time. It is a time for backyard cook outs and lazy summer evenings spent on the porch (or deck if you live in the suburbs) with a refreshing drink and the company of family and friends. Casual events such as these call for casual toasts along the general variety. But in the course of summer we may find some special occasions that call for special toasts. Here are some of both.

> "*Here's to all good things in life:*
> *Love, health, happiness and of course, good friends*
> *May we have many more good times together.*"

> "*Here's to the heat!*
> *Not the heat that burns down bars and shanties*
> *But the heat that pulls down bras and panties.*"

I would rate this toast as PG-13. It is a good summertime toast for adults in a party atmosphere.

“I’ve drank to your health with others.
I’ve drank to your health alone.
I’ve drank to your health so many times
That I’ve almost ruined my own.”

“Here’s to you as good as you are.
Here’s to me as bad as I am.
As good as you are and as bad as I am,
I’m as good as you are, as bad as I am.”

“Let us wipe out the past, trust in the future, and rejoice in the glorious Now.”

“Let us treat every day as if it were our last because some day we will be right.”

“Life consists not in holding good cards, but in playing those you hold well.”

“Laugh and the world laughs with you.
Cry and the world laughs at you anyhow.”

“‘Tis hard to tell which is best,
Music, food, drink, or rest.”

“May you always distinguish between the weeds and the flowers.”

“Who loves not women, wine, and song,
remains a fool his whole life long.”
(John Henry Voss)

“May we never want a friend to cheer us, or a bottle to cheer him.”

> *"When friends and other friends contrive*
> *To make their glasses clink,*
> *Then not one sense of all the five*
> *Is absent from the drink.*
> *For touch and taste and smell and sight*
> *Evolve in pleasant round,*
> *And when the flowing cups unite*
> *We thrill to sense of sound.*
> *Folly to look on wine? Oh fie*
> *On what the teetotlers think . . .*
> *There's five good reasons why*
> *Good fellows like to drink."*

> *"May the roof above us never fall in, and the friends gathered below never fall out."*

> *"May you be hung, drawn and quartered*
> *Hung in the hall of fame,*
> *Drawn by a golden chariot,*
> *And quartered in the arms of the one you love best."*

Of course summer brings with it an assortment of insects, which are bound to be present if you propose your toast out of doors. In case they do, you may want to include them.

> *"Who'd care to be a bee and sip*
> *Sweet honey from the flower's lip*
> *When he might be a fly and steer*
> *Head first into a can of beer."*

> *"Here's to the chigger,*
> *The bug that's no bigger*
> *Than the point of a pin;*
> *But the bump that he raises*
> *Itches like blazes*
> *And that's where the rub comes in."*

"Here's to the flea that jumped over me and bit the behind of my missus."

"Here's to the happy, bounding flea;
You cannot tell the he from the she,
But he can tell, and so can she!"
(Roland Young)

I don't know what it is about the lowly flea that has generated so many toasts, but here is one that even incorporates Latin.

"Great fleas have lesser fleas,
And these have less to bite 'em;
These fleas have lesser fleas,
And so ad infinitum.
The great fleas themselves in turn,
Have greater fleas to go on.
While these again have greater still,
And greater still, and so on."

"A little health, a little wealth,
A little house and freedom.
With some few friends for certain ends
But little cause to need 'em."

"Health to my body, wealth to my purse
Heaven to my soul, and I wish you no worse."

"Here's to us that are here, to you that are here, and the rest of us everywhere."
(Rudyard Kipling)

"Life is a jest, and all things show it—
I thought so once but now I know it."
(John Gay)

*"May our faults be written on the seashore,
and every good action prove a wave to wash them out."*

"May we all live in pleasure and die out of debt."

Nothing sums up summertime better than fishing, golf, and beer. Here are some toasts for these favorite summer pastimes.

Fishing Toasts

*"Here's to our fisherman bold;
Here's to the fish he caught;
Here's to the one that got away,
And here's to the ones he bought."*

*"A fisherman, by and by,
Will very seldom tell a lie;
Except when it is needed to
Describe the fish that left his view."*

*"Here's to the fish that I may catch;
So large that even I,
When talking of it afterward,
Will never need to lie."*

*"Here's to the fisherman!
He riseth in the early morning
And disturbeth the whole household.
Health to me,
And death to fish;
They're wagging their tails
That will pay for this."*

On Golf

Golf contains all of the elements essential for a good participatory sport: motorized carts, funny clothes, weapons, and beer. In golf your clubs are your weapons, and nothing means more to a golfer than his clubs. A good set of expensive clubs will assure even the worst golfer that his friends will not make fun of him for being such a lousy player. A good set of clubs should cost as much as a used car. Every golfer's bag should contain a driver, a mashie, and a niblick. The driver is also known as "the guy in charge of maneuvering the cart," the mashie is the person who has every episode of M*A*S*H on tape, and the niblick is not something which should be discussed in public. The golf bag can contain other clubs as well, but it is up to each golfer to give them names. That is why you will hear golfers calling their clubs names like Big Bertha, Old Betsy, the Terminator and You Worthless Piece of #@&%!.

Here is one for the animal rights activist or vegetarian on your next fishing trip.

"Enjoy the stream, O harmless fish,
And when an angler for his dish,
Through gluttony's vile sin,
Attempts, the wretch, to pull thee out,
God give thee strength, O gentle trout,
To pull the rascal in."

"May the holes in your net be no bigger than your fish."

"Let's lift our glass to the creative fisherman—every time he talks about the one that got away, it grows another foot."

Golf Toasts

"Here's to your woods, here's to your irons,
Here's to your putter, too.
May every shot you hit with them,
Fall in the hole for you."

"I used to think that golf was just
like man's best friend, the dog.
But 'dog' spelled backwards comes out 'god'
While 'golf' just comes out 'flog.'"

"I love golf, it makes me happy,
It makes me feel alive.
But I hit the ball all over the course
I need a cart with four-wheel drive."

"To the great sport of golf, long may it reign,
Even though sometimes it can be a big pain."

Beer Toasts

In any language, summer means beer. Actually, that is not entirely true. In Norwegian, summer means "that brief period of time in July when the temperature goes over 50°." But metaphorically speaking, summer and beer go together like chips and dip, like hot dogs and relish. Now that I think about it, chips, dip, hot dogs, relish, and beer pretty much is my summer.

Summertime is hot and hot weather calls for ice cold beer. When toasting your friends with a cold beer please use caution. If you become too schmaltzy with your toast you will look like one of those goofballs in a Light beer commercial, and, goodness knows, that is not a pretty sight. If, however, you use any of the following toasts, you can be assured that you will never be mistaken for a commercial of any type.

"None be so deaf as those who will not hear.
None so blind as those who will not see.
But I'll wager none so deaf nor blind that he
Sees not nor hears me say come drink this beer."
(W. L. Hassoldt)

"Beer makes you smarter. It made Bud Wiser."
(Jim Irvin, my dad, who told me this joke at least 300 times as I was growing up.)

"Let's drink the liquid of amber so bright;
Let's drink the liquid with foam snowy white;
Let's drink the liquid that brings all good cheer;
Oh, where is the drink like old-fashioned beer?"

"You can't buy beer,
You can only rent it."

Frozen Mugs

It's time to put your frosted mugs in the same closet with your pet rock and mood ring. Frozen mugs are out.

There are several good reasons for this. In the history of European beer, no country has ever featured frozen mugs. Lager was invented to be stored cold . . . that's what lager means. But the first brewers of lager didn't have refrigeration, per se. They stored the casks of beer in caves dug into the sides of mountains. They served lagers chilled, but not icy cold. You're just muting the tastes if you serve beer icy cold.

Another thing to remember when serving from frozen mugs is that ice forms on the inside of your frosty mug. By freezing your mugs, all you're doing is diluting the body and the flavor of the beer.

Why Beer Is Nature's Most Perfect Beverage

1. It was meant to be consumed in quantity. Unlike other beverages, beer is seldom sold one can at a time. It is sold by the six-pack, the twelve-pack, and the twenty-four-piece case. If you do happen to be able to buy a single bottle of beer, it is generally a quart bottle.
2. Health experts tell us to drink eight glasses of water a day. Coincidentally, the main ingredient in beer is water. In fact, beer is over 95 percent water. The other five percent are nutritious things like barley, hops, and yeast; all tasty ingredients found in bread. Instead of drinking eight glasses of water a day and eating bread, just have ten or twelve beers.

(continued)

“*Here,*
With my beer
I sit,
While golden moments flit;
Alas!
They pass
Unheeded by;
And as they fly,
I,
Being dry,
Sit, idly sipping here
My beer.”
(George Arnold)

“*Come, sit we by the fireside*
And roundly drink we hear,
Till that we see our cheeks all dyed
And noses tanned with beer.”
(Robert Herrick)

“*Ale's a strong wrestler,*
Flings all it hath met;
And makes the ground slippery,
Though it not be wet.”

“*Beer! Beer! Beer!*
We students adore you,
Beer! Beer! Beer!
We love to see you foam;
When we for wine abjure you,
We miss you we assure you,
For it's only with clear sparkling beer
That students feel at home.”

Memorial Day Toasts

Memorial Day used to be known as Decoration Day. It also used to be held on May 30 instead of being shifted around to accommodate a three-day weekend. Traditionally, Memorial Day is a day to remember all of the men and women who have given their lives to protect our country. The original designation of Decoration Day spelled out the custom of decorating the graves of servicemen and women with flowers and flags. Memorial Day is now home of the Indianapolis 500 motor race.

"To the memory of those
Who died for freedom."

"To our flag—may its stars light the way
And its stripes guide our steps in the
Everlasting cause of peace."

"To the land we live in, love, and would die for."

Flag Day Toasts

Flag Day is observed on June 14 in celebration of the adoption of the stars and stripes as the official flag on that day in 1777. It is not a legal holiday in the sense that banks do not close, mail is still delivered, and nobody gets the day off. But that doesn't mean it isn't a good day for a toast.

"May we always remember what red, white, and blue
really stand for—
love, purity, and fidelity."

"To her we drink, for her we pray,
Our voices silent never;
For her we'll fight, come what may,
The Stars and Stripes forever."
(Stephen Decatur)

"The union of lakes, the union of lands,
The union of states none can sever;
The union of hearts, the union of hands,
And the flag of our union forever."

Why Beer Is Nature's Most Perfect Beverage

3. You do not need any special equipment to enjoy beer. While champagne requires champagne glasses and wine calls for wine glasses, beer can be enjoyed right in its original package. Beer tastes as good when consumed right from the bottle or can as it does when poured in a paper cup.

Fourth of July Toasts

Independence Day is this country's greatest national holiday. It is celebrated with parades, flags, and, of course, fireworks. No other holiday is as closely identified with fireworks as the Fourth of July. Well, maybe Chinese New Year, but that's beside the point.

The Fourth of July is also a big day for picnics and cookouts. Family and friends gather across the land to celebrate our independence and have one heck of a party. And wherever there's a party, you can be sure there will be toasts.

> *"Here's to the memory*
> *Of the man*
> *That raised the corn*
> *That fed the goose*
> *That bore the quill*
> *That made the pen*
> *That wrote the Declaration of Independence."*

> *"To our country! Lift your glasses!*
> *To its sun-capped mountain passes,*
> *To its forest, to its streams,*
> *To its memories, its dreams,*
> *To its laughter, to its tears,*
> *To the hope that after years*
> *Find us plodding on the way*
> *Without so much tax to pay."*

> *"We've toasted all names and all places,*
> *We've toasted all kinds of game,*
> *Why not just for loyalty's sake*
> *Drink one to our nation's name."*

> *"To the Fourth of July—like oyster soup, it cannot be enjoyed without crackers."*

> *"To the United States, where each man is protected by the Constitution regardless of whether he has ever taken the time to read it."*

Fourth of July Drinks

Some things never change. Some things shouldn't change: parades on the Fourth of July, town fireworks, and Independence Day picnics. Everyone wants to celebrate on this birth-of-the-nation holiday, and if you're in charge of the entertainment, offer up some of these patriotic cocktails.

Patriotic Punch

Good to look at and better to drink, this punch is wonderfully refreshing for a summer day. Adjust the alcohol and juice proportions according to the crowd, the day, and the degree of patriotic fervor.

1 liter vodka
2 quarts grapefruit juice
2 quarts cranberry juice

Chill ingredients. Combine in a punch bowl with ice or an ice ring. Approximately 25 servings.

"The Frenchman loves his native wine;
The German loves his beer;
The Englishman loves his 'alf and 'alf;
Because it brings good cheer.
The Irishman loves his whisky straight,
Because it gives him dizziness
The American has no choice at all,
So he drinks the whole damned business."

"May our counsels be wise,
And our commerce increase,
May we ever experience
The blessings of peace."

"Let the tree of liberty thrive round the world
and every one of God's children in its bounty."

"To America:
'With all its faults and blemishes, this country gives a man elbowroom to do what is nearest his heart.'"
(Eric Hoffer)

Labor Day Toasts

Labor Day was first celebrated in 1894 and was designed to honor the American worker. Since it is an official holiday and most American workers have the day off, I always thought they should have called it No-Labor Day, but ideas like this are probably the reason I am not the guy in charge. Here are some toasts celebrating the worker in all of us followed by some specific toasts for different occupations.

"May the work that you have
Be the play that you love."

"Here's to success, which can set its roots deep only through soil enriched by countless failures."

More Fourth of July Drinks

Independence Punch (Non-alcoholic)

2 quarts cranberry juice
1 quart raspberry soda
1 pkg. frozen raspberries

Chill juice and soda. Thaw raspberries. Combine in a punch bowl with ice or an ice ring. Approximately 15 servings.

American Beauty

1 1/2 oz. brandy
1 oz. dry vermouth
1/2 tsp. white crème de menthe
1/2 tsp. grenadine
1 oz. orange juice
1 oz. port

Combine ingredients except port in a shaker half filled with ice. Shake well. Strain into a cocktail glass. Float the port on top.

Fourth of July

1 oz. grenadine
1 oz. vodka
1 oz. blue Curaçao

Pour ingredients, in order given, into a cordial or shot glass, so that they form separate layers.

"*To the dignity of labor*
And the benefit of its ends."

"*To all who work to live:*
'A truly American sentiment recognizes the dignity of labor and the fact that honor lies in honest toil.'"
(Grover Cleveland)

"*A day's work is a day's work, neither more nor less, and the man who does it needs a day's sustenance, a night's repose and due leisure, whether he be a painter or a ploughman.*"
(George Bernard Shaw)

Occupational Toasts

When you toast to Labor Day, you should also include a toast to the jobs and occupations of the men and women who keep this country on the move. As your social gathering progresses, try toasting all of the different occupations represented by the people in attendance. Here are a few occupational toasts to get you started.

Accountant

"*Here's to the man who keeps my books,*
Watching money like an eagle,
I only wish I really knew
That your tactics were all legal."

Advertising

"*The world of advertising people is often referred to as 'the jungle.'*
I give you our very own Tarzan of the Apes."

Architect

"*Here's to the architect. As Frank Lloyd Wright once said, 'The physician can bury his mistakes, but the architect can only advise his client to plant vines.'*"

Artist

"*No great artist ever sees things as they really are.*
If he did he would cease to be an artist."
(Oscar Wilde)

Baker

"*We wish you life, we wish you health,*
Wherever you may go.
We need not wish you wealth because,
You're rolling in the dough."

Banker

"*Here's to the banker, who, in the words of Mark Twain, is a fellow who lends his umbrella when the sun is shining and wants it back the minute it begins to rain.*"

"*May I present to you a person who knows all there is to know about banks—except breaking and entering.*"

Butcher

"*You chop our pork,*
You grind our chuck,
You even trim our roast.
So it is with everlasting thanks,
That we propose to you this toast."

"*Here's to our butcher, our carver of meat,*
It is to you we hail.
All we ask in return from you,
Is to keep your thumb off of the scale."

Barber

"*He cuts our hair*
And shaves our face,
And talks and talks
With ease and grace."

Old-Fashioned Hard Work

Some occupations like butcher, baker, and even candlestick maker have been around since the middle ages. But not all of the jobs from those days are still in existence. For instance, you will not find many vocational schools teaching courses for careers as:

Fishmongers
Pewterers
Court jesters
Girdlers
Armourers
Tallow chandlers
Salters
Ironmongers

Cook

"May we always have more occasion for the cook than the doctor."

Computer Specialist

"Here's to our very own computer whiz who still uses all his fingers and toes for the simpler problems of arithmetic."

Dentist

*"'Twould make a suffering mortal grin,
and laugh away dull care,
if he could see his dentist in
another dentist's chair."*

Doctor

"To our neighborhood doctor whose only professional problem is to have patience with his patients."

Electrician

*"Amperes, currents, AC DC power,
We love electricians but not their rate per hour."*

Farmer

*"Good luck to the hoof and the horn
Good luck to the flock and the fleece
Good luck to the growers of corn
With blessings of plenty and peace."*

Gardener

*"May the weeds wilt before you;
May the vegetables rise up to feed you;
And may the bugs stay always on the other side of the fence."*

*"Here's to the gardener—
the only person who spreads more fertilizer than the politician."*

Homemaker/Housewife/Domestic Engineer

No matter what title this person is assigned, they are among the hardest workers in the world. They labor from sun up to sundown, except for the time they take off to watch *Oprah*, to make a house a home. Here is a toast to those who make life more comfortable.

> "*In the words of Louisa May Alcott, 'Housekeeping ain't no joke.'*
> *Thanks for keeping our house warm and loving and fun.*"

Lawyer

> "*I give you our legal eagle and counselor who in the course of his trials has opened many cases—not all in the courtroom.*"

Miner

> "*May all your labors be in vein.*"

Orthodontist

> "*To the orthodontist, a man who must keep his spirits high after looking down in the mouth all day.*"

Police

> "*Here's to the policeman who passes our way.*
> *Here's to the mailman who calls every day.*
> *Here's to the babies who continually say;*
> *'Mom, which is my daddy—the blue or the gray?'*"

Politician

> "*Here's to an honest politician—a man who when bought, stays bought.*"

Printing

> "*You can always tell a barber*
> *By the way he parts his hair;*
> *You can always tell a dentist*

Thanksgiving Drinks

Mayflower Cocktail

1 1/2 oz. sweet vermouth
1/2 oz. dry vermouth
1/2 oz. brandy
1 tsp. Pernod
1 tsp. Triple Sec
dash orange bitters

Combine ingredients in a shaker half filled with ice. Shake well. Strain into a cocktail glass.

Americana

1/4 oz. Tennessee whiskey
1 tsp. fine sugar
dash bitters
champagne, chilled

Combine the whiskey, sugar, and bitters in a collins or highball glass until the sugar is dissolved. Fill with champagne.

Shirley Temple

(Non-alcoholic)
ginger ale
1/2 tsp.grenadine
maraschino cherry,
orange slice

Pour ginger ale into an old-fashioned glass over ice. Add grenadine and stir gently. Garnish with a cherry and orange slice.

When you're in the dentist's chair;
And even a musician—
You can tell him by his touch;
You can always tell a printer,
But you cannot tell him much."

Note: This toast can be used to salute virtually any occupation by substituting the word printer for the word plumber, painter, theoretical physicist, etc.

Psychiatrist

"*Here's to the psychiatrist—a person who doesn't have to worry as long as other people do.*"

Sales

"*Here's to opening accounts and closing deals!*"

Scientist

"*To science and all that it has brought to us. We are reminded of the words of Albert Einstein who said, 'The whole of science is nothing more than a refinement of everyday thinking.'*"

Teacher

"*Here's to the best kind of teacher we know;*
Who adds class to the classroom,
making normal students want to become exceptional scholars.
What parents could ever ask for anything more?"

Waiter

"*We drink your health, O waiter!*
And may you be preserved
From old age, gout, or sudden death!
At least till supper's served."

(Oliver Herford and John Cecil Clay)

Thanksgiving Toasts

Thanksgiving is one of the most popular holidays we have in this country. It is an Everyman's holiday that stands for overeating, football, and a four-day holiday weekend. How could anyone not fully agree with this?

Thanksgiving is a time for families and feasting; both of which can be perfectly matched with a toast.

> *"Let us toast to our blessings and good fortune on this Thanksgiving Day."*

> *"To the harvest time of year*
> *When Plenty pours her wine of cheer,*
> *And even humble boards may spare*
> *To poorer poor a kindly share."*

> *"May our pleasures be boundless*
> *While we have time to enjoy them."*

> *"Here's to the turkey I'm about to eat and the turkeys I'll eat it with."*

> *"For what we are about to receive, may the Lord make us truly thankful."*

> *"To our national birds—*
> *The American Eagle,*
> *The Thanksgiving Turkey;*
> *May one give us peace in all our states—*
> *And the other a piece for all our plates."*

> *"When turkey's on the table laid,*
> *And good things I may scan,*
> *I'm thankful that I wasn't made*
> *A vegetarian."*
> *(Edgar A. Guest)*

Thanksgiving Drinks

Giving thanks is something we all could be better at, and Thanksgiving gives us a chance to realize our good intentions, and enjoy a feast. A cocktail called the "Thanksgiving Special" should be carried to the cook, who deserves a good portion of the thanks for the day.

Thanksgiving Special
1 oz. gin
3/4 oz. apricot-flavored brandy
3/4 oz. dry vermouth
splash lemon juice

Combine ingredients in a shaker half filled with ice. Shake well. Strain into a cocktail glass.

Happy Apple
2 oz. rum
3 oz. apple cider
1/2 oz. lime juice

Combine ingredients in a shaker half filled with ice. Shake well. Strain into an old-fashioned glass. Garnish with a lime twist.

"For turkey braised,
The Lord be praised."

"Here's to the blessing of the year,
Here's to the friends we hold so dear,
To peace on earth, both far and near.
Here's to the good old turkey
The bird that comes each fall
And with his sweet persuasive meat
Makes gobblers of us all."

"Bless, O Lord
These delectable vittles,
May they add to the glory
And not to our middles."
(Yvonne Wright)

"We've got ANOTHER holiday to worry about.
It seems Thanksgiving Day is upon us."
(Charlie Brown in 'A Charlie Brown Thanksgiving')

Thanksgiving is a very special time of the year and deserves a special grace as well as special toasts. This one was written by Danny Thomas, yes, that Danny Thomas, when he was in the sixth grade.

"For the air we breathe,
And the water we drink,
For a soul and a mind with which to think,
For food that comes from fertile sod,
For these, and many things, I'm thankful to my God."

Christmas/Hanukkah/Kwanzaa Toasts

Special holidays call for special toasts, and December is the home of the year's most special holidays. Many families have their own holiday toasts that have passed down from generation to generation.

In our family, I can still recall the words of my father who would raise a glass on Christmas Day and say, "Hey, my glass is empty here."

If your family doesn't currently have a heart-warming toast like this to fall back on, perhaps you can find one from the following selections.

Christmas Toasts

"*Christmas is here,*
Merry old Christmas,
Gift-bearing, heart touching, joy bringing Christmas,
Day of grand memories, king of the year."
(Washington Irving)

"*I know I've wished you this before*
But every year I wish it more.
A Merry Christmas."

"*To Christmas—hang up love's mistletoe over the earth,*
And let us kiss under it all the year round."

"*Blessed is the season which engages*
The whole world in a conspiracy of love."
(Hamilton Wright Mabie)

"*At Christmas play and make good cheer*
For Christmas comes but once a year."
(Thomas Turner)

"*As fits the holy Christmas birth,*
Be this, good friends, our carol still—
Be peace on earth, be peace on earth,
To men of gentle will."
(William Makepeace Thackeray)

Christmas Drinks

Christmas is for gathering, so a wonderful punch bowl seems ideal for the whole family. Irresistible Egg Nog is a treat with or without rum. Wassail, the traditional old English holiday drink, was originally made with ale, roasted apples, toasted bread, raisins, and currants. Too much for today's taste, but here is a marvelous modern version. The name is derived from the old Gaelic toast, Was Hael!, Be Well! Indeed. And merry, merry Christmas.

Egg Nog

6 eggs
1 cup sugar
1/2 tsp. salt
1 cup rum
1 1/2 tsp. vanilla
1 quart light cream or milk
nutmeg

Beat eggs until light and foamy. Add sugar, salt, and vanilla. Add rum and cream. Stir well. Chill. Sprinkle with nutmeg before serving. Makes approximately 12 half-cup servings.

"Many happy returns of the day to you—
No sorrow nor sadness
But all joy and gladness.
Many happy returns on this Christmas Day!"

"Be merry all, be merry all,
With holly dress the festive hall,
Prepare the song, the feast, the ball,
To welcome Merry Christmas."

"To a person so generous that it makes me want to say, 'Yes, my friends, there is a Santa Claus.'"

"In the immortal words of Tiny Tim, 'God bless us, every one.'"

(Note: Just to clear up any possible confusion, I am referring to the character from the classic Charles Dickens book, *A Christmas Carol*, not the scraggly-haired, falsetto-voiced crooner who got married on *The Johnny Carson Show*.)

"Here's to the holly with its bright red berry.
Here's to Christmas, let's make it merry."

"Here's wishing you more happiness
Than all my words can tell,
Not just alone for Christmas
But for all the year as well."

"Christmas . . .
A day when cheer and gladness blend,
When heart meets heart
And friend meets friend."
(J. H. Fairweather)

"*I wish you a Merry Christmas*
And a Happy New Year,
A pocket full of money
And a cooler full of beer."

"*I have always thought of Christmas as a good time; a kind, forgiving, generous, pleasant time; a time when men and women seem by one consent to open their hearts freely; and so I say 'God bless Christmas.'*"
(Charles Dickens)

"*Here's to the white of the mistletoe,*
And to its many leaves so green;
And here's to the lips of ruby red,
Waiting 'neath to complete the scene."

"*Here's to friends we've yet to meet,*
Here's to those here; all here I greet;
Here's to childhood, youth, old age,
Here's to prophet, bard and sage,
Here's to your health—may all be bright
On this so special Christmas night."

"*Now thrice welcome Christmas*
Which brings us good cheer,
Minced pies and plum porridge."

"*Joy to the world, and especially to you.*"

"*Here's to the season when fowl killing promotes peace and good will.*"

Christmas is a major holiday for the Irish (probably ranking right behind St. Patrick's Day), so it makes sense that the Irish would have provided us with some of the most colorful of the Christmas toasts. Here are a few of them.

More Christmas Drinks

Sparkling Orange Egg Nog
(Non-alcoholic)
1 quart orange juice, chilled
1/4 cup lemon juice
3 eggs
2 Tbs. sugar
dash cinnamon
dash cloves
1 pint vanilla ice cream
16 oz. ginger ale, chilled

Beat eggs until light and foamy. Add 2 cups of the orange juice, lemon juice, sugar, and spices and stir well. Chill. Just before serving add ice cream and remaining 2 cups of orange juice and beat with a hand mixer. Add ginger ale and mix briefly. Sprinkle with nutmeg.

Joy to the World
1 1/2 oz. light rum
1/2 oz. bourbon
1/2 oz. dark crème de cacao

Pour ingredients into a mixing glass nearly filled with ice. Stir. Strain into a cocktail glass.

"Holly and ivy hanging up
And something wet in every cup."

"May yours be the first house in the parish to welcome St. Nicholas."

"May you be as contented as Christmas finds you all the year round."

"May you be poor in misfortune this Christmas
And rich in blessings
Slow to make enemies
Quick to make friends
And rich or poor, slow or quick,
As happy as the New Year is long."

"A Christmas wish–
May you never forget
What is worth remembering
Or remember what is best forgotten."

"May you never be without a drop at Christmas."

"May your sheep all have lambs
But not on Christmas night."

"May your corn stand high as yourself, your fields grow bigger with rain, and the mare know its own way home on Christmas night."

"Peace and plenty for many a Christmas to come."

An old Irish tradition is to leave the door unbolted on Christmas Eve and place a candle in the window so that the Virgin Mary can find her way to Bethlehem. This is the toast that accompanies that tradition.

> *"May the Virgin and her Child lift your latch on Christmas night."*

Hanukkah Toasts

Hanukkah (also spelled Hanukah and Chanukah) is the Jewish Festival of Lights, which is celebrated for eight nights in December. It commemorates the victory of Judas Maccabeus and the rededication of the Temple in Jerusalem The Festival of Lights is marked by the lighting of candles in a menorah, an eight-branched candlestick, to commemorate the miracle of a small vial of oil that burned for eight days.

Here are eight sample toasts (one for each night) that can be given to celebrate this holiday. They may stand alone or accompany the traditional Jewish toast of Le Chiam (To Life).

> *"May these be our gifts at Hanukah; deep peace and lasting love that we will share together with the ones we are fondest of."*

> *"May the warmth of Hanukah bring us hope to lift our hearts and love to light our way."*

> *"As we celebrate the miracles of long ago may we have great pride in our heritage, great joy in our freedom and real love in our homes."*

> *"Time of light, time of hope, time of courage, time of gratitude. May this time of remembering, prepare us for a time of peace."*

Etiquette Tip: Orphans' Holidays

One of the most thoughtful things you can do is to invite "orphaned" friends to your home to share your food and company on holidays when they cannont be with their own families.

They should be told that they are not expected to bring gifts. Nevertheless, it is a kind gesture for the visiting "orphan" to send a floral arrangement or centerpiece to the hostess ahead of time.

A visitor can feel like an interloper no matter how hard everybody works to enfranchise him. It is the responsibility of the person who invited him to pay special attention at these times and to offer the use of the family phone so that he can call his own family at whatever the distance.

Kwanzaa

Kwanzaa is based on seven principles:

1. Umoja—unity
2. Kujichagulia—self determination
3. Ujima—collective work and determination
4. Ujamaa—cooperative economics
5. Nia—purpose
6. Kuumba—creativity
7. Imani—faith

"At the festival of lights, may our faith be renewed and our hearts rejoice in Adonai's love for our people."

"May each day of Hanukah be a very happy one
and the spinning dreidel bring us lots of luck and fun."

"May the lights of Hanukah shine brightly for us all
as we celebrate in peace and love."

"May these be our gifts at Hanukah; warm hearts and shining faces
surrounding us to make our home the happiest of places."

Kwanzaa Toasts

Kwanzaa, or Kwanza, is a secular festival in celebration of the African heritage of African-Americans. It begins on December 26 and lasts for seven days. Kwanzaa was developed by Maulana Karenga and was first observed in 1966. It is based in part on traditional African harvest festivals but particularly emphasizes the role of the family and community in African-American culture. Each day is dedicated to a particular principle (unity, self-determination, collective work and responsibility, cooperative economics, purpose, creativity, and faith), and on each day one of the candles on a seven-branched candelabrum is lighted. The celebration also includes the giving of gifts and a karamu, or African feast.

As with some other holidays, official Kwanzaa toasts may not exist. But also as with other special occasions, quotes, verse, and prose may be converted into toasts given before a celebratory meal. Here are some lines that could easily be converted to toasts.

"I am because we are, because we are, I am."
(Recited during the Kwanzaa feast.)

"Harambee!! (let's pull together)"

"Matunda Ya Kwanzaa! (first fruits of the harvest)"

"Habari Gani - Kwanzaa (what's the news)"

There is also a Black Pledge, which is recited along with a Maya Angelou poem at the feast (Karamu). The pledge is as follows:

> *"We pledge to bind ourselves to one another, to embrace our lowliest, to keep company with our loneliest, to educate our illiterate, to feed our starving, to clothe our ragged, to do all good things, knowing that we are more than keepers of our brothers and sisters. We ARE our brothers and sisters.*
>
> *In Honor of those who toiled and implored God with golden tongues, and in gratitude to the same God who brought us out of hopeless desolation, we make this pledge."*

More on Kwanzaa

There are also seven symbols during Kwanzaa:

1. Mkeka—a straw mat, for tradition and history
2. Mazao—fruits and vegetables, for celebrating harvest
3. Kinara—a seven-branched candle holder for seven principles
4. Muhindi—an ear of corn for each child, for fertility and potential
5. Zawadi—gifts, to encourage creativity
6. Kikombe Cha Umoja—the unity cup, used in prayers and blessings
7. Mahumaa—seven candles: three red, three green, one black, for the seven principles

CHAPTER 4

The Toast of the Town

Many people have delivered toasts: famous people, infamous people, nonfamous people, and people you have never heard of. Here are some samples of each.

Toasts of the Famous

Many famous people made famous toasts, which weren't famous when they made them but are famous now. The most famous of the famous quotes was uttered by a fictional character named Rick Blaine who lived in Casablanca during the 1940s. I am sure you have quoted him many times when you uttered his toast,

> *"Here's looking at you kid."*
> *(Humphrey Bogart in* Casablanca*)*

Sometimes famous people have said things which were not really toasts at the time they said them but could easily be incorporated into toasts by adding words like, "In the words of [ ], I propose this toast." Or, "To quote [ ], a man who knew a lot about drinking, I toast you with the following words . . . " Here are some famous quotes that you can turn into toasts.

> *"I can tell I've had enough to drink when my knees start to bend backwards."*
> *(W.C. Fields)*

> *"I drink champagne when I am happy and when I'm sad. Sometimes I drink it when I'm alone. When I have company I consider it obligatory. I trifle with it if I'm not hungry and drink it when I am. Otherwise I never touch it—unless I'm thirsty."*
> *(Lily Bollinger)*

> *"I saw a notice which said 'Drink Canada Dry' so I've started."*
> *(Brendan Behan)*

> *"Beauty is in the eye of the beerholder."*
> *(W.C. Fields)*

"Drink is your enemy–love your enemies."
(W.C. Fields)

I had the opportunity to meet Ed McMahon once when I was doing a television show in New York City, and in addition to being a really nice guy, Ed was a champion toaster. He toasts every dinner he enjoys with friends with these simple words:

"Here's to the festival of life."

This is a profound statement and a wonderful toast. We should celebrate each minute of life and toast our good fortune of being a part of it.

"I never drink water–look at the way it rusts pipes."
(W.C. Fields)

"Candy is dandy,
But liquor is quicker."
(Ogden Nash)

"Drink! For you know not whence you came, nor why;
Drink! For you know not why you go, nor where."
(Omar Khayam)

"Fifteen men on the Dead Man's Chest
Yo ho ho and a bottle of rum!
Drink and the devil had done for the rest,
Yo ho ho and a bottle of rum!"
(Long John Silver in Robert Louis Stevenson's Treasure Island*)*

"Here's to your good health and your family's good health.
May you live long and prosper."
(Joseph Jefferson, 'Rip Van Winkle')

Namesakes

You don't have to be Adam and Eve to have a drink named after you, but they do seem particularly appropriate. "To Life!" is the toast for these two who started it all. Napoleon, a short man who was larger than life, has a dessert and a cocktail bearing his name. Two historically important American figures have drinks named after them, clever Betsy Ross and gallant Robert E. Lee. And three entertainers: the beautiful Mary Pickford, the great Charlie Chaplin, and the wise Will Rogers, who made life his art.

Mary Pickford Cocktail

1 oz. light rum
1 oz. pineapple juice
1/2 tsp. grenadine
1/2 tsp. Maraschino

Combine ingredients in a shaker half filled with ice. Shake well. Strain into a cocktail glass and garnish with a cherry.

“Live long and prosper.”
(Mr. Spock)

“In vino veritas (In wine there is truth.)”
(Pliny the Elder)

“God only made water, but man made wine.”
(Victor Hugo)

“Man, being reasonable, must get drunk;
The best of life is but intoxication.”
(Lord Byron)

“I'd hate to be a teetotaler. Imagine getting up in the morning and knowing that's as good as you're going to feel all day.”
(Dean Martin)

“When there is plenty of wine, sorrow and worry take wing.”
(Ovid)

“Give strong drink unto him that is ready to perish, and wine unto those that be of heavy hearts. Let him drink, and forget his poverty, and remember his misery no more.”
(Proverbs 31:4-7)

“My grandmother is over eighty and still doesn't need glasses. Drinks right out of the bottle.”
(Henny Youngman)

“If you drink, don't drive. Don't even putt.”
(Dean Martin)

“Champagne for my sham friends; real pain for my real friends.”
(Francis Bacon)

Actually, this toast sounds much better if you turn it around a little so that it reads, "Champagne for my real friends and real pain for my sham friends." This is probably what Bacon had in mind when he wrote it but he may have been drinking at the time.

> *"Come quickly, I am tasting stars!"*
> (Dom Perignon, when he first discovered champagne)

> *"A man is never drunk if he can lay on the floor without holding on."*
> (Joe E. Lewis)

> *"I have taken more out of alcohol than alcohol has taken out of me."*
> (Winston Churchill)

> *"I've made it a rule never to drink by daylight and never to refuse a drink after dark."*
> (H.L. Mencken)

> *"Sometimes too much drink is barely enough."*
> (Mark Twain)

> *"You can't drown yourself in drink. I've tried: you float."*
> (John Barrymore)

> *"There are more old drunkards than old doctors."*
> (Ben Franklin)

> *"Wine is the most healthful and most hygienic of beverages."*
> (Louis Pasteur)

(Pasteur was also credited with first uttering the line, "Does this milk taste funny to you?")

Top Ten Party Secrets:

1. Separate the food and drinks. This creates movement or "party flow."
2. Invite guests with different interests.
3. As the host, try to control your alcohol intake.
4. Avoid finger foods that leave something in your hand.
5. Buy good liquor: your friends are worth it.
6. Theme drinks are fun, but make sure to have alternatives.
7. Buy plastic cups, not paper. Paper cups will eventually drip.
8. Have the makings of a pot of coffee ready.
9. End the party on a high note. Your guests will leave while they are having a good time, and they'll remember it as a successful party.
10. Clean up immediately after everyone leaves. Even though you're tired, it's still better than waking up to the mess in the morning.

More Namesake Drinks

Adam and Eve
1 oz. Forbidden Fruit Liqueur
1 oz. gin
1 oz. brandy
splash lemon juice

Pour all ingredients into a shaker half filled with crushed ice. Shake well. Strain into a cocktail glass.

Napoleon
2 oz. gin
1/2 oz. Dubonnet Rouge
1/2 oz. Grand Marnier

Stir all ingredients in a mixing glass half filled with ice. Strain into a cocktail glass.

Charlie Chaplin Shooter
1 oz.sloe gin
1 oz. apricot-flavored brandy
1/2 oz. lemon juice

Combine ingredients in a shaker nearly filled with ice. Shake well. Strain into a shot glass.

"Drunkenness is simply voluntary insanity."
(Seneca)

"When I read about the evils of drinking, I gave up reading."
(Henny Youngman)

"It provokes the desire, but it takes away the performance."
(Shakespeare)

"Drink the first. Sip the second slowly. Skip the third."
(Knute Rockne)

"First you take a drink, then the drink takes a drink, then the drink takes you."
(F. Scott Fitzgerald)

"Better sleep with a sober cannibal than a drunken Christian."
(Herman Melville)

"I'd rather have a free bottle in front of me than a pre-frontal lobotomy."
(Tom Waits)

"I drink when there is an occasion, and sometimes when there is no occasion."
(Miguel de Cervantes)

"He that drinks fast, pays slow."
(Ben Franklin)

"The whole world is about three drinks behind."
(Humphrey Bogart)

> "*When I drink, I think; and when I think, I drink.*"
> *(Francois Rabelais)*

> "*Whenever someone asks me if I want water with my Scotch, I say I'm thirsty, not dirty.*"
> *(Joe E. Lewis)*

> "*Actually, it only takes one drink to get me loaded. Trouble is, I can't remember if it's the thirteenth or fourteenth.*"
> *(George Burns)*

Toasts of the Infamous

Not too many infamous people are remembered for their quotes or toasts because, as a whole, bad guys are not too smart and dumb guys do not leave many memorable quotations. Here are a few of the better things ever said by the infamous that can be used as toasts.

> "*Thank you all for coming to the party tonight, and as I say that I am reminded of the words of Joseph Stalin who said, 'Gratitude is a sickness suffered by dogs.'*"

OK, this might not be the best example.

If you ever find yourself proposing a toast to Communism, you may wish to cite the words of Mao Zedong who said:

> "*Communism is not love.*
> *Communism is a hammer which we use to crush the enemy.*
> *Bottoms up.*"

Actually, Chairman Mao never said "bottoms up." I just added that to make it a toast, as you can do with almost anything anybody has ever said.

> *Ferdinand Marcos once said about government, 'It is easier to run a revolution than a government.'*

This would have been a good toast to kick off a revolution, but, unfortunately, Marcos could not run either a revolution or a government. I think the words of his wife Imelda Marcos might make a better toast "Does this shoe come in a size five?"

Sometimes a bad guy says something that almost makes sense. The words of the Marquis de Sade would be the perfect toast to kick off an orgy.

> *Sex is as important as eating or drinking and we ought to allow the one appetite to be satisfied with as little restraint or false modesty as the other.*
>
> *(Marquis de Sade)*

And if we are ever in a situation where a toast to the country of Canada is called for, we can always look to the words of Al Capone who said, "I don't even know what street Canada is on."

Good Toasts from People You Never Heard Of

You may, in fact, have heard of several of the people credited with creating the toasts in this chapter, since in their own social circles they may have been famous. Others are from people with whom I am virtually certain that you have no knowledge. Look at them all as ammunition in your machine gun of toasts and use them to your advantage.

> *. . . And malt does more than Milton can*
> *To justify God's ways to man.*
>
> *(A.E. Housman)*

"Back and side go bare, go bare:
Both foot and hand go cold;
But, belly, God send thee good ale enough,
Whether it be new or old."
(John Still)

"A soft drink turneth away company."
(Oliver Herford)

"Bacchus' blessings are a treasure,
Drinking is the soldier's pleasure;
Rich the treasure, sweet the pleasure,
Sweet is pleasure after pain."
(John Dryden)

"Here's to the maiden of bashful fifteen;
Here's to the widow of fifty;
Here's to the flaunting, extravagant quean,
And here's to the housewife that's thrifty!
Let the toast pass;
Drink to the lass;
I'll warrant she'll prove an excuse for the glass."
(Richard Brinsley Sheridan)

"If I ever marry a wife,
I'll marry a landlord's daughter,
For then I may sit in the bar,
And drink cold brandy and water."
(Charles Lamb)

"Work is the curse of the drinking class."
(Mike Romanoff)

The Perfect Martini

The perfect Martini is the Holy Grail of mixed drinks. The cocktail's origins are obscure, its history debatable, and its preparation endlessly controversial. Given that gin and vermouth are the only two ingredients, it may be hard to grasp the dispute, but not to Martini aficionados. Decades-long debates survive about the preparation and the proportion of gin to vermouth, which ranges from 1 part vermouth to anywhere between 5 and 15 parts gin. Obviously, the less vermouth, the drier the drink, and it is this chilled, crisp dryness that makes the ultimate Martini.

The Martini is presented with a cocktail olive, a pitted green olive without pimento, or a twist of lemon peel. Served with a cocktail onion, the drink is called a Gibson. Today, the Vodka Martini has supplanted its elegant predecessor, but the quest for the perfect drink continues. The mystique of the Martini wouldn't be the same without it.

“*And Noah he often said to his wife when he sat down to dine,*
'I don't care where the water goes if it doesn't get into the wine.'”
(C.K. Chesterton)

“*Drink wine, and live here blitheful while ye may;*
The morrow's life too late is, live today.”
(Herrick)

“*If on my theme I rightly think,*
there are five reasons why men drink,—
good wine, a friend, because I'm dry,
or lest I should be by and by,
or any other reason why.”
(John Sirmond)

“*Who loves not women, wine, and song.*
Remains a fool his whole life long.”
(Johann Heinrich Voss)

“*Best while you have it use your breath,*
There is no drinking after death.”
(John Fletcher)

Toasts from TV and Movies

American culture seems to revolve around the electronic media, and a good many toasts that we may use in everyday life have their roots in these art forms. While most of the toasts given in movies and on television shows are of the simple, “Here's to you” variety, there are quite a few classics. We have already mentioned the famous Humphrey Bogart line from “Casablanca” when he lifted his glass to Ingrid Bergman and said, “Here's looking at you, kid.” But here are some of the lesser known toasts from the world of entertainment.

"*Here's to swimmin' with bow-legged women.*"
(Quint in Jaws, *1975)*

"*Here's to plain speaking and clear understanding.*"
(Kasper Gutman in Maltese Falcon, *1941)*

"*Here's to pencil pushers. May they all get lead poisoning.*"
(Eddie Valient in Who Framed Roger Rabbit, *1988)*

"*Lads! Here's to stinking rich!*"
(Wally in Time Bandits, *1980)*

"*May the best of your past be the worst of your future.*"
(Hal in Long Kiss Goodnight, *1996)*

"*A toast. To all of you . . . to hell with you, to all of me.*"
(Harry Fabian in Night and the City, *1992)*

"*Here's to the Army and Navy and the battles they have won; here's to America's colors, the colors that never run.*"
(Wang Chi in Big Trouble in Little China, *1986)*

"*I am the queen of England. I may have the body of a weak feeble woman. But I have the heart and stomach of a concrete elephant. So first I'm going to have a little drink, and then I'm going to execute the whole lot of you.*"
(The Queen in Blackadder II, *1985)*

"*Drink up. The world's about to end.*"
(Ford Prefect in The Hitchhiker's Guide to the Galaxy, *1981)*

More Martinis

Martini

Since a Martini is so personal, it is tempting to offer the simplest recipe of 3 ounces gin and vermouth to taste. The following have exact proportions with which to begin an individual Martini odyssey.

2 1/2 oz. gin
1/2 oz. dry vermouth

In a mixing glass half filled with ice, add the vermouth first, then the gin. Stir. Strain into a cocktail glass. Serve with one or two olives or a twist of lemon.

James Bond Martini

3 oz. gin
1 oz. vodka
1/2 oz. Lillet
lemon peel

Combine ingredients in a shaker with ice. Shake. Strain into a cocktail glass. Add a slice of lemon peel.

"*Know why they put them little umbrellas in those tropical drinks? It's so that when it rains it don't thin out the liquor!*"

(Faye Riley in *batteries not included, *1987)*

"*Looks like I picked the wrong week to quit drinking.*"

(McCroskey in Airplane!, *1980)*

I loved *Animal House* and have watched it dozens of times. Here are two of the best lines from the movie which make excellent toasts.

"*Cut the crap. Give me a drink.*"

(Marion Wormer in Animal House, *1978)*

"*My advice to you is to start drinking heavily.*"

(Bluto in Animal House, *1978)*

"*They may be drinkers, Robin, but they're still human beings.*"

(Batman in Batman *the TV series, 1966)*

"*Meet me down in the bar! We'll drink breakfast together.*"

(Bellows in The Big Broadcast of 1938, *1938)*

"*We shall drink to our partnership.*"

(Dr. Pretorius in Bride of Frankenstein, *1935)*

"*I am the last poet. I see America drinking the fabulous*
cocktails I make.
Americans getting stinky on something I stir or shake.
The sex on the beach,
The schnapps made from peach,
The velvet hammer,
The Alabama slammer.

I make things with juice and froth,
The pink squirrel
The three toed sloth.
I make drinks so sweet and snazzy
The iced tea,
The kamakazi,
The orgasm,
The death spasm,
The Singapore sling,
The dingaling.
America you've just been devoted to every flavor I got,
But if you want to get loaded
Why don't you just order a shot?
Bar is open."

(Brian in Cocktail, *1988)*

"*Mekka Lekka Hi*
Mekka Heinie Ho."

(Jombi on Pee Wee's Playhouse *TV show)*

This wasn't really designed as a toast but it makes a great one among friends because nobody else will understand it.

"*Drink up while it's cold, ladies.*"

(Captain Hadley in The Shawshank Redemption, *1994)*

"*Listen doll girl, when you drink as much as I do, you gotta start early.*"

(Delong in Cry Danger, *1951)*

"*A wiseguy never pays for his drinks.*"

(Lefty in Donnie Brasco, *1997)*

"*I never drink wine.*"

(Count Dracula in Dracula, *1931)*

Royalty at the Bar

Kings and queens, princes and princesses, even a queen's cousin have drinks named after them. A quick survey reveals that royal recipes have no patterns: no liquor seems more noble than any other. So the link between royal personages and their namesake drinks remains a mystery. History, no doubt has an answer. But no matter. Raising a toast with a "Queen Elizabeth" or a "Prince Edward" is as close as any of us is likely to get to the royals.

Queen Elizabeth

1 1/2 oz. gin
1/2 oz. dry vermouth
1 tsp. Benedictine

Combine ingredients in a shaker half filled with ice. Shake well. Strain into a cocktail glass.

Duchess

1 1/2 oz. Pernod
1/2 oz. dry vermouth
1/2 oz. sweet vermouth

Combine ingredients in a shaker half filled with ice. Shake well. Strain into a cocktail glass.

“I never drink wine. Aw, what the hell!”
(Dracula in Dracula: Dead and Loving It, *1995)*

“Okay hard drinkers, let's drink hard. I'm buyin'.”
(Seth Gecko in From Dusk Till Dawn, *1996)*

“My dear girl, there are some things that just aren't done, such as drinking Dom Perignon '53 above the temperature of thirty-eight degrees Fahrenheit. That's just as bad as listening to the Beatles without earmuffs!”
(James Bond in Goldfinger, *1964)*

“I'd like to propose a toast, to my son. He is eighteen today. He has just ordered his first drink. Before he drinks it, I'd like to wish him a long life, a wife as fine as his mother, and a son as fine as he's been. To my son!”
(Bull Meechum in The Great Santini, *1979)*

“I envy people who drink. At least they know what to blame everything on.”
(Sid Jeffers in Humoresque, *1946)*

“We're gonna drink this one to Ozzie. A good man who tried to save my ass by injecting me into yours.”
(Lt. Tuck Pendleton in Innerspace, *1987)*

“A toast to my big brother George. The richest man in town.”
(Harry in It's a Wonderful Life, *1946)*

The following lines are also from movies but they aren't actually toasts. They are, however, perfect additions to toasts. All you have to do to convert them is to add a recipient for the toast

(Here's to you . . .) and add an ending (All the best to you.) Here's how it works:

First we designate the recipient of the toast. "Here's to my best friend Louie,"

Then we find a movie quote from Louie's favorite movie or a quote that fits his personality:

> "*There is a time for daring and a time for caution, and a wise man knows which is called for.*"
> *(Keating in* Dead Poet's Society, *1989)*

Then end the toast with a comment or wish: "Here's to a wise man indeed. Here's to Louie."

Here are some more entertainment quotes that can be woven into your toasts.

> "*There comes a time in every woman's life when the only thing that helps is a glass of champagne.*"
> *(Katherine 'Kitty' Marlowe in* Old Acquaintance, *1943)*

> "*If Plato is a fine red wine, then Aristotle is a dry martini.*"
> *(Chet in* Kicking and Screaming, *1995)*

> "*We want the finest wines available to humanity, we want them here, and we want them now!*"
> *(Withnail in* Withnail and I, *1987)*

> "*There are many things my father taught me here in this room. He taught me, keep your friends close, but your enemies closer.*"
> *(Michael Corleone in* The Godfather: Part II, *1974)*

Still More Namesakes

Will Rogers
1 1/2 oz. gin
1/2 oz. dry vermouth
1 Tbs. orange juice
1 dash Triple Sec

Combine all ingredients in a shaker nearly filled with ice. Shake well. Strain into a cocktail glass.

Cowboy Will's
(Non-Alcoholic)
1 1/2 oz. orange juice
1/2 oz. tonic
1 tsp. fine sugar

Combine all ingredients in a shaker nearly filled with ice. Shake well. Strain into a cocktail glass.

Betsy Ross
2 oz. brandy
1 1/2 oz.port
dash Triple Sec

Combine ingredients in a mixing glass nearly filled with ice. Stir well. Strain into a cocktail glass.

"*Ah. Fortune smiles. Another day of wine and roses.*
Or, in your case, beer and pizza!"
(Two-Face in Batman Forever, *1995)*

"*We can't have the happiness of yesterday without the pain of today.*
That's the deal."
(Joy Gresham in Shadowlands, *1993)*

"*May the best of your past be the worst of your future.*"
(Hal in Long Kiss Goodnight, *1996)*

"*Louis, I think this is the beginning of a beautiful friendship.*"
(Rick Blaine in Casablanca, *1942)*

"*Good friends are one of life's blessings.*
Don't give them up without a fight."
(Ole Golly in Harriet The Spy, *1996)*

"*Bring us a pitcher of beer every seven minutes until someone passes out. Then bring one every ten.*"
(Thornton Melon in Back to School, *1986)*

CHAPTER 5

Toasts from Coast to Coast to Coast

The Americans are a funny lot. They drink whiskey to keep them warm, then they put ice in it to make it cool; then they put some sugar in it to make it sweet and then they put a slice of lemon in it to make it sour. Then they say, 'Here's to you' and drink it themselves.

—B. N. Chakravarty

There is a lot to be said about the above observation. In America we sometimes get confused and develop tunnel vision. We tend to forget that there are at least seven other countries in the world who do things differently than we do. Because of that oversight, I think it is important to take a look at toasts from around the world.

One of the nice things about toasting is that it is universal. Virtually every country and every culture across the globe celebrates occasions large and small with a toast. Some cultures, like the Irish, are world famous for their toasts, while other cultures may only have one toast that they use for every occasion. Here are some toasts from countries around the world.

English Toasts

The universal English toast is a simple yet poetic:

"Cheers!"

This monosyllabic toast wishes the recipient good health, wealth, and happiness all wrapped up in one word. Of course, most of the English have never seen the popular American TV show by the same name, but it is just as well because nobody in that sit-com spoke with an English accent so they would probably be difficult to understand.

Another typical English toast is an equally simple:

"All the best!"

Again, with a minimum of effort the English are able to convey best wishes to all involved in the toast. This concise yet effective use of the mother tongue is exactly why England has produced some of the greatest writers of all time. And speaking of great

English writers, a man who was no stranger to a good toast was none other than the Bard of Avon, William Shakespeare. Shakespeare wrote wonderful toasts into many of his plays. Here are just a few.

> "*I drink to the general joy of the whole table.*"
> (*MacBeth*)

> "*I have half-a-dozen healths to drink to these young ladies.*"
> (*King Henry VIII*)

> "*Be large in mirth; anon we'll drink a measure the table 'round.*"
> (*MacBeth*)

> "*Let us drink down all unkindness.*"
> (*The Merry Wives of Windsor*)

> "*Romeo, I come. This do I drink to thee.*"
> (*Romeo and Juliet*)

(Note: This may not be the best toast to offer in a group, since Juliet died right after she said it. It is not generally considered to be one of your average good luck toasts.)

Toasts to England are different than English toasts. Here are some salutes to the land of kings and queens, which you probably won't hear in your everyday pub visit.

> "*England my country, great and free!*
> *Heart of the world, I drink to thee!*"

> "*St. George he was for England,*
> *And before he killed the dragon*
> *He drank a pint of English ale*
> *Out of an English flagon.*"

On Pubs

The best place to propose a toast in England is in a pub and, fortunately, there is a convenient pub on every corner for your toasting pleasure. Pubs specialize in warm beer with alcoholic contents approaching that of tranquilizers. They are served in "pints" (equaling .284 bushels) and in "half pints" (equal to 17.8 cubic swallows). Sometimes you will find them served by the "liter," which equals one metric hangover. The beer is dark, bitter, and ghastly, but after the tenth one you hardly notice. Of course you can get things other than beer in a pub. You can also order ale, stout, or something called "sparkling hard cider," which tastes like fizzy bad white wine.

The best thing about pubs in England is their names. They all have quaint names like the Pork and Thistle, the Rinse and Spit, the Scratch and Sniff, and the Butt and Cleavage.

French Toast

Here is the classic French Toast (4 servings):

Slightly beat four eggs.

Add ½ teaspoon salt and 1 cup of milk. Beat some more.

Add ½ teaspoon of vanilla extract for flavor.

Dip into this mixture 8 slices of bread.

Brown bread on both sides on a hot, well buttered griddle.

Serve the toast sprinkled with sugar or cinnamon and with maple syrup on the side.

Eat while wearing a beret and speaking with a French accent.

> *"First pledge our Queen this solemn night,*
> *Then drink to England, every guest;*
> *That man's the best Cosmopolite*
> *Who loves his native country best."*
> *(Sir Alfred Tennyson)*

> *"In English beer,*
> *With an English cheer,*
> *To the right little*
> *Tight little island."*

British poet Abraham Cowley also had an opinion on raising a glass. He said:

> *"Fill up the bowl then, fill it high.*
> *Fill all the glasses then—for why,*
> *Should every creature drink but I?*
> *Why, man of mortals, tell me why."*

French Toasts

The French are renowned for drinking a lot of top-quality wine, and nothing goes better with good wine than a good toast. Unfortunately, most French toasts are written in French. Here are a couple that I was able to have translated.

> *"À vôtre santé [ah-vote-reh sahn-tay]*
> *(To your health)"*

This is followed by the response toast of;

> *"À la vôtre! [ah-la-vote-reh]*
> *(And to yours!)"*

> *"Plus je bois, mieux je chante.*
> *(The more I drink, the better I sing)"*

In addition to giving toasts before a meal, the French have two occasions to present toasts during the meal. When the last drop of wine is poured from the bottle, it is common to say, "Marié cette année où pendu la prochaine," which translates to "Married this year or hung the next." I guess this refers to the fate of the person receiving the last drop of wine, and to be perfectly honest with you, neither option sounds like a good one.

The second toast opportunity during a meal comes between courses when a small glass of liquor is tossed back in one gulp in order to "cleanse the stomach." While drinking this shot, the Frenchman says, "cul sec," which translates to "bottoms up." If he has been drinking heavily, he may be heard to utter "cul de sac," which translates to "I live on a dead-end street."

One of my favorite toasts for a business outing comes from *The Three Musketeers*, which was written by Alexander Dumas who was French. Therefore, I think this classic qualifies as a French toast.

"Let us drink to the prosperity of your establishment."

Italian Toasts

The Italians, much like the French, produce excellent quality wines. Unlike most other nationalities, however, the Italians are ready to party at the drop of a hat. If you don't believe me just go over to Italy, walk down the street, and drop your hat. You will be amazed at the results. Party, party, party.

Many writers have expressed the spirit of Italy much better than I. Edward Bulwer-Lytton said, "Midnight, and love, and youth, and Italy!" I guess what he means by this is that Italy is the equivalent of all the good things in life.

The Italians are one of those cultures which seems to have just a few toasts that fit every occasion. For instance, "Alla tua Salute" translates as "To your health," and as my mother used to say, if you have your health, you have everything. Another popular toast is "Cin Cin." This translates to "All things good for you." And if neither of those toasts fit the occasion, all you need to say is, "Propino tibi!" This translates as "I drink to you."

On German Food

Germany may be known for many things: efficiency, luxury automobiles, and quality beer. What they are not known for is their haute cuisine. German food is, in a word, bad. Don't get me wrong, I have had some fine German meals, but for the most part German cuisine relies on over cooked meat, sauerkraut, red cabbage, and spaetzel, which are small noodles. This food, along with the requisite beer, tends to produce a volume of methane, which in turn produces the farfagnügen you have heard so much about.

German Toasts

What France and Italy are to wine, Germany is to beer. They make a lot of beer in Germany, and I dare say it is possibly the best beer in the world. When drinking beer, it almost becomes necessary to raise a toast with every glass of beer. And, at the rate most beer drinkers consume the amber liquid, this calls for a toast approximately every fifteen minutes. The Germans, always a culture of efficiency, have a single toast that works well everywhere, "Prosit!" which translates to "To your health." I guess that when you drink as much beer as they do, it is important to toast to your health every fifteen minutes. Either that or they should say, "Wo sind die Toiletten?" which translates to "Where are the bathrooms?"

Russian Toasts

Quick, what beverage is Russia most famous for? If you answered Yoo Hoo (the chocolate beverage) you are wrong. If, however you answered vodka, you win a free sack of potatoes.

Russia produces the best vodka in the world. They also consume it at the rate of a bottle a day. This may be one of the reasons that they are having a difficult time coping with the concept of capitalism.

Joseph Stalin, a famous Russian, once said that "Gaiety is the most outstanding feature of the Soviet Union." I don't know about you, but of all the pictures I have seen of Russia and the Russian people, I don't think the word "gaiety" ever entered my mind. But, apparently if you drink enough vodka, gaiety hits you like a slap with a wet mackerel.

Like their European counterparts, the Russians tend to stick with one all-purpose toast. Also, like their neighbors, they believe in drinking to your health. They sum it up by saying,:

> "*Za vashe zdorovia [zah-vash-drove-yeh]*"

The easiest way to remember this toast is to commit it to memory as the answer to a question. Pretend that you know a man named Za Vash and he drove ya to the mall. If anyone asks how you got there you can tell them Za Vash Drove Ya.

Polish Toasts

How many Poles does it take to make a toast? Well, just one. What did you think this was going to be, one of those lame light bulb jokes? The Poles, like everybody else on the planet, love a good toast, and like most other cultures they toast to your health. The traditional Polish toast is:

> “*Na Zdrowie! [nahz-drov-ee-eh]*”

This looks and sounds similar to the Russian toast, but that is probably because they are such close neighbors.

When I was a young boy I lived in a neighborhood of Cleveland, Ohio that had many Polish residents, and these people were toasting each other all the time. They toasted to the holidays, to new babies, and even to the completion of the incredible Polish sausage that they made in their kitchens and smoked in their backyards. Unfortunately, when I was five years old I neither understood Polish nor was I able to write them down even if I did understand them.

I did uncover this one, however, which I am told is a basic Polish toast.

> “*Zdrowie twoje, w gardlo moje.*
> *(To your health, down my throat.)*”

This drink should be tossed into the mouth and swallowed in one gulp which, depending on the potency of the liquid being quaffed, is quite a feat in itself. If you do not speak fluent Polish and are wondering how this toast should be pronounced, try saying it along with me.

> “*Zdrowie twoje, w gardlo moje.*
> *z-drove-ay tfoye, v guard-whoa moy-e*”

Hooked on phonics works for me!

The Russians Are Coming

If a drink has “Russian” in the title, vodka is its inspiration. Most “Russian” drinks take their cue from the popular “Black Russian,” vodka and coffee liqueur. They are pared down, no-nonsense drinks with a single, to-the-point taste. These drinks may be coffee or mocha or strawberry, but they are elevated from the prosaic by the presence of vodka, which may be tasteless, but never, never pointless.

White Russian
1 1/2 oz. vodka
1/2 oz. coffee liqueur
1/2 oz. cream

Combine ingredients in a shaker half filled with ice. Shake well. Strain into an old-fashioned glass over ice.

Black Russian
1 1/2 oz. vodka
1/2 oz. coffee liqueur

Pour vodka and liqueur into an old-fashioned glass nearly filled with ice. Stir well.

Japanese Toasts

The Japanese, inventors of sake, a rice wine that will make you see double, also enjoy a good toast. They, however, prefer to drink to the emptying of a glass than to the health of the drinker. The most often used Japanese toast is, "Kan pai," which literally means "bottoms up." A more recognized Japanese toast is the one that was uttered by Kamikaze pilots during World War II as they left on their suicide missions. The toast literally meant "our last farewell" and was repeated three times. It is,

> "*Banzai! Banzai! Banzai!*"

This should not be confused with the Japanese toast of, "Bonsai," which means, "I have a very tiny tree growing in a dish."

Chinese Toasts

In China toasts are delivered to many people at one time, principally because when you have over a billion people all crammed into one country you tend to do everything with many people at one time. This could be one of the reasons why China was never known as the land of romance.

The Chinese also consume some rather unusual foods like 1,000-year-old eggs, and a little bird that is cooked and consumed whole! They don't make this delicacy in my local Chinese restaurant and I am thankful for that, but they do give the occasional toast, which sounds just like a Japanese toast but is spelled, "Kan pei!"

And just like their neighbors to the east, this toast translates to "Bottoms up!" A group toast in China is most often given for victory in a venture. It goes, "Yam seng!" and means "drink to victory."

Solo drinking is not done in China. The act of drinking itself is a social act and a cup is not raised in public without another person acknowledging it and returning the toast. If a person wants to toast another with a Kan pei, they must first get the other person's attention, raise his glass in a toast gesture, and wait for the other party to return the salute. Formally, the cup is raised with two hands, but informally a toast may be presented with one hand.

After the toaster Kan peis, they drain the contents of the cup in the true meaning of bottoms up.

At a Chinese dinner party, many Kan peis are offered and it is custom to turn your cup or glass upside down after the toast to prove that you, in fact, drank the contents. Apparently the Chinese don't trust each other when it comes to drinking. They also tend to use small cups for toasting so that they can toast many times during the dinner without getting "toasted" themselves.

Australian Toasts

Australia is known as the land down under, but when it comes to drinking and toasting they will put you under the table. Aussies love to party and they keep their toasts simple. The most common toast comes from the motherland in the form of:

> "*Cheers!*"

But they also call on their seafaring history with a toast of:

> "*Down the Hatch!*"

And on their fun loving spirit with:

> "*Here's looking up your kilt!*"

Hawaiian Toasts

Even though Hawaii is a member of the United States, the natives keep the Hawaiian language alive through frequent usage and street names that are unpronounceable to the visitor. The Hawaiian language contains only twelve letters: A, E, H, I, K, L, M, N, O, P, U, and W. Needless to say, *Wheel of Fortune* never caught on very well in Hawaii.

When pronouncing Hawaiian, every letter is pronounced, including back to back vowels. I guess the rule in Hawaiian grammar is, "When two vowels go walking, they both end up talking."

Traditional Hawaiian toasts are obviously given in Hawaiian but they have similar meanings to toasts from around the globe. For

À la Française

The French have a certain style that Americans find, well, seductive.

And drinks with a French connection are often alluring. Some remind us of Paris's most provocative places.

French Connection

2 oz. cognac
1 1/2 oz. Amaretto

Combine ingredients in a shaker half filled with ice. Shake well. Strain into a cocktail glass.

Montmartre

1 1/2 oz. gin
1/2 oz. sweet vermouth
1/2 oz. Cointreau

Combine ingredients in a shaker half filled with ice. Shake well. Strain into a cocktail glass.

Moulin Rouge

1 1/2 oz. sloe gin
1/2 oz. sweet vermouth
dash bitters

Pour ingredients into a mixing glass nearly filled with ice. Stir. Strain into a cocktail glass.

instance, the toast "Kamau!" translates to "Here's how," and the phrase "Hauoli maoli oe!" means "to your happiness."

According to my brother Tim, who now lives on the island of Maui, the native Hawaiians sometimes toast each other while drinking a concoction known as awa but pronounced ava. In the Hawaiian language, a w is pronounced like a v. This was first brought to light under the administration of Voodrow Vilson.

Awa is distilled from the awa plant and tastes like liquid mud. It also does not muddle your thinking or make you drunk in the most common sense of the word. What it does instead is to render your limbs useless by turning your bones into gelatin. People on an awa buzz cannot walk or use their arms and look like they are having a seizure, but they can think clearly and carry on intelligent conversation.

Irish Toasts

Attempting to cover the topic of Irish toasts in a finite amount of space is like trying to describe the ocean in ten words or less. There are as many !rish toasts as there are Irish pubs, and that is a lot. Among other things, the Irish invented Guinness, which is quite possibly the finest beer ever made. The best Guinness is served in Dublin, Ireland where it is brewed. To taste fresh Guinness accompanied by a real Irish toast is close to heaven itself.

Many Irish toasts are attributed to St. Patrick, the patron saint of Ireland. As you know, he is responsible for driving all of the snakes from the country. For ridding Ireland of snakes St. Patrick was awarded a sainthood and his very own holiday. Meanwhile, over in Austria, the Pied Piper of Hamlin did the same thing with the country's rat population but all he received in return was an NSF check. This caused him to lead all of the children into the sea for which he received neither toasts nor a holiday.

> *"St. Patrick was a gentleman who, through strategy and stealth,*
> *Drove all the snakes from Ireland. Here's toasting to his health.*
> *But not too many toastings lest you lose yourself and then,*
> *Forget the good St. Patrick and see all those snakes again."*

Irish toasts are very poetic and picturesque, much like the country from which they originate. Here are some of my favorites.

"May the face of every good news and the back of every bad news be toward us."

"May the roof above us never fall in,
And may we friends gathered below never fall out."

"May you have warm words on a cold evening,
A full moon on a dark night,
And the road downhill all the way to your door."

"Health and long life to you;
The woman of your choice to you;
A child every year to you;
Land without rent to you;
And may you die in Ireland."

"O Lord God divine
Who turned the water into wine
Please forgive we foolish men
We are going to turn it back again"

"May you have food and raiment
A soft pillow for your head,
May you be forty years in heaven,
Before the devil knows you're dead."

"May the strength of three be in your journey."

"Here's that we may always have a clean shirt
A clean conscience,
And a guinea in our pocket."

A Nice Gesture

Hawaiians sometimes "toast" each other silently by using the hand signal made by taking a fist and extending the thumb and pinkie out to the sides as though you were ordering five beers and you had lost your middle three fingers in an industrial accident. This signal means "hang loose," which roughly translates to "I'm not wearing any underwear."

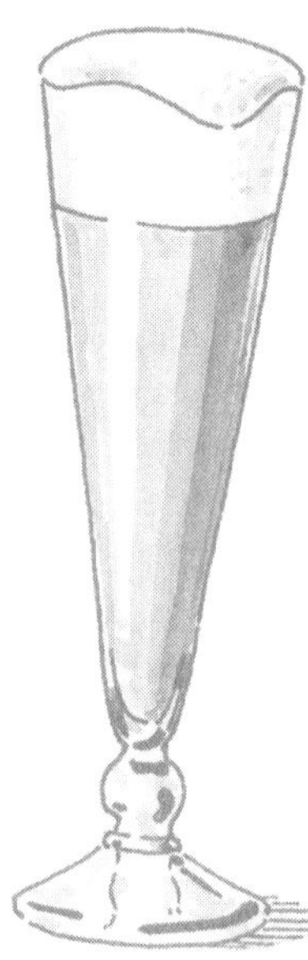

"Here's a health to your enemies' enemies!"

"May the grass grow long on the road to hell for want of use."

"May you be poor in misfortune,
Rich in blessings,
Slow to make enemies,
And quick to make friends.
But rich or poor, quick or slow,
May you know nothing but happiness from this day forward."

"Here's health and prosperity to you and all your posterity,
And them that doesn't drink with sincerity
that they may be damned for all eternity."

"Ireland was Ireland when England was a pup
And Ireland'll be Ireland when England's all washed up
So it's up the long ladder and down the short rope
To hell with King Henry and God bless the pope."

Since fish are plentiful in Ireland, several of their toasts revolve around the fish.

"The health of the salmon to you,
A long life, a full heart, and a wet mouth."

"The health of the salmon and of the trout,
That swim back and forward near the Bull's Mouth;
Don't ask for saucepan, jug or mug,
Down the hatch—drink it up!"

Irish toasts also take on a religious flavor with not only good health being wished upon the recipient but also the Lord's blessing.

"May those that love us, love us.
Those that hate us, may God Turn their hearts.
And if he does not turn their hearts,
May he turn their ankles, so that we may
know them by their limping."

"Like the goodness of the five loaves and two fishes,
Which God divided among the five thousand men,
May the blessing of the King who so divided,
Be upon our share of this common meal."

"May there always be work for your hands to do
May your purse always hold a coin or two.
May the sun always shine on your windowpane.
May a rainbow be certain to follow each rain.
May the hand of a friend always be near you.
May God fill your heart with gladness to cheer you."

"May the lord keep you in his hand and never close his fist too tight on you.
And when it comes to making choices, never let it me misunderstood how a true Irishman ranks his as evidenced by this toast."

"Here's to the lasses we've kissed me lads,
here's to the lips we've pressed, for of
kisses and lasses, like liquor in glasses,
the last is always the best!"

Guinness

The beverage of choice in Ireland is Guinness, a thick, dark substance that can best be described as a beer milk shake. I especially recommend it with your breakfast cereal. The Guinness brewery in Dublin produces 2 million pints of the stout every day, only half of which is exported. If I have done the math correctly, that means that every person in Ireland has to drink a lot of beer every day. In addition to Guinness and the other fine beers made in Ireland, they also produce some of the finest Irish whiskey ever made. When you combine Irish whiskey with Irish beer, you can begin to understand why these people believe in leprechauns.

Jewish Toasts

Jewish toasts are some of the most fun toasts around. They just seem to make you smile when you say them. Take, for instance, the classic toast, "L'chayim," which means "To life." If you pronounce the word properly you should wind up with a smile on your face. You will also wind up with some phlegm, but hopefully it won't be on your face.

The really fun Jewish toast is "Mazel tov," which means "Congratulations." Mazel tov is an acceptable toast for weddings, bar mitzvahs, graduations, or for any occasion to which the sentiment of congratulations is in order. When Mazel tov is really fun is at a wedding. When they toast at a wedding, not only do they enjoy a drink but then they get to smash the glass by stepping on it. Actually, I don't think the toast has anything to do with the breaking of the glass except that they both happen at a wedding.

In researching this book, I decided to contact as many representatives of the various international and ethnic categories as I could. For Jewish toasts I relied on the knowledge of my friend Jeff Blackman, a professional speaker from Chicago. Jeff enlightened me on two toasts.

First, he gave me a quick lesson in conversational Jewish. For instance "nachis" (pronounced nok-us) means pride, good fortune, and overflowing joy such as you would experience at a birth, a wedding, or a no-fault divorce. "Simcha" (pronounced sim-ka) means a blessed event like a birth, a wedding, or a no-fault divorce. "Tuchis" is a yiddish word for tush or butt. So a Jewish toast could be:

> "*Wishing you great nachis, bountiful simcha, and some occasional tuchis.*"

Greek Toasts

Greeks are another party-loving culture. If you have ever been to a Greek restaurant, you know that they celebrate everything with a toast. Even when they bring the flaming appetizer saginaki to your table, they have an accompanying toast.

Saginaki is a square of cheese that is heated and brought to your table where it is doused with the Greek liquor ouzo and set on fire. As the cheese goes up in flames, everyone in the restaurant hollers, "Oopa!" which I believe is Greek for "Yikes, my cheese is on fire." (Ha, ha, ha, I got you on that one. Oopa actually means "Hooray.")

When the wine is poured—typically a Greek rose called roditys—glasses are raised to the toast of "Ygia-sou!" (pronounced ee-ya-soo) or "Cheers!" Or you may hear the Greek toast of "Stin ygia sou!" (pronounced steen-ee-ya-soo), which means "To your health!"

Scottish Toasts

The only people who rival the Irish for the abundance of toasts are their neighbors to the east, the Scottish. The Scots invented, among other things, Scotch. Not only did they invent Scotch but they drink Scotch on every possible occasion.

Most Scottish toasts were written in Scottish, or more correctly, Gaelic. This is a very complicated language that was spoken throughout the British Isles until someone discovered that English was a lot easier to learn. The traditional Scottish/Gaelic toast is:

> "*Slainte*"

Pronounced Slan—Jah, it means, as do most toasts, here's to your health. If you propose the toast of Slaite in any Scottish pub while raising your wee dram of Scotch whisky (just for the record, there is no "e" in Scotch whisky; like other drinks, however, it will produce "p") you will be welcomed. If you buy a round for everybody in the pub before you propose the toast, you will be welcomed back.

The legendary poet laureate (literally, poet with a gig) of Scotland is Robert Burns. Everywhere you travel in Scotland you will hear his name revered as the master of the language. Unfortunately for the rest of us, the language of which Mr. Burns was a master was Gaelic, so while his toasts may sound very poetic, they don't make much sense to the rest of us without a translator. Here are some of Robert Burns's most famous toasts with a translation provided by me. Since I have never spoken Gaelic, I cannot vouch for the accuracy of these translations, but I came as close as I could.

> "*Some hae meat, and canna eat,*
> *And some wad eat that want it;*
> *But we hae meat, and we can eat*
> *And sae the Lord be thank it.*"

Translation:

> "*Good food, good meat*
> *Good God, let's eat.*"

Here's one that is pretty much self-explanatory:

> *"A man may drink and no be drunk;*
> *A man may fight and no be slain;*
> *A man may kiss a bonnie lass,*
> *And aye be welcome back again."*

One of Robert Burns' shorter toasts is:

> *"Freedom and Whisky gang thegither—*
> *Tak off your dram."*

The first line makes sense except for his poor spelling of the word "together," but "Tak off your dram" either means "lift up your glass," or "take off your pants." Either way it's a fun toast.

There were other Scottish toasters besides Robert (call me Robbie) Burns. Dean Ramsay, who sounds like he should be in a television soap opera but in reality was an Episcopalian clergyman, wrote these toasts which don't need much translation:

> *"May the honest heart ne'er feel distress."*

> *"May the winds of adversity ne're blow in your door."*

Many Scottish toasts have been handed down for centuries and are not only lyrical in a Scottish kind of way but also convey lovely sentiments once you understand them. For instance:

> *"Here's grand luck an' muckle fat weans."*

In this instance, "muckle fat weans" translates to "big fat children," although I happen to think that Muckle Fat Weans would be a perfect name for a blues singer.

Here's another one of my favorites:

> *"Here's tae us! Wha's like us?*
> *Da' few and they're deed"*

Which I am sure you already figured out means:

> *"Here's to us! Who's like us?*
> *Damn few and they're dead."*

Here are some more traditional Scottish toasts, suitable for any occasion.

> *"May the best ye've ever seen*
> *Be the worst ye'll ever see."*

> *"Then let us toast John Barleycorn,*
> *Each man a glass in hand;*
> *And may his great posterity*
> *Ne'er fail in old Scotland."*

And if you really want to toast in a traditional Scottish manner, try this traditional regimental toast given by the Royal Scots.

> *"Slainte mhath, h-uile latha, na chi 'snach fhaic. Slainte."*

If you just can't muster this mouthful, here it is in English:

> *Good health, every day, whether I see you or not. Health."*

Latin Toasts

One of the problems with a dead language is that the only people proficient in speaking it are . . . dead. Latin, once the most universal language of the world, is now considered a dead language, spoken only by snobbish scholars and priests.

Former vice president Dan Quayle, upon visiting Latin America, once said that he wished he had paid more attention in Latin class so that he could speak to the people of Latin America. This wouldn't of course have helped him. Not everybody in Latin America speaks Latin, only the snobbish scholars and priests.

Still, imagine how you could impress people at the next toga party you attend if you could give a real Latin toast. Here are some from which you can choose:

"Propino tibi"

This toast translates to "I drink to you," if, of course, your name is Tibi.

"Dum vivimus vivamus"

"Let us live where we live" is the translation of this toast, but this seems like a pretty dumb toast. Of course you are going to live where you live otherwise you wouldn't be living there. What else are they going to live, where you don't live? If you live where you don't live you will be considered a squatter and subject to local laws.

"Ad finum esto fidelis"

"Be faithful to the end" is the translation of this toast, but I am not sure to the end of what.

"Tempus fugit"

Everyone knows that this phrase translates to "Time flies," and while I am not a Latin scholar I think that if you move the "tempus" part to the previous toast that you would have:

"Ad finum esto fidelis tempus"

This could possibly translate to "Be faithful to the end of time."

"Carpe diem"

This is another popular Latin toast, which we all know translates to "Seize the day." Again, if we changed a word we could have a more current toast in:

"Carpe vodka (Seize the martini)"

Mexican Toasts

Mexico is the home of tequila, and tequila just naturally lends itself to toasts. Unfortunately, too much tequila lends itself to speaking a language you don't even understand. Tequila is made from the juice of the maguey plant, which is grown in Jalisco. This is not important. What is important is that tequila packs a heck of a wallop. Traditionally it is consumed straight up following a tradition of licking salt from the back of your hand and biting onto a wedge of lime. The salt kills the taste of the tequila and the lime keeps you from throwing up. What a fun drink. Tequila can also be used to make a margarita, which is a much more tasty drink. Since every Margarita contains a shot of tequila, equal care must be given so as not to over consume to the point that you wake up wearing your boxer shorts and a baseball hat in the middle of the desert.

The traditional Mexican toast is "Salud!" which is Spanish for "health." I find it intriguing that the Mexicans would drink to health with tequila, which can take your health away in no time if you drink it in volume.

Danish Toasts

In Denmark and other Scandinavian countries the traditional toast is very simply:

> "*Skål! (pronounced skoal)*"

No matter where you go in Finland, Norway, Sweden, or Denmark, you will always be on top of things if you offer a friendly toast of Skoal! The place where you could go wrong is if you start to drink the traditional Scandinavian liquor called akvavit. Akvavit (pronounced aqua veet and sometimes spelled acquvit) means "the water of life" and is a clear schnapps-type liquid that packs the punch of a six pack of tequila.

Dinner parties in Denmark are sometimes topped off with a nightcap called the little black one. The host takes a small coin and places it in a coffee cup. Hot coffee is then poured over the coin until it can no longer be seen. Then akvavit is poured into the cup until it dilutes the coffee to the point where the coin can again

Mexican Mayhem

It's easy to slip into the mood of a Mexican party. Wear a sombrero. Drink a "Sombrero." Remember Chiquita Banana? Drink a "Chiquita" with bananas. Salsa, hot green and mild red, supplies the spice. Tequila, with cola, with juice, and even with coffee, delivers the spirit.

Tequila Punch

1 litertequila
4 bottles chilled sauterne
1 bottle chilled champagne
8 cups diced fruit
fine sugar to taste

Pour tequila, wine, and fruit into a punch bowl. Add ice and champagne just before serving. Makes approximately 40 servings.

Cactus Bite

1 1/2 oz. tequila
1 oz. lemon juice or juice of 1/2 lemon
2 tsp. Cointreau
2 tsp. Drambuie
1/2 tsp. fine sugar
dash bitters

Combine ingredients in a shaker half filled with ice. Shake well. Strain into a cocktail glass.

be see. The drink is then consumed with two results. First, between the coffee and the akvavit you wind up with a guest who is drunk but wide awake, and second, if you don't swallow it, you get a free coin at the end of your drink.

The traditional Scandinavian method of toasting is called, oddly enough, skoaling, and it follows a set pattern. The host of the party will begin the skoaling by toasting the women present, one at a time. Meanwhile, the hostess toasts the other men in attendance, one at a time. The odd thing is that the guests do not return the toasts. This means that in an average size dinner party you have the host and hostess skoaling around like nobody's business while the guests remain sober.

Next, the men finally get into the act of skoaling by toasting the ladies present, but the ladies do not return the toast. Now you have a bunch of sober Scandinavian ladies in the midst of a drunk host and hostess and men who are on their way. Next, the gentlemen toast each other, and the ladies, if they are so inclined, finally get to toast the other ladies. If you ask me, this kind of behavior is leading to nothing but trouble, but I am not Scandinavian so I am not too worried about it.

CHAPTER 6

Toasts for Serious Drinking

No poems can live long or please that are written by water-drinkers.

—HORACE

Let me begin this chapter by stressing that I am not necessarily in favor of serious drinking. I think drinking should be fun, therefore, I prefer humorous drinking. But every so often you will find yourself placed in a position where the cocktails flow like lava, and before you know it everything in its path has been burned to a crisp.

Most serious drinking occurs amongst the young. When you are twenty-one you are basically bulletproof and can drink for extended periods of time with no serious side effects, except for the obvious inebriation. But as you get older, you find that excess liquor will give you heartburn, insomnia, and make you act like the people you used to make fun of.

Serious drinking will nearly always be accompanied by serious toasting. And of the toasts given by serious drinkers, very few are acceptable for publication. Therefore, I have cleaned up the toasts included in this chapter to the best of my ability while still trying to maintain their original intent. Here then are toasts for serious drinking.

Bar Toasts

No, Sir; there is nothing which has yet been contrived by man, by which so much happiness is produced as by a good tavern or inn.

—JAMES BOSWELL

It is no secret that most of the alcoholic beverages consumed in this country are consumed in bars and taverns, so it just naturally follows that a large number of toasts are given in a bar as well.

The prime time for bar toasts seems to be that period that has come to be known as happy hour. This is the time after the day's work is done and before the evening's dinner is begun when many of us find our way to our favorite way station for refreshment and friendship. Even Herbert Hoover, the thirty-first president of the United States, called the cocktail hour, "The pause between the errors and trials of the day and the hopes of the night."

Bar toasts, unlike other social toasts, are usually delivered to and with people whom you may have met for the first time, in other words, strangers. But a stranger who shares a toast with you is a stranger no more. Try some of these bar toasts the next time you find yourself alone in a tavern and looking to make some new friends.

"Drink today, and drown all sorrow,
You shall perhaps not do't tomorrow.
Best while you have it, use your breath;
There is no drinking after death."
(Francis Beaumont and John Fletcher)

"He who goes to bed, and goes to bed sober,
Falls as the leaves do, and dies in October
But he who goes to bed, and does so mellow,
Lives as he ought to, and dies a good fellow."

"Here's to the man who takes the pledge,
Who keeps his word and does not hedge,
Who won't give up and won't give in
Till the last man's out and there's no more gin."

"May the joys of drinking never supersede the pleasure of reasoning."

"Here's to you that makes me wear old clothes;
Here's to you that turns my friends to foes,
But seeing you're so near—here goes
Here it goes under my nose
God knows I need it."

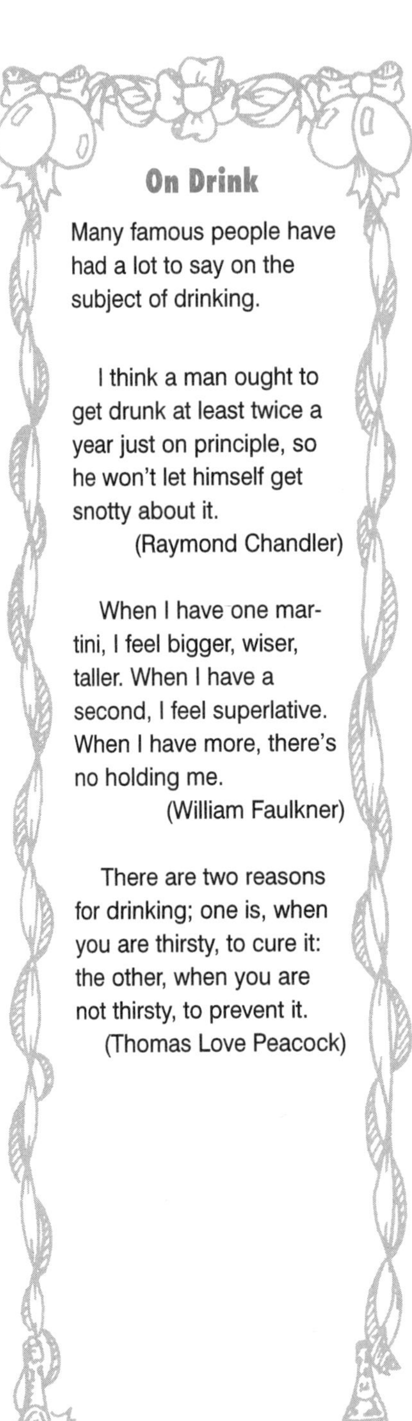

On Drink

Many famous people have had a lot to say on the subject of drinking.

I think a man ought to get drunk at least twice a year just on principle, so he won't let himself get snotty about it.
(Raymond Chandler)

When I have one martini, I feel bigger, wiser, taller. When I have a second, I feel superlative. When I have more, there's no holding me.
(William Faulkner)

There are two reasons for drinking; one is, when you are thirsty, to cure it: the other, when you are not thirsty, to prevent it.
(Thomas Love Peacock)

"A toast to the Three Great American Birds:
May you always have an Eagle in your pocket,
A Turkey on your table,
And Old Crow in your glass."

"If wine tells truth, and so have said the wise;
It makes me laugh to think how brandy lies."
(Oliver Wendell Holmes)

"I always keep a stimulant handy in case I see a snake—which I also keep handy."
(W.C. Fields)

"In the words of William Morris, "I drink to the days that are.""

"To the corkscrew—a useful key to unlock the storehouse of wit, the treasury of laughter, the front door of fellowship, and the gate of pleasant folly."
(W.E.B. French)

"For whether we're right or whether we're wrong,
There's a rose in every thistle
Here's luck—
And a drop to wet your whistle."
(Richard Hovey)

"Here's may we never drink worse."

"Mingle with the friendly bowl,
The feast of reason and the flow of soul."
(Alexander Pope)

"Here's to lying, stealing, cheating and drinking.
When you lie, you lie to save a friend,
When you steal, you steal a young girl's heart,
When you cheat, you cheat death,
And when you drink, you drink with us!"

"'The greatest happiness of life is the conviction that we are loved, loved for ourselves, or rather in spite of ourselves."
(Victor Hugo)

"'Tis not so bad a world,
As some would like to make it;
But whether good or whether bad,
Depends on how you take it."

"I went to Frankfort, and got drunk
With that most learn'd professor, Brunck;
I went to Worms, and got more drunken
With that more learn'd professor, Ruhnken."
(Richard Porson)

"You shall and you shan't,
You will and you won't,
You're condemned if you do,
And you are damned if you don't."

"Here's to those who love us well,
Those who don't may go to hell."
(James Keene)

"A glass in the hand's worth two on the shelf—Tipple it down and refresh yourself!"

“Better to pay the tavern keeper than the druggest.”

“On land or at sea
One need not be wary;
A well-made martini
Prevents beri-beri.”

“Clink, clink your glasses and drink;
Why should we trouble borrow?
Care not for sorrow,
A fig for the morrow.
Tonight let's be merry and drink.”

“Come fill the bowl, each jolly soul!
Let Bacchus guide this session;
Join cup to lip with “hip, hip, hip”
And bury all depression.”

“What harm in drinking can there be?
Since punch and life so well agree?”
(Thomas Blacklock)

“Come landlord, fill the flowing bowl
Until it does run over.
For tonight we'll merry be, merry be, merry be,
Tomorrow we'll get sober.”

“Let schoolmasters puzzle their brains
With grammar and nonsense and learning;
Good liquor I stoutly maintain,
Gives genius a better discerning.”
(Oliver Goldsmith)

"The man that isn't jolly after drinking
Is just a driveling idiot, to my thinking."
(Euripides)

"Bottoms up
Tops down;
Wear a smile
Not a frown."

"Here's to the group at the local bar,
We come here once a week.
But it's not the beer, it's not the food,
It's the friendship that we seek."

This toast was written at a bar called The Shack in Playa Del Rey, California. Whenever I am in town, this is where I hang out with my friends Roy and Linda Phillippe and their circle of cronies. Here's another one written the same night.

"The pitcher is empty, we're all out of beer,
So go and order another.
We will drink to your health and we'll drink to your birth,
And we'll even drink to your mother."

"One drink is plenty;
Two drinks too many,
And three not half enough."
(W. Knox Haynes)

"Well, if it isn't gin,
Was meant to do us in,
The chances are it's lemonade or dates."
(A.P. Herbert)

Churchill on Tradition

Winston Churchill was the youngest First Lord of the Admiralty when he ascended to that post in 1912. He immediately made many changes, which prompted one of his admirals to say that Churchill was "scuttling the traditions of the Royal Navy".

Churchill replied by saying, "I'll tell you what the traditions of the Royal Navy are—rum, sodomy, and the cat-o'-nine-tail lash." Aren't you glad that you didn't have to join the Royal Navy to get rum?

"The first glass for myself, the second for my friends; the third for good humor, and the fourth for mine enemies."
(Sir W. Temple)

"Then fill the cup, fill high! Fill high!
Nor spare the rosy wine,
If death be in the cup, we'll die—
Such death would be divine."
(James Russell Lowell)

"Up to the lips and over the gums,
Look out liver, here it comes."

"Here's to the girls of the American shore,
I love but one, I love no more;
Since she's not here to drink her part,
I drink her share with all my heart."

"There are several reasons for drinking,
And one has just entered my head;
If a man cannot drink when he's living
How the hell can he drink when he's dead?"

"They that drink deepest live longest."

"'Tis a pity wine should be so deleterious,
for tea and coffee leave us much more serious."
(Lord Byron)

"To some people drinking is more than just the consumption of alcohol, it is the abstinence from water. One of those people is W.E.B. French."

"O Water! Pure, free of pollution
I vainly wished that I dared trust it.
But I've an iron constitution,
And much I fear that water'd rust it."

"Take the glass away;
I know I hadn't oughter;
I'll take a pledge—I will—
I never will drink water."

Toasts Among Friends

The vast majority of a person's drinking time is spent with friends, therefore, it logically follows that the majority of a person's toasts should also be spent on friends. Since we have established that every event and every occasion is an opportunity for a toast, then it would make sense to give a toast to your friends whenever you get together. Here are some friendly toasts to get you started.

"Here's to a true friend: someone who knows everything about you and likes you just the same."

"Friendship is the wine of life.
Let us drink of it and to it."

"A day for toil, an hour for sport,
but for a friend life is too short."
(Ralph Waldo Emerson)

"May our injuries be written in sand and our friendships in marble."

Average Americans

Over the past twenty years, Americans have averaged 1.32 gallons of beer per year, per person. They have also averaged .33 gallons of wine per year and .75 gallons of hard spirits. This translates to approximately 7 bottles of beer, 3.5 glasses of wine, and 32 mixed drinks in one year. If you have one beer per month, one glass of wine per quarter, and three mixed drinks per month, congratulations! You are above average!

"Here's to the friend
Who listens to my advice,
Who rejoices in my success,
Who scorns my enemies,
Who laughs at my jokes,
Who ignores my ignorance."

"May thy life be long and happy,
Thy cares and sorrows few;
And the many friends around thee
Prove faithful, fond and true
Happy are we met, happy have we been,
Happy may we part, and happy meet again."

"May the contents of our glasses
brighten our minds,
and strengthen our resolution."

"When wine enlivens the heart
May friendship surround the table."

"May friendship, like wine, improve as time advances,
And may we always have old wine, old friends, and young cares."

"In the words of Mark Twain, "To get the full value of joy, you must have someone to divide it with." I am proud to be able to share my joy with my friends."

"To my friends:
Friends we are today,
And friends we'll always be,
For I am wise to you, and you can see through me."

"Friendship is an arrangement by which we undertake to exchange small favors for big ones."
(Baron de Montesquieu)

"There are three kinds of friends; best friends, guest friends, and pest friends. I'll leave it up to you to decide which category you fall into.
Instead of loving your enemies, treat your friends a little better."
(Ed Howe)

"True friendship comes when silence between two people is comfortable."
(Dave Tyson Gentry)

"I consider (name) as a true friend and will only break the silence to say, "All the best to you my friend.""

"A friend may well be reckoned the masterpiece of Nature."
(Ralph Waldo Emerson)

"Laughter is not at all a bad beginning for a friendship, and it is far the best ending for one."
(Oscar Wilde)

"Here's to a friendship that has always been filled with laughter."

"As I toast to your friendship over these many years, I recall the words of Robert Louis Stevenson who said, "As long as we are loved by others I should say that we are almost indispensable; and no man is useless while he has a friend.""

Crazy Names

As you know, bars offer a wide variety of adult beverages with which you can quench your thirst. The martini is a popular drink as is the Seven and Seven or the rum and Coke. Lately, however, more and more drinks have been popping up that have exotic and even somewhat racy names. Here are the ten oddest names of drinks that I have ever found.

Sex on the Beach
Screaming Orgasm
'57 Chevy with a White License Plate
Slippery Nipple
Buttery Nipple
Alien Urine Sample
Sex on my Face
Mind Eraser
Duck Fart
Gilligan's Island

I also found other drinks with even stranger names, but I was too embarrassed to order them in public let alone put them in print. Suffice it to say that most of them were named after body parts or acts of love.

"The holy passion of friendship is of so sweet and steady and loyal and enduring a nature that it will last through a whole lifetime, if not asked to lend money."
(Mark Twain)

"God gives us our relatives—thank God we can choose our friends."
(Ethyl Watts Mumford)

"Benjamin Franklin said that there are three faithful friends—an old wife, an old dog, and ready money. Franklin never knew you my friend or he would have added one to the list."

"Your friend is the man who knows all about you, and still likes you."
(Elbert Hubbard)

"There is an old time toast which is golden for its beauty. "When you ascend the hill of prosperity may you not meet a friend."
(Mark Twain)

"A friend is a person with whom I may be sincere. Before him I may think aloud."
(Ralph Waldo Emerson)

"I honestly don't know what I would do without a friend like you. I guess I'd have to take a cab to the airport."

"Friends don't let friends dance drunk."

"Here is a toast to my friend. Let me just say that two people have never felt more close and friendly than when they are on the same diet."

"To friendship; the only cement that will hold the world together."

"Genuine friendship is like good health. You never fully realize the value of either until it is lost. Here's to good friendship and good health for a good long time."

"Friendship is like money, it's easier made than kept."

"We may not know what the future holds but we know who holds the future. Here's to you and me my friend."

"To my friend I pass on this advice for all men over fifty. Keep an open mind and a closed refrigerator."

"Here's to eternity—may we spend it in as good company as this night finds us."

"To our friendship, which like the wine in this glass, has mellowed and gotten better and better over time."

"There is no possession more valuable than a good and faithful friend."
(Socrates)

"A real friend is one who walks in when the rest of the world walks out."
(Walter Winchell)

"Friendship improves happiness, and abates misery, by doubling our joy, and dividing our grief."
(Joseph Addison)

Man's Best Friend

It has been said that a dog is man's best friend. In fact, Groucho Marx once said, "Outside of a dog, a book is man's best friend. Inside of a dog it's too dark to read."

I have always question the validity of the man's best friend description of a dog. Granted, I love dogs, I own dogs, I like most dogs better than most people, but when it comes to friendship, a dog receives a failing grade in three major areas.

1. Your dog may always be happy to see you but they will not give you a ride to the airport.
2. Neither will they bail you out of jail.
3. A dog never buys the beer.
4. If you have human friends who also fit this category, drop them and get a dog.

Drinking Games

When good friends get together for a night of cocktails, the evening can sometimes progress beyond simple toasts. Sometimes you think it is a good idea to play a few drinking games between toasts. These games come in a wide variety of styles but here is one that I found to be fairly interesting.

I Never

All that is required for this game is a group of close friends and a supply of beverages. Everyone sits around a table or even on the floor and the first person makes a true statement about something they have never done. For instance, they might say, "I have never been to Europe". At that point, if anybody playing the game has_done the thing the first player has not, i.e., go to Europe, that person must

(continued)

“*One bottle for the four of us,*
Thank God there's no more of us.”

“*Friendship is the marriage of the soul.*”
(*Voltaire*)

“*To perfect friends who were once perfect strangers.*”

“*Old friends are scarce,*
New friends are few;
Here's hoping I've found
One of each in you.”

“*Friends help you move.*
Real friends help you move bodies.
Here's to my real friends.”

“*Friends have all things in common.*”
(*Plato*)

“*May we never have friends who, like shadows, follow us in sunshine only to desert us on a cloudy day.*”

May the friends of our youth be the companions of our old age.”

“*Here's to you, old friend, may you live a thousand years,*
Just to sort of cheer things in this vale of human tears;
And may I live a thousand too—a thousand—less a day,
'Cause I wouldn't care to be on earth and hear you'd passed away.”

“*Here's to cold nights, warm friends, and a good drink to give them.*”

"Pour deep the rosy wine and drink a toast with me.
Here's to the three: Thee, Wine, and Camaraderie."

"To our best friends, who hear the worst about us but refuse to believe it."

"To goodbyes—that they never be spoken.
To friendships—may they never be broken."

"When climbing the hill of prosperity, may we never meet
a friend coming down.
Here's to the friends of tomorrow."

"In friendship we find nothing false or insincere; everything is straightforward and springs from the heart."
(Cicero)

Do you have a friend that you have known for as long as you remember? You may not see each other very often, but when you do you should definitely use the opportunity to propose a toast.

"To a friend who remembers all of the details of our childhood, and has the discretion not to mention them."

If you have the opportunity to propose a toast for friends within your church circle, you can impress them with this biblical quote.

"Forsake not an old friend, for the new is not comparable to him. A new friend is as new wine; when it is old, thou shalt drink it with pleasure."
(Ecclesiastes 9:10)

"The world is happy and colorful,
And life itself is new.
And I am very grateful for
The friend I found in you."

Drinking Games

drink. The game livens up when the participants begin to confess more and more intimate things that they have not done. "I have never had sex with an inflatable doll." If anybody in the room has done this, they must drink. Only two rules apply. First, everybody has to be completely honest or the game won't work. Second, when a person takes a drink because they have performed the act that the other player has described, no questions are asked. Instead, glasses are raised in a silent toast of recognition.

"A health to you,
A wealth to you,
And the best that life can give to you.
May fortune still be kind to you,
And happiness be true to you,
And life be long and good to you,
Is the toast of all your friends to you."

If you can commit the following verse to memory, it will provide you with one of the best toasts for your best of friends. If you can't remember it, print it on three-by-five cards and pass it out when you make the toast. It will guarantee that you don't stumble, and it will give your friends a lasting memento of your feelings.

"To my friend,
I love you not only for what you are, but for what I am when I am with you. I love you not only for what you have made of yourself, but for what you are making of me. I love you because you have done more than any creed could have done to make me good, and more than any fate could have done to make me happy. You have done it without a touch, without a word, without a sign. You have done it by being yourself. Perhaps that is what being a friend means, after all."

If you are chronically self-absorbed, it may be difficult for you to make a toast because you would have to be talking about somebody else. If you are the poster child for egomania, here is a toast you can give, and get, at the same time.

"Nothing but the best for you;
That is why you have me for a friend."

"A glass is good, a lass is good,
And a warm hearth in cold weather.
The world is good and people are good,
And we're all good people together."

Surviving a Hangover

There is nothing worse than that end-of-the-world, my-head-is-going-to-explode kind of feeling often associated with hangovers. One prevailing theory about hangovers is that dehydration is the culprit because, as the body processes liquor, it uses up a great deal of water. Another hypothesis describes a hangover as a minor withdrawal episode from an addictive substance. Of course, at the time, you couldn't care less, you just want to feel better—no matter what.

Here are several remedies after you've already made the fatal mistake of tasting too much. None of them will make the room suddenly stop spinning, or will stop the little men with golf shoes from walking around inside your stomach, but they should put you into stable condition, eventually.

- Drink a glass of orange juice and two aspirins before you go to bed. If you don't like aspirin, use Advil or Tylenol. It sounds impossible, and it won't stop all the pain instantly, but this works. A glass of water would suffice if orange juice at the time seems too grotesque. You will wake up feeling much, much better.
- The fashionable remedy is the Bloody Mary. A little tomato juice, a little vodka, some Tabasco, salt and pepper, and some lemon, and you're good to go. If you've got a little horseradish, it's even better. Grit your teeth and drink it.
- The Palm variety remedies use orange juice and booze. Some prefer the Palm Springs version, which is the Mimosa—your favorite Florida orange juice and champagne. Otherwise, you might want the Palm Beach variety—a screwdriver, or orange juice with a little vodka.
- Coffee and grappa, anyone? Or maybe an Irish coffee with those pancakes?
- How about a Scotch milk punch? Mix 2 oz. of Scotch and 6 oz. of milk, and add one teaspoon of sugar and a sprinkle of nutmeg. Stir very well. Some people have this stuff on the breakfast table after a big night to pour into their morning coffee. Whatever works.
- How about a little hair of the dog—5 oz. of tomato juice and 4 oz. of beer with a little salt and pepper, lemon juice, and Tabasco.
- This is the toughest-man-in-the-world remedy. Mix two raw eggs in a blender with 8 oz. of tomato juice, a tsp. of lemon juice, salt, pepper, and Worcestershire sauce. And then slam it down.

Although it is not recommended that you have one for the road if drinking alcoholic beverages, I think it is perfectly acceptable to propose one final toast of the evening, which could be delivered with coffee if so desired. It just puts a nice finish on a pleasant evening spent with friends.

> *"Goodbye, dear ones, and if you need a friend,*
> *How happy I will be,*
> *Should you get tired of life's rough way*
> *Just come and lean on me.*
> *I'll take you on the smoothest road*
> *That God to man e'er gave;*
> *And will go by the longest way*
> *That takes us to the grave."*

Old friends are always the best friends. And if your best friends are old, they should be able to take a joke or two with some of the following toasts:

> *"Here's to (name) who is at that age where he doesn't care where his wife goes, just as long as he doesn't have to go with her."*

> *"The trouble with life is that just about when somebody (name)'s age starts to get a handle on things, they start to lose their grip."*

> *"I have been friends with (name) for a long time. I remember when the police used to tell him to slow down. Now he gets the same advice from his doctor."*

> *"(Name) is like the Liberty Bell; old, heavy and slightly cracked."*

*"Here is a toast that was inadvertently taught to me by my third grade teacher when I had difficulty spelling the word friend, which I always wanted to spell f-r-e-i-n-d. She told me, "Always remember, we'll be fri**end**s to the **end**." And the same holds true for you, my friend. All the best."*

I have heard many people say that their spouse is their best friend, and I suppose this is good. But you will have to admit that there are some things your best friend knows about you that would be better for your spouse not to know. But if you are one of the lucky ones who is married to your best friend, here is a special toast just for you.

"A toast to my better half and my best friend. You know more about me than any other person on earth and yet you still like me. I must have found the perfect mate."

Or, if you like toasts that rhyme, you can try this one.

"Here's to my mate and my best friend,
The one on whom I can always depend.
We've been together through thin and thick
We're together so much it makes others sick.
But I love you my friend and I will for all time,
For my love is yours, and your love is mine."

Beer Hunter

Start with a six pack of cold beer. Remove all of the cans from their plastic harness and stand them up in a shoebox. Next, have everyone turn their backs while you shake up one can really, REALLY hard. Shake it until you think it's going to blow. Put the can back with the others. Next, turn your back and allow somebody else to mix up the six cans. One at a time, the players select a beer, hold it to their face and pull the tab. If they opened a non-shaken beer they get to drink it. If they get the shaken beer, they get a towel.

Fraternity Toasts

Fraternities are college institutions that were formed to teach young male students how to consume their body weight in beer. To get into a fraternity a student has to "pledge". When pledging, the new fraternity member must undergo embarrassing, degrading, and soul destroying rituals to prove their worth to the other drunken members of the frat. I was never in a fraternity when in college for the simple reason that I thought fraternity guys were a bunch of sheep who copied each other. Instead, I wore tie-dyed clothing, wore long hair and puka shells, and listened to Grateful Dead albums. I was a rugged individualist just like everybody else.

I stress the point that I was never in a fraternity because I do not know any real fraternity toasts. I am also assuming that each fraternity has their own secret toast. Perhaps they don't and I never needed to tell you that I didn't join a fraternity because nobody ever asked me, but I just wanted to be totally forthright and honest with you.

When you combine a bunch of lonely fraternity boys with a few kegs of low-quality beer, you hear toasts like these.

> "*Lets drink 'till we're drunk*
> *Then lets drink some more*
> *Lets drink till we all*
> *Fall down on the floor*"

> "*We drink to the girls that do.*
> *We drink to the girls that don't.*
> *We drink to the girls that say they will*
> *And then they say they won't.*
> *But the girls we toast from early morn*
> *Until the late of night*
> *Are the girls that say they never have,*
> *But just for us they might.*"

If fraternities stand for anything they stand for brotherhood and camaraderie. All of the members of the fraternity are expected to stick together through thick or thin, and occasionally their toasts reflect this kinship.

Here is a classic toast that is heard from fraternity houses from coast to coast. Unfortunately, I have no clue as to its origin or what it could possibly mean.

"*Ziggy Zaggy*
Ziggy Zaggy
Hoy, hoy, hoy.
Ziggy Zaggy
Ziggy Zaggy
Hoy hoy hoy
Ziggy Zaggy
Ziggy Zaggy
Hoy, hoy, hoy"

At the end of this stupid toast, all glasses are raised and their contents are consumed.

Finally, use the following toast at the beginning of any serious fraternity drinking bout. It contains all the elements of a good toast. It is short. It is easily memorized. And it has something to do with sports.

"*Gentlemen, start your livers!*"

Sorority Toasts

Unlike fraternities, sororities do not exist solely for the inebriation of their members. They exist so that the female members can borrow clothes from their fellow sisters. Needless to say, I have never been in a sorority either, but based upon watching *Animal House* over 200 times, I think I have a good grasp on what happens there.

When sorority members toast, they toast to friendship and sisterhood. They also toast to men and sex but not as often as they counterparts in fraternities. Here are some toasts that should work in any sorority.

"*Here's to the men of all classes*
Who through lasses and glasses
Will make themselves asses"

A Greek Game

Were you in a fraternity or sorority in college? If so, you are probably familiar with fraternity and sorority names. See if you can pick the real names from the fictitious ones.

Alpha Delta Kappa
Alpha Lambda Delta
Alpha Beta Supermarket
Kappa Alpha Theta
Kappa Kappa Gamma
Tappa Kegga Beer
Phi Kappa Phi
I Felta Thigh
Phi Alpha Delta
Phi Fo Fum

“Here’s to us, and everybody else.
But mostly us.”

“Here’s to it and to it again;
If you don’t do it when you’re to it,
You may not get to it to do it again.”

Toasts for the Guys

Man is the only animal that laughs, drinks when it is not thirsty, and makes love at all seasons of the year.

—VOLTAIRE

Men are always ready to toast with other men as long as they don’t have to get serious and/or sentimental. Men will toast to a football team they have never heard of before they will toast to love.

Most male-oriented toasts will revolve around sports, drinking, or sex. The ideal guy toast would be one that incorporated all three of those elements,

“Here’s to our team, they fought real hard,
We knew that they could take it.
So now let’s party and get real drunk
And then let’s all get naked.”

For the most part, toasts for guys will involve the fairer sex. Here are a couple of the gentler ones.

“Here’s to the girl with the big blue eyes,
Here’s to the girl with the milk-white thighs.
Our eyes have met; our thighs, not yet.
Here’s hoping!”

“In the words of Plutarch, “When the candles are out all women are fair.””

> *Here's to turkey when you're hungry,*
> *Champagne when you're dry,*
> *A pretty woman when you need her,*
> *And heaven when you die.*

Bachelor Parties

It's a funny thing that when man hasn't got anything on earth to worry about, he goes off and gets married.

—ROBERT FROST

Bachelor parties have long been an excuse for a bunch of men to sit around, drink beer, and get a close-up look at a stripper. Even though the bachelor party is supposed to be the groom's last night of freedom, it is hardly ever spent pursuing those things that he will not be able to do after he is married.

Married men will get together with their friends and drink beer until the end of time. And thanks to the plethora of Gentlemen's clubs, they can even see strippers close up on their lunch hours. But after he is married, there are many other things that a man will never again be able to do. These are the events upon which the bachelor party should be designed.

A true bachelor party would feature men sitting around the living room with their feet on the furniture and their coaster-less beers leaving sweat rings on the tables. It would also feature a lot of gassy foods, which would produce the manly sound that he will no longer be able to emit in his own home.

The food for a bachelor party should consist of things which are packaged in bags, and if any hors d'oeuvres are cooked, they should be eaten directly from the pan or pot in which they were heated. But enough of my picture of an ideal bachelor party, here are some toasts that should work well in any group of drunken men where one of them is about to tie the knot.

> *Say it with flowers, say it with sweets.*
> *Say it with kisses, say it with eats.*
> *Say it with jewelry, say it with drink.*
> *But whatever you do don't say it with ink.*

Etiquette Tip: Bachelor Parties

From Paddy Chayefsky's 1955 television drama *The Bachelor Party* to Lerner and Loewe's *My Fair Lady* ("Get Me to the Church on Time"), and certainly before, there has been a tradition in our popular culture of "one last fling" for the groom-to-be.

According to legend, this can turn into a stag party replete with drinking, reminiscing, and half-clad women jumping out of unbaked cakes. There is no etiquette for such an affair, but a wide selection of municipal statutes may apply.

In practice, it is best to schedule bachelor parties several days prior to the wedding so that the groom can recover. The party is thrown in a private dining room by the best man or sometimes by the groom's father if his father also is best man.

Drinks Named After Tools

The only drink currently named after a household tool is the screwdriver. This drink made of vodka and orange juice got its name from the Texas oil men who invented it and used their screwdrivers to stir the drink. I think we should have more drinks named after the tools. Here are some ideas.

The Pliers—Fresh squeezed juice of 1 lemon, 1 lime, and anything else you could squeeze with a pair of pliers.

The Plunger—It doesn't make any difference what is in this drink. Nobody in their right mind would order a drink called The Plunger.

The Ball Peen Hammer—A 12 oz. Tumbler of cheap bourbon. It will give you a headache similar to the one you would get from repeatedly hitting yourself with a ball peen hammer.

The Monkey Wrench—Rum, Banana Liquor, Ice, served in a tin cup

*"Pins and needles, needles and pins,
When a man marries, his troubles begin."*

*"Drink, my buddies, drink with discerning.
Wedlock's lane where there is no turning;
Never was owl more blind than lover;
Drink and be merry, lads; and think it over."*

"Marriage is a wonderful institution, but who wants to live in an institution?"
(Groucho Marx)

*"Here's to the freedom and pleasures of the single life...
May my memory now fail me!"*
(Michael Macfarlane)

*"A game. A book, a fire, a friend,
A beer that's always full,
Here's to the joys of a bachelor's life,
A life that's never dull."*

"To the bachelor, a man who can have a girl on his lap without having her on his hands."

*"'Tis better to have loved and lost,
than to marry and be bossed."*

*"Directed to the groom-to-be;
We've known this guy since football days
When he'd win one for the Gipper.
But now I'd say it's getting late,
So let's bring out the stripper."*

Sporting Events

Toasts have been a part of sporting events since the days of the Roman Empire when fans of the chariot races would offer this toast, "Veni, vidi, vici." which translates to "My money's on Ben Hur." Since that time toasts have been given for virtually any sporting event. Here are a few of them.

Baseball

"*Let's raise a glass to a baseball player who would steal second,*
but would never steal your girl . . . yeah right."

Basketball

"*Here's to basketball;*
the only place where you can go to court without a lawyer."

Bungee Jumping

"*You jumped off a bridge today*
With a cord around your feet.
Had it broken you'd have gone splat,
And that would be no treat."

Cricket

"*Cheers, mate, let's have your ticket*
And hope we don't have a sticky wicket."

Croquet

"*Here's to a dedicated croquet player.*
When he's playing croquet, nothing else mallets."

Fishing

"*Lift a toast to a fisherman and a truthful man.*
Well, lift a toast to a fisherman."

Football

"*Tackle, block, illegal use of hands.*
That's not on the field,
That's just in the stands."

Basketball Terminology

Basketball has a lot of special terminology. This makes it difficult for the novice fan to absorb all of the sport's nuances until he learns the language. Here are some definitions to help you along.

Personal foul—a foul committed by one player upon another.

Impersonal foul—This is a foul committed by one player upon a total stranger.

Technical Foul—This is a foul called against a player who is "technically" doing something wrong. A technical foul could be called against a player who does not high five other players after a good shot, or any player who is playing in shoes which are not the brand he endorses.

Flagrant Foul—This foul is committed on purpose and with intent to injure. It should not be confused with the Fragrant Foul, which is committed by a player wearing too much cologne.

Golf

"*Here's to our friend who just missed a hole in one . . . by seven strokes.*"

"*To golf, the only game where par is good but below par is better.*"

"*To the best round of golf we have ever had . . .*
unless the rest of you guys are going to tell the truth."

Hockey

"*Here's a toast to the game of hockey; that thing they play in between fights.*"

"*From one goalie to another,*
Let's get the puck outta here."

"*May your life be as exciting as a hockey game,*
With little time spent in the penalty box."

Martial Arts

"*A toast for a martial arts expert. A belt for a black belt.*"

Sailing

"*Drink up—to America's Cup.*"

Scuba Diving

"*Here's to a great dive—may you sink lower than ever.*"

Shooting

"*A toast to an expert shooter. It's hard to find a man of your caliber.*"

Surfing

"*Duuuuuuude*"

"*A tasty wave,*
Shooting the curl,
I drink this toast,
And hope I don't hurl."

Tennis

"To our tennis match. May it be the only place that we never find love."

Volley Ball

*"If you spiked our drinks like you spike the ball
We won't be walking very far at all."*

Water Polo

"In memory of all the horses that have drowned in this game."

Sporting event toasts can also include the big events. Toasts are very appropriate for the Super Bowl to the Masters.

Toasts for Girls

Girls have their own celebrations, just like guys. Most of the time female celebrations are more subdued and refined than guys celebrations. For instance, you will find a relatively small number of girls who throw up at a bachelorette party, while at the bachelor party across town you haven't officially had a good time until you have thrown up.

Once in a while, however, girls will get nutty. They will hire a limousine, get a case of champagne, and paint the town red. When this happens, there is no telling what kinds of toasts the ladies will be giving. The following samples are probably very tame by comparison.

Bachelorette Parties

Bachelorette parties generally happen in public, at a restaurant, comedy club, bar, or, if you have a fun-loving attitude, a male strip joint. Hey, you know the guys are doing it so you may as well have fun too.

"A toast to the blushing bride.
Next week at this time she'll be going for a ride."

"Here's to [bride]: She knows all of her husband's favorite foods...and where to order them!"

"By the time you swear you're his,
Shivering and sighing'
And he vows his passion is infinite, undying—
Lady, make a note of this: One of you is lying!"

"Girls will be girls,
And boys will be boys.
But if they disobey us,
They can't play with any of our toys."

Girls Night Out

The only time women get wilder than they do at a bachelorette party is when they stage something called a Ladies Night Out. When ladies have a night out they usually do it to complain about men. Each woman, in turn, will tell her latest horror story involving a man, and the rest of the women will commiserate and raise a toast to their sister. I don't know if prizes are awarded at the end of the evening for the woman who had the worst experience, but I think a simple trophy called The Lorena Bobbit Award would be well received.

Since numerous toasts will be delivered during the evening, the challenge is for each woman to come up with new and clever toasts. Here are some starters to get you thinking.

"Here's to the men we love.
Here's to the men who love us
And if the men we love don't love us,
Then forget the men. Here's to us."

"A drink to the ideal husband—any other woman's"

"I like to have a martini,
Two at the very most.
After three I'm under the table
After four, I'm under the host"
(Dorothy Parker)

"Women and elephants never forget!"
(Dorothy Parker)

"Be bold in what you stand for and careful what you fall for."
(Ruth Boorstin)

"Here's to that most provoking man
The man of wisdom deep
Who never talks when he takes his rest
But only smiles in his sleep."

"Oh here's to the good, and the bad men too,
For without them saints would have nothing to do!
Oh, I love them both, and I love them well,
But which I love better, I can never tell."

"Don't accept rides from strange men—and remember that all men are as strange as hell."
(Robin Morgan)

"Here's to the men, God bless them!
Worst of my sins, I confess them,
Is loving them all, be they great or small,
So here's to the boys! God bless them!
To men—who divide our time, double our cares,
And triple our troubles."

Etiquette Tip: Bachelorette Parties

Prior to the wedding, the maid of honor and bridesmaids may fête the bride at a bachelorette luncheon or tea (once again, the bridesmaids get the raw end of the deal).

Fortunately, modern practice has been evolving (or is it devolving?) the bachelorette party to the same status as bachelor party. Reconfigured as a "girls' night out," such affairs include drinking, reminiscing, and whatever it is that half-clad males look good popping out of.

An even more modern technique is for the friends of the bride and groom to throw them a joint last fling.

"*To men—creatures who buy playoff tickets months in advance*
But wait until Christmas Eve to buy presents."

"*May you always be happy,*
And live at your ease;
Get a kind husband
And do as you please."
(J.S. Oglivie)

"*Sometimes you have to kiss a lot of frogs before you find a prince.*"

Some times the girls night out will turn sentimental. Tears are shed, hugs are given, and more drinks are consumed. During this sentimental period, women give toasts that sound as though they came directly from a greeting card, and it probably did. Women spend so much time shopping for cards that some of the verses must stick in their subconscious. See if these toasts don't sound like they should come wrapped in a picture of two friends walking in the rain.

"*May we get what we want out of life and what we deserve out of life—and may they be the same thing!*"

"*Here's to it*
and to it again.
If you ever get to it
and can't do it
lead me to it
and I'll do it!"

"*May the most you wish for be the least you get.*"

Responsible Drinking: More Does Not Make It Better

But alcohol is a drug, pure and simple, and it is foolish not to be aware of its dangers. It affects our bodies and brains, our judgment, coordination, and perception. The amount of alcohol that brings on these impairments is entirely individual. And it doesn't matter what you drink: a cocktail, a beer, a five-ounce glass of wine and a three-ounce glass of sherry all have about .6 ounces of pure alcohol in them. An overdose can be fatal.

Drunk drivers are involved in nearly half of all American traffic fatalities and the innocent are often the victims. Over 20,000 people are killed in the United States each year because of drunk driving-related accidents. Awareness and responsibility are the only factors that will make a difference.

And law enforcement. The laws vary from state to state, but police are working hard to get drunk drivers off the road. Their primary weapon is the Breathalyzer, which can count your BAC, blood alcohol content, or the percentage of alcohol in your blood. A BAC percentage as low as .05 has been found to increase the normal risk of accident by two to three times. So while you may not feel that your reflexes or judgment are impaired, if you are drinking you should not be driving. Period.

In most states a .10 BAC is considered evidence of driving under the influence of alcohol (DWI). In some states, the level is .08. The penalties range from a suspension of your driver's license for as little as a few days up to a year. Convictions include fines ranging from $100 to $500 and brief imprisonment—for the first offense. Punishment increases with repeated offenses. The BAC and the penalties are changing all the time, so check the laws of your state.

"Responsible drinking" is not an oxymoron. Moderation is the key to most pleasures. It is our responsibility as hosts, friends, and even citizens to keep people from driving drunk. In many states, it is our *legal* responsibility to do so.

To drink in moderation is not to have less fun, but to savor the drink we do have. We raise our glasses for so many joyous and solemn occasions—to the bride and groom, to the job well done, to the friend we have lost, and to the pure pleasure of the drink itself.

More does not make it better.

Hangovers in History

Throughout history, man has sought the perfect hangover cure. In ancient Egypt, they believed boiled cabbage would make your hangover disappear. In South America the Warau Indian women cured the hangovers of their men by tying them in their hammocks and not freeing them until they were well again. Even the ancient Assyrians had a plan. They thought that pulverized swallow's beak mixed with myrrh was the perfect solution. This may explain why there aren't a whole lot of ancient Assyrians around today. Today, medical experts recommend aspirin for headache pain and plenty of liquids to cure the dehydration caused by the over consumption of liquor.

Toasts for the Morning After

Serious drinking can lead to serious hangovers, and the best cure for a hangover is a bit of the hair of the dog that bit you. Personally, I find dog hair to be very disgusting and quite difficult to swallow. In fact, I don't know why anyone would follow this advice. I prefer to have another cocktail to get better, which, of course, should be accompanied by another toast.

"Here's to the good time I must have had."

"Sing a song of sick gents
Pockets full of rye,
Four and twenty highballs,
We wish that we might die."

"Lord, how my head aches! What a head have I!
It beats as it would fall in twenty pieces."
(Shakespeare, Romeo and Juliet)

"Here's to the blood bank,
I'm going there to have my eyes drained."

"The glances over cocktails
That seem to be so sweet
Don't seem quite so amorous
Over Shredded Wheat"
(Frank Muir)

CHAPTER 7

Toasts for Life's Special Little Moments

While life has many special events worthy of special toasts, we have many more little moments in our lives that tend to go unnoticed. These are the events to which we would like to pay homage.

Part of the fun of being a human being is that we can celebrate. Oh sure, dogs and cats celebrate, but how much fun can you really have wagging your tail or coughing up a hairball? We, as homo sapiens, have the capacity to truly enjoy every minute of our lives.

Not to wax philosophical, but did you know that human beings are the only creature in the world blessed with the ability to laugh? That's right, only humans are able to fully enjoy the subtleties of life through the gift of laughter. This explains why a vast majority of standup comedians in the world today are humans. So take time from your day to celebrate everything. If your shoelaces do not break when you put on your shoes, celebrate. If you find your car keys right where you left them, celebrate. And if you go through an entire evening at home without once receiving a phone call from a telemarketer, celebrate.

While many generic toasts will work nicely for just about every occasion, we've included some custom toasts to help you extract the greatest pleasure from all of life's special little moments.

Balancing Your Checkbook

I was a lousy accountant. I always figured that if you came within eight bucks of what you needed you were doing okay. I made up the difference out of my own pocket.

—Bob Newhart

Balancing your checkbook is no small feat. Nothing else in the world comes close to the feeling of sheer ecstasy you get when your bank statement matches the one you receive from the bank exactly. Wow, what a rush. You, with your $3.95 calculator, were able to arrive at the same number as your multimillion dollar bank was able arrive at with their supercomputers. You should be proud of yourself.

In the few times that I was actually able to achieve this state of fiscal nirvana, I treated myself to a refreshing beverage. If it ever happens again, I will be ready to give myself a toast, too.

*"OK, you went over the limit a bit,
And your thoughts I dare not pronounce.
But the bank says that the limit you've hit,
So sit back and watch those babies bounce."*

*"Your mathematical skills have taken a lickin'
Thank goodness your checkbook is balanced with Quicken."*

Winning the Lottery

According to the *Guiness Book Of World Records*, the largest lottery jackpot was $118,000,000 paid in California on April 17, 1991. Since the advent of the super lottery called PowerBall, that amount may have been surpassed. It is not the size of the lottery jackpots that has always amazed me, but the fact that most of the lottery winners vow to continue working at their job in the textile mill. What are these people thinking? Do they really think that if they are sitting on several million dollars that they are really going to miss the $125 in wages they pull in each week? If you know somebody who won the lottery, please give them this piece of advice: stop working and have some fun!

If you know a lottery winner, make sure that you give them a nice bottle of wine combined with a special toast. Since they have all the money now, you know whom to turn to when you need a loan.

*"When it comes to luck, it couldn't get any dumber
I still can't believe you picked the right number
Congratulations!"*

"We wish you good luck until we are tired of it."

*"May Dame Fortune always smile on you,
But never her daughter, Miss Fortune."*

"May your luck ever spread—like jelly on bread."

"28, 17, 9, 5, and 3.
I can't believe you finally hit you lucky S.O.B."

"A jolly good smoke, a nicely turned joke,
A handful of trumps when at play.
A drop of old wine, champagne that's fine,
And a run of good luck from today."

"You've got a good system to winning this game,
You've got it all down to a T.
You think they'll sign a big check in your name,
Tough luck pal, the winner is ME."

"You've got the luck of the Irish,
You've hit on the lottery.
I hope my luck is as good as yours,
When I ask you to lend some to me."

Getting a New Car

While drinking and driving a car definitely do not mix, toasting and buying a car mix quite well. I makes no difference if you buy a new car, a used car, or a second car, it is an occasion that warrants a celebration. Here are some samples you may wish to quote, or use them to stimulate your own imagination to come up with new car toasts of your own.

"A car that is free from rattle and clank,
You've got one now for your own.
Four tires, three speeds, and a five loan
Now take that long ride to the bank."

"Here's to today and the hell with the past,
You finally bought a car that will last."

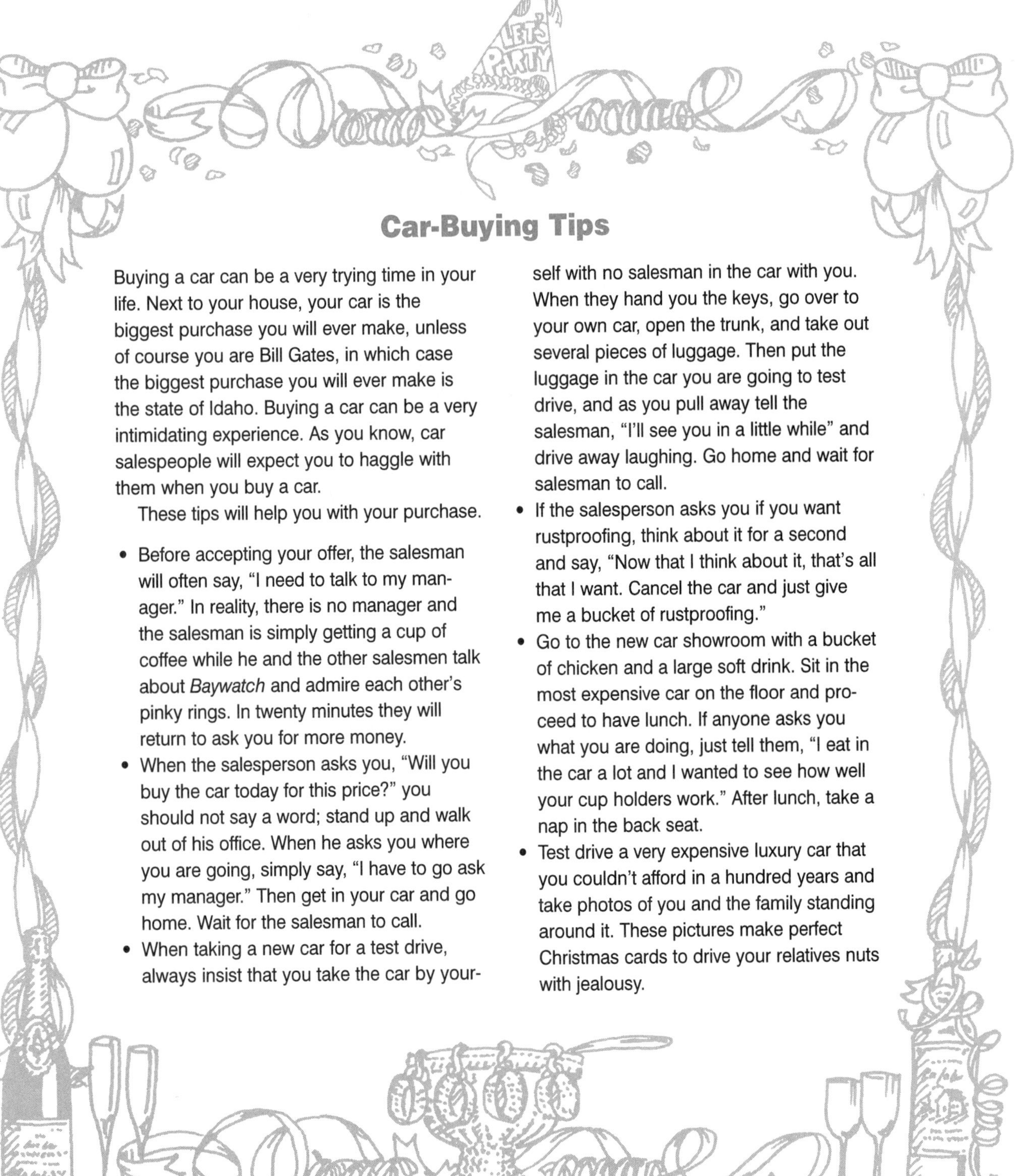

Car-Buying Tips

Buying a car can be a very trying time in your life. Next to your house, your car is the biggest purchase you will ever make, unless of course you are Bill Gates, in which case the biggest purchase you will ever make is the state of Idaho. Buying a car can be a very intimidating experience. As you know, car salespeople will expect you to haggle with them when you buy a car.

These tips will help you with your purchase.

- Before accepting your offer, the salesman will often say, "I need to talk to my manager." In reality, there is no manager and the salesman is simply getting a cup of coffee while he and the other salesmen talk about *Baywatch* and admire each other's pinky rings. In twenty minutes they will return to ask you for more money.
- When the salesperson asks you, "Will you buy the car today for this price?" you should not say a word; stand up and walk out of his office. When he asks you where you are going, simply say, "I have to go ask my manager." Then get in your car and go home. Wait for the salesman to call.
- When taking a new car for a test drive, always insist that you take the car by yourself with no salesman in the car with you. When they hand you the keys, go over to your own car, open the trunk, and take out several pieces of luggage. Then put the luggage in the car you are going to test drive, and as you pull away tell the salesman, "I'll see you in a little while" and drive away laughing. Go home and wait for salesman to call.
- If the salesperson asks you if you want rustproofing, think about it for a second and say, "Now that I think about it, that's all that I want. Cancel the car and just give me a bucket of rustproofing."
- Go to the new car showroom with a bucket of chicken and a large soft drink. Sit in the most expensive car on the floor and proceed to have lunch. If anyone asks you what you are doing, just tell them, "I eat in the car a lot and I wanted to see how well your cup holders work." After lunch, take a nap in the back seat.
- Test drive a very expensive luxury car that you couldn't afford in a hundred years and take photos of you and the family standing around it. These pictures make perfect Christmas cards to drive your relatives nuts with jealousy.

"*Ashes to ashes*
Dust to dust
Your new car is shiny,
Just don't let it rust."

"*Beemer, Jaguar, Mercedes-Benz.*
With a car like that, we'll always be friends."

"*A new car makes you feel alive,*
Especially one with four-wheel drive."

"*To you and your sweetheart*
Who'll sit side by side,
May your life be as smooth,
As your new car's first ride."

Losing Weight

Losing weight has become a national obsession in America. We are never happy with our excess pounds and have listened to just about anybody for dieting advice. When we reach our desired weight—even for only a brief period of time—it is time to celebrate. Here are some toasts you can use. (Note: rather than calorie-laden alcoholic beverages, you may wish to use beverages like bottled water, skim milk, or diet soda for these toasts.)

"*You're looking good, you're slim and trim, you've sure got what it takes.*
Now to keep your newfound form, no more large chocolate shakes."

"*More and more there's less and less of you.*
Congratulations!"

The Stock Market

Over the past few years, success in the stock market has been the cause of many toasts. People who know virtually nothing about investing have been making money in spite of themselves. This new found money has resulted in toasts like this:

> "*We say good-bye to the new car loans*
> *We're now paying cash thanks to old Dow Jones.*"

> "*May your portfolio be the only thing that grows fat with age.*"

> "*Here's to my stockbroker—may your life be full of bulls.*"

> "*To money—the finest linguist in the world.*"

> "*To prosperity! As John Ray once said, 'Money cures melancholy.'*"

If you have never made a toast to the stock market it may be because you do not know anything about it and find it confusing. I know I was very intimidated at first, but I soon discovered that investing in the stock market is easy once you know your way around. Here is a brief overview.

The Stock Market Made Easy

When you buy stock in a company they give you pieces of paper called shares. You take these shares and share them with all the members of your family. That is why they call them shares. Sometimes you will discover that the shares you invested your life savings in have become worthless because the company, United Amalgamated Universal Acme Products, was engaged in the illegal business of smuggling Rottweilers into the country and was thus forced to shut down and declare bankruptcy. When this happens you will no doubt experience severe chest pains.

Diet Tips

If you are looking to shed a few unwanted pounds, here are some ideas to help you lose the weight.

- Only eat foods that you don't like.
- Eat dinner in front of a full length mirror, naked. If you have to look at yourself in the altogether, you will soon lose your appetite. Only use this technique at home. Restaurants usually frown upon it.
- Put all of your food in a blender: everything—potatoes, steak, ice cream. Plop the entire meal in the blender and set it on puree. You'll still have all of your vitamins, but they'll be in a form you just can't stomach.
- Each day, only eat foods that start with the same letter of the alphabet. On day A you can eat apples, asparagus, and artichoke. On day B you can have broccoli, beef, and beer. The hardest day is X.

These pains can be alleviated through the use of a special heart adhesive available only to stock holders. It is commonly referred to as ticker tape.

Some stocks will issue their shareholders a dividend. This, as we all know from basic arithmetic, is the amount into which you jam the divisor, thus creating the quotient. That is why you hear so much talk about stock quotients, sometimes shortened to stock quotes.

Most stocks are divided into categories. The best stocks are called blue chip stocks. They got this name because in the game of poker the blue chips are worth more than the white chips or the red ones. Stocks in agricultural companies are know variably as corn chips or potato chips. Stocks in electronics industries are known as computer chips.

Recovery from an Illness

When someone you know is getting better from an illness, you may not want to ply them with liquor just to present a toast. As we have mentioned before, toasts can be delivered with almost any liquid, and in this case I would recommend something more bland like broth, juice, or good old bottled water. After all, it's the sentiment that counts.

Here are some toasts that are chocked full of sentiment and perhaps even a laugh or two.

> "*You're sick right now, you're feeling low,*
> *You're losing all your tan.*
> *But pretty soon you'll be much better,*
> *And not have to use a bed pan.*"

> "*Illness comes by many roads, but always uninvited.*
> *Here's to a quick repair of the road you're on now.*"

> "*My parents always enjoyed good health,*
> *In fact, they loved it.*"
> (Gracie Allen)

"Be careful about reading health books. You may die of a misprint."
(Mark Twain)

"Here's to you.
With friends like you, who needs enemas?"

"Here's to your health . . . or at least what's left of it."

"May this be the last time that a doctor ever earns a dollar out of you."

"Here's a health to every one;
Peace on earth, and heaven won."

Barn Raising

Chances are that unless you are Amish you will probably never attend a barn raising. But since this is the *Everything Toasts Book*, I want you to be prepared for every contingency. So if you are planning a trip through Pennsylvania, Ohio, or Indiana, you may want to memorize these toasts just in case you get invited to the Amish equivalent of a paint party.

"Our barn is up,
Our glasses we clink.
It's just too bad,
We're not allowed to drink."

"Let's raise the barn, and put on the door;
This is our only toast, we don't know any more."

Cast Party

There are two kinds of cast parties. One is the type that is put on for the cast of a play, and the other is a party given for someone who has broken an arm or leg and now must wear a cast. Here are some toasts to cover them both.

For Something That's Broken

"Here's to tough breaks. May they heal quickly."

"Your arm's in plaster,
You're on the mend.
While you're healing remember,
We're friends to the end."

"Here's to your cast
It won't last.
Heal fast."

For the Cast of a Play

"What should the theater be? The theater should be full."
(Guiseppe Verdi)

"Here's to the critics, or, as Walter Winchell once said, 'A dramatic critic is a newspaperman whose sweetheart ran away with an actor.'"

"As this show ends, let's remember the words of Samuel Goldwyn, 'Don't pay attention to critics—don't even ignore them.'"

For Something that Got Broken During a Play

"The play's a hit, we're selling out,
Everyone we know has seen it.
But the next time we tell you to 'break a leg'
Please know we don't really mean it."

Your Team Won!

Nothing makes you feel better than backing a winner. We all love to be on the side of victory so we support sports teams who do what we can't, namely, play the sport.

"*To the spirit of winning as best summarized by Vince Lombardi who said, 'Show me a good loser and I'll show you a loser.'*"

"*Lombardi also said, 'Winning isn't everything, it's the only thing.'*"

"*Losing the Super Bowl is worse than death.*"

"*With death you don't have to get up the next morning.*"
(George Allen)

"*In the spirit of winning let us all remember that it is not whether you win or lose that counts, it's the point spread.*"

"*As we toast this victory, let us recall the words of Damon Runyon who said, 'The race is not always to the swift, nor the battle to the strong—but that's the way to bet.'*"

"*To our team who won and played fair. I guess there's a first time for everything.*"

"*Hip hip, hurray, we won today,*
Let's rejoice and raise a glass.
We didn't merely beat this team,
We really kicked their ass."

Your Team Lost!

As a wise old sage once said, "It's not whether you win or lose that counts, it's the point spread." It never feels good to lose, but if you and your friends are drowning your sorrows after a loss, use the occasion to toast to better days again.

> *We've lost again, we just can't win,*
> *Our team just had bad luck.*
> *Unless of course, It's all their fault*
> *And the team just really sucks.*

This toast, which I have heard used in different cities at different times, is ideal for those cities where both of your major sports teams tend to stink. Most recently, neither the Chicago Bears, nor the White Sox have been playing very well, so in Chicago the toast would go,

> *Go bears! And take the White Sox with you!*

> *I would prefer even to fail with honor than to win by cheating.*
> *(Sophocles)*

Apparently, Sophocles was not a big bettor in his day. I think this toast should be hung in the locker rooms of every team ever accused of throwing a game, and every team that is even thinking about it.

> *There is no failure except in no longer trying.*
> *(Elbert Hubbard)*

Losers in History

The record in professional football for the most number of consecutive losses belongs to the Tampa Bay Buccaneers who lost twenty-six games in a row in the 1976-77 seasons.

CHAPTER 8

Toasts and Eggs— Mealtime Toasts

When you first think about the concept of giving a toast, the first image that comes to mind is of a toast being given in conjunction with a meal, usually a dinner. Another beauty of toasting is that it is not restricted to dinner toasts but can be enjoyed with any meal of the day.

Your first toast of the day should happen at breakfast as you and your spouse stare at each other over a bowl of soggy cereal. Normally you would use this together time to read the newspaper or watch some annoying morning show on TV. I suggest that you use this time to propose a toast to your beloved. If you do not have a beloved, you can propose a toast to your roommate or to your dog. If you have neither a roommate nor a dog, why not give a toast to that guy with blow-dried hair on the annoying morning show.

Sunrise Toasts

If you are an early riser, you may wish to make your first toast of the day as the sun comes over the horizon, or over the neighbor's house, depending upon where you live.

"To the sun; a blanket for the poor man."

"Let us make hay while the sun shines;
Then at night we'll make oats or possibly alfalfa."

"Here's to a new morning, that time of day when,
According to the words of Alexander Animator
The rising generation retires,
And the retiring generation rises."

"Here's to a steaming cup of Joe.
Without it I'm going to wake up slow."

"Busy old fool, unruly Sun,
Why dost thou thus,
Through windows and through
Curtains call on us? Must to thy motions lovers' seasons run?"
(John Donne)

(Note: This may sound pretty dopey, but if you are a man celebrating the sunrise with a woman, this toast will make you sound like Captain Romance.)

For the busy executive who can't spare a lot of time for his or her toasts, this sunrise toast says it all.

"Here's to the sun.
Gotta run."

Breakfast Toasts

The first meal of the day calls for a toast. In fact, I think that is the origin of the word toast. In the early 1800s, a man named Luke of Earle discovered that if he put his bread next to an open flame for several minutes, the bread would catch fire and turn black. But, after several years of experimentation, Luke of Earle found out that if he moved the bread away from the flame that it would not ignite but simply turn brown. This was the best thing the world had ever seen. (Note: Shortly after Luke invented toast, his neighbor invented sliced bread, which we still recognize as the benchmark for the best thing that ever happened.)

Luke instantly raised his cup of Sanka and said, "I'd like to propose a salute to my new invention which I will call toast." And from that time forward, this salute was called a toast.

When giving a breakfast toast, you can use either alcoholic or nonalcoholic beverages. If you are giving the toast on a weekend and don't have to drive anywhere for awhile, you can propose a breakfast toast with champagne, a mimosa (half champagne and half orange juice served chilled in a wine glass), a Bloody Mary, or a Screwdriver.

If you have to go to work, you may not wish to get too "toasty" in the morning. In this case you can propose your toast with juice, coffee, tea, or any other responsible breakfast beverage. Here are some breakfast toasts you may wish to try.

"As we break our fast, let us toast to a love that will last."

"Eggs and bacon, bacon and eggs;
I toast my wife, who's got beautiful legs."

Recipe for Ultimate Bloody Mary

This cocktail is named for Mary Tudor, also known as Mary I. Mary was the queen of England and Ireland from 1553–1558. She was a devout Catholic and hated Protestants so she mercilessly persecuted them. It was this action that earned her the nickname, Bloody Mary. Here is my recipe for the best Bloody Mary you have ever had.

1 ½ ounces of the chilled top shelf vodka of your choice
3 ounces of V-8 vegetable juice
½ ounce lemon juice
Dash of Worcestershire sauce to taste
Dash of Tabasco Sauce to taste
Dash of celery salt

Combine ingredients in a cocktail shaker and pour over ice in a tall glass with a salted rim. Serve with a stalk of celery, a dill pickle, or an olive. I happen to like them with all three.

"Here's to Mikey, he'll eat anything."

"May your troubles be handled as smooth as silk,
And your day be as crisp as cereal with no milk."

"Juice, coffee, toast, and tea.
Here's to you, and here's to me."

"May we breakfast with health,
Dine with Friendship,
Crack a bottle with Mirth,
And sup with the goddess Contentment."

"A toast to bread,
as without bread,
we'd have no toast."

I remember reading this toast on my father's coffee cup, which he used to dunk his donuts.

"As you travel on through life brother,
Whatever be your goal,
Keep your eye upon the donut,
And not upon the hole."

Several old proverbs contain the essence of good toasts. Here are some examples that you can customize to fit the occasion.

"A misty morning may prove a good day."
(Scottish)

"The early morning is the time to find the people at home."
(Hawaiian)

"The morning hour has gold in its mouth"
(German)

Midday Toasts

Midday toasts can also be called coffee break toasts because that is the usual occasion with which they coincide. When you gather in the coffee room with your fellow workers, it would be nice to offer up a toast to the camaraderie of your coworkers or to the success of the day. Try it. Sure, your fellow employees may look upon you a little strangely the first time you try it, but after a few days of coffee break toasts you may find that it becomes a tradition that sparks friendship and good will. Here are some you can try.

> “*Raise your cups and clink your mugs,*
> *We're taking coffee instead of drugs.*”

> “*Here's to coffee, the morning transfusion.*”

Here is a Turkish proverb which makes a good midday toast.

> “*Coffee should be black as Hell, strong as death, and sweet as love.*”

Here is the intellectual approach

> “*In the words of Alexander Pope I propose this toast;*
> *Coffee, which makes the politician wise,*
> *And see thro' all things with his half-shut eyes.*”

Luncheon Toasts

Lunch does not usually connote toasts unless it is in the guise of a business lunch. The business lunch–also called the three martini lunch–is usually held among business people, one of whom wants to sell something to the other. These lunches frequently take place in expensive restaurants featuring portions of meat large enough to block the cleanest of arteries. They are also usually expensive, but that is not a consideration because business lunches are billed to expense accounts.

If you are fortunate enough to take part in a business lunch, you want to make sure that you have access to the proper toast. As you clink martini glasses with your associate, you may wish to try out some of these proven business toasts.

"I raise a glass to business, to commerce, and to friendship, for without the last, the other two are meaningless."

"In the words of Henry Ford, 'A business that makes nothing but money is a poor kind of business.' Here's to a business relationship that goes the extra mile."

"There's no such thing as a free lunch. May I have your business?"

"Here's to you—the customer is always right."

"I toast to a sumptuous lunch, a productive meeting, and a prosperous future."

"As Robert Louis Stevenson once said, 'Everyone lives by selling something.'"

"The three martini lunch is the epitome of American efficiency. Where else can you get an earful, a bellyful, and a snootful at the same time?"
(Gerald R. Ford)

The opposite of the business lunch is the friendly lunch. Not to insinuate that business lunches cannot be friendly, but friendly lunches usually mean that no business will be conducted, at least not openly. Subliminal messages may be conveyed at a friendly lunch, but for the most part the conversation is limited to sports, fashion, the opposite sex, or politics.

Here are some toasts you can give when you are out to lunch with your friends.

"Lunch is lunch,
And dinner is dinner;
But lunch with my friends,
Is a guaranteed winner."

Raise a glass, let's give a toast,
To the friends that I love most.

To the middle of the day. May the worst part of the day
be behind us
and the best of the day still to come.

Sunset Toasts

Sunset is the most romantic time of the day. As you watch the sun slip over the horizon you reflect on the accomplishments of the day and make plans for tomorrow. Sunsets are beautiful creations of nature that fill the skies with a myriad of brilliant hues of orange, red, and yellow. A little know fact is that the beauty of a sunset is directly proportional to the amount of pollution in the atmosphere. This means that theoretically the most colorful sunsets in the world are not in Hawaii or the South Pacific but over the steel mills of Gary, Indiana. Of course, the pollution is so thick over Gary that you can't see the sun at noon let alone at sunset.

Wherever you watch the sunset, the best way to experience it is in a comfortable beach chair with a beverage in your hand and your best friend at your side.

May the clouds in your life be only a background for a lovely sunset.

May the beam of the glass never destroy the ray of the mind.

All good things must come to an end;
Here's to an even better tomorrow.

Dinner Toasts

Dinner time is prime toasting time. For many, dinner (also called supper in some parts of the land) is the main meal of the day. It is a time when the whole family can gather around the table and share their stories of the day. In my house, it is a time when we can all gather around the television set and eat our microwaved dinners in silence.

At your next informal family gathering, why not surprise everybody at the table and offer a toast before you dig into your meatloaf and mashed potatoes.

> “*To soup—may it be seen and not heard.*”

> “*To Mom's cooking—may my wife never find out how bad it really was.*”

> “*May we always have more occasion for the cook than for the doctor.*”

> “*As Mark Twain once said, 'To eat is human, to digest divine.'*”

> “*To the magic that turns groceries into meals.*”

> “*Eat, drink and be merry; for tomorrow we diet.*”

> “*O hour of all hours, the most blessed upon earth,*
> *the blessed hour of our dinners!*”
> *(Edward George Lytton)*

> “*In the words of Shakespeare, 'unquiet meals make ill digestions.'*”

> “*On the table spread the cloth,*
> *Let the knives be sharp and clean;*
> *Pickles get and salad both,*
> *Let them each be fresh and green.*”

Dinner is also the most social meal of the day. Friends can gather for dinner at restaurants and homes and treat the meal as the main social activity of the evening, sometimes lasting for hours. Dinner toasts can encompass almost any kind of sentiment, but most often they reflect good times, good food, and good friends. Here are a few that will fit many occasions.

"I'd rather have a dinner while I'm living than a monument when I'm dead, for the dinner will be on my friends, while the monument would be on me."

"A health to you,
A wealth to you,
And the best that life can give to you.
May fortune still be kind to you.
And happiness be true to you,
And life be long and good to you,
Is the toast of all your friends to you."

"Friendship is the wine of life.
Let's drink of it and to it."

"Here's to a true friend;
Someone who knows everything about you and still likes you."

"May we have more and more friends,
And need them less and less."

"To friends: as long as we are able
To lift our glasses from the table."

"A little health, a little wealth,
A little house and freedom.
With some few friends for certain ends
But little cause to need 'em."

"Here's to all good things in life:
Love, health, happiness and of course, good friends
May we have many more good times together."

"May you live as long as you want to, and want to as long as you live."

"Good company, good wine, good welcome, make good people."
(Shakespeare)

Toasts with and for Wine

Wine is most often consumed as an accompaniment to a fine dinner. In fact, many wines are designed specifically to be enjoyed with food. The food complements the wine and the wine complements the food.

Wine was first made on earth in 2,000,000 B.C. by Ernest and Julio Grallo. Upon discovering that their grape collection was trod upon by a herd of woolly mammoths, Ernie and Julie tried to drown their sorrows by drinking the juice that was created. As they first tasted the sweet nectar of the grape, they looked at each other with the same thought, "If we let this stuff set for a while it may get us drunk."

Over the years, man learned to make wine, bottle wine, age wine, and tax wine. Wine is a ritual drink in many religions. And, if you drink too much of it you will become religious as you pray, "Please God, let me stop throwing up and I promise I'll never drink wine again."

Wine is a large part of European culture where it is consumed with every meal. This is due partly to the fact that Europeans cook parts of animals that were never intended for human consumption. A glass or two of a good red wine tends to make you forget that the escargots, tripe, and sweet breads you are eating are, in reality, snails, cow stomach, and sheep brains.

Wine comes in two basic varieties, red and white. Red wine is served at room temperature while white wine is served chilled. If you ever see someone putting ice cubes into a glass of fine red wine, you have both the legal right and obligation to kill them. Wine also comes in two basic kinds of packaging, bottles with corks and bottles with screw tops. Generally speaking, bottles with corks contain a higher quality wine. Wine in bottles with screw caps, on the other hand, can be consumed right out of its own container without any need for pretense or expensive stemware. A third kind of wine now comes in a box. Wine that comes in a box should be treated with the same reverence one would give to aerosol cheese.

More has been written about wine than any other beverage. Wine was around in Biblical times and flourishes today. It is the beverage of aristocrats and commoners, of romance and repast. Here are a few of the many toasts written and proposed with wine in mind.

"God, in his goodness, sent the grapes
To cheer both great and small;
Little fools will drink too much,
And great fools none at all."

"Good wine makes good blood;
Good blood causeth good humors;
Good humors cause good thoughts;
Good thoughts bring forth good works;
Good works carry a man to heaven.
Ergo: Good wine carrieth a man to heaven."
(James Wowell)

"Wine should be eaten, it is too good to be drunk."
(Jonathan Swift)

"This bottle's the sun of our table.
Its beams are rosy wine;
We, planets that are not able
Without its help to shine."
(Richard Brinsley Sherida)

Red Wines

Red wines are called red wines because of their color. This logic does not follow through to white wines. They are not white. White wine usually varies in hue from light straw to tawny amber. It is never white. It is more from the yellow family. But I guess that yellow wine wouldn't have nearly the sales appeal.

Red wines have names like Cabernet Sauvignon and Pinot Noir. If you are confused over which red wine to buy, the rule of thumb states that you are safer with a wine who's name you cannot pronounce. Grenache or Petit Syrah are usually better tasting than Thunderbird or Harold's Best.

Red wines were meant to be consumed with red foods like raw meat, cranberries, kidney beans, and Christmas cookies. Red wine goes equally well, however, with Hershey bars, beanie wienies, and industrial strength cheese.

"A warm toast.
Good company.
A fine wine.
May you enjoy all three."

"Comrades pour the wine tonight
For the parting is with dawn;
Oh, the clink of cups together,
With the daylight coming on!"
(Richard Hovey)

"Here's to mine and here's to thine!
Now's the time to clink it!
Here's a bottle of fine old wine,
And we're all here to drink it."

"Here's to the man
Who owns the land
That bears the grapes
That makes the wine
That tastes as good
As this does."

"It's a naïve wine without any breeding,
but I think you'll be amused by its presumption."
(James Thurber)

"Count not the cups; not therin lies excess
In wine, but in the nature of the drinker."

"Drink wine, and live here blitheful while ye may;
The morrow's life too late is—live today!"

“*Give of your wine to others,*
Take of their wine to you.
Toast to life, and be toasted awhile,
That, and the cask is through.”
(James Monroe McLean)

“*For of all labors, none transcend*
The works that on the brain depend;
Nor could we finish great designs
Without the power of generous wines.”

“*Then fill the cup, fill high! Fill high!*
Nor spare the rosy wine,
If death be in the cup, we'll die –
Such death would be divine.”
(James Russell Lowell)

“*Fill up boys, and drink a bout;*
Wine will banish sorrow!
Come, drain the goblet out;
We'll have more tomorrow!”

“*Drink to me only with thine eyes,*
And I will pledge with mine;
For I would have to pawn my watch
If you should drink more wine.”

“*God made man,*
frail as a bubble.
God made love,
Love made trouble.
God made the vine,
Was it a sin
That man made wine
To drown trouble in?”
(Oliver Herford)

White Wines

White wines include familiar varietals like Chardonnay, Riesling, and the fun to say Gewurztraminer (literally, I Have Sausage In My Shoes). My favorite white is Chateau Blanc. This is a fancy name for 'House of Blanche' after the inventor's wife, but they couldn't fit the last two letters on the label.

White wines can be consumed with anything but are most frequently associated with white foods like cheese, chicken, rice, and Wonder bread.

Toasts with Champagne

Wine is wine but champagne is wine taken to another level. There is something magical about the tiny bubbles that slowly float to the top of the shapely champagne glass. They mesmerize the mind and enhance the sensibilities. Champagne is a sparkling white wine, traditionally made from a mixture of grapes grown in the old French province of Champagne. Champagne was first developed by the seventeenth century monk named Dom Perignon. He went on to greater fame by making the most expensive champagne on the market.

The only real champagne comes from France. All other sparkling wines must, by law, be called sparkling wines. So even though you think you are drinking champagne, unless it came from the Champagne region of France, you are drinking sparkling wine. As far as I am concerned, if the wine bubbles, it's close enough to toast with as if it were real champagne.

The trickiest part of drinking champagne is getting the bottle open. Unlike still wines, champagne is not opened with a corkscrew. Oh, it could be, but I certainly wouldn't want it to take place in my house. Champagne is fitted with a very tight-fitting cork which is held in place by a wire bail. This double security system is one of the things that adds to champagne's intrigue. If you have seen a bottle of champagne opened in the movies, you always hear a loud "pop" and see the precious liquid spewing forth from the bottle. What you do not see is that the cork that flew out of the bottle has imbedded itself in someone's forehead. Champagne corks can be lethal weapons in the wrong hands. Please do not let yourself become the victim of a driveby corking. Follow these simple instructions to safely open your bubbly.

1. Remove the foil from the top of the bottle.
2. Untwist the wire bail and set it aside. Notice how it looks like a little stool for a Barbie doll.
3. Hold the champagne bottle at a 45-degree angle away from your body. You do not need a protractor, just make your best guess at what 45 degrees is.
4. Firmly hold the bottle with one hand while you grasp the cork with the other. Slowly twist the bottle in one direction while maintaining a firm grip on the cork.

5. You will start to feel the cork loosen. Keep your hand on it so it doesn't fly out and kill your dog.
6. Gently let the cork pop out of the bottle under its own pressure. You should not hear a loud pop. You should also not have any champagne foaming out of the bottle. If there is one thing you definitely do not want to do with fine champagne it is to waste it.
7. Pour the champagne into glasses, toast, and enjoy. Repeat the process until you run out of champagne.

"The miser may be pleased with gold,
The lady's man with pretty lass;
But I'm best pleased when I behold
The nectar sparkling in the glass."

"Tiny bubbles, in the wine,
make me feel happy, make me feel fine."
(Don Ho)

"To champagne, the wonderful beverage that makes you see double and feel single."

"Here's to champagne, the drink divine,
That makes us forget all our troubles;
It's made of a dollar's worth of wine
And three dollars' worth of bubbles."

This toast was originally written over ninety years ago when a dollar was really a dollar. If you are able to purchase a four-dollar bottle of champagne today, I would not suggest that you drink it. Here is the same toast updated for the twenty-first century.

"Here's to champagne, the drink divine,
That makes us forget all our troubles;
It's made from ten dollars worth of wine
And twenty dollars worth of bubbles."

Of course, we also have to add in the cost of marketing and advertising, label design, distribution, R&D, and import taxes, so you are really paying a lot for bubbly wine. I hope you enjoy it.

> "*O thrice accursed*
> *Be a champagne thirst,*
> *When the price of beer's all we've got.*"

> "*To champagne—*
> *Nectar strained to finest gold,*
> *Sweet as love, as virtue cold.*"

> "*To the glorious, golden vintage of France,*
> *Whose bubbling beauties our spirits entrance;*
> *When with friends tried and true this nectar we quaff*
> *We wish for a neck like a thirsty giraffe.*"

> "*Some take their gold*
> *in minted mold,*
> *and some in harps hereafter.*
> *But give me mine*
> *In bubbles fine*
> *And keep the change in laughter.*"
> *(Oliver Herford)*

> "*The bubble winked at me and said,*
> *'you'll miss me, brother, when you're dead.'*"
> *(Oliver Herford)*

After-Dinner Toasts

You may ask yourself what the difference is between a dinner toast and an after-dinner toast. Without getting into the subtle nuances that separate the two, let me just say that one occurs before dinner, and the other occurs after.

A proper after-dinner toast takes place after dinner but before dessert. This allows the toaster to raise a glass of port wine—often served with dessert with which to offer the toast. If the toaster waits until after dessert, he or she may have to toast with an empty glass since dinner and dessert are now officially over.

After-dinner toasts are given to the success of the dinner and to the graciousness of the host and hostess.

> *"May your goblets overflow with love and your*
> *plates be piled high with happiness."*

Since this toast is given after dinner and therefore after other toasts involving alcoholic beverages, it may become either sentimental or feisty. Here are examples of both.

> *"Here's to you and here's to me*
> *May we never disagree*
> *If we do*
> *To hell with you*
> *Here's to me"*

Sometimes the after-dinner toast is simply a reminder that more coffee is needed. Like this:

> *"I used to know a clever toast,*
> *But now I cannot think it,*
> *So fill your glass to anything,*
> *And damn your souls, I'll drink it!"*

The Last Toast of the Day

The final toast of the day can take place in bed, right before going to bed, or right before passing out. These toasts are designed to be given in bed to your loved one.

> *"Because I love you truly*
> *Because you love me too,*
> *My very greatest happiness*
> *Is sharing life with you."*

Ordering Wine in a Restaurant

It is easy to be intimidated when attempting to order wine in a fancy restaurant. This is because the sommelier (literally, "foreign guy with an accent") knows more about wine than you could ever hope to know, and he will use this power to his full advantage. If you do not take his suggestion of an '89 Ruby Cabernet, he will feel personally insulted and go back to the kitchen and snicker his little French snicker as he and his fellow sommeliers spit in the bottle. To avoid this embarrassment, always ask the sommelier what he would recommend, then snicker at him and order whatever you want. This will throw him off guard.

When ordering wine in a diner you will order directly from a waitress named Yolanda. Your choices will be limited to red or white, and your wine will be served with a straw. But then you don't have to worry about Yolanda snickering at you.

"Here's to the prettiest, here's to the wittiest,
Here's to the truest of all who are true,
Here's to the neatest one, here's to the sweetest one,
Here's to them all in one—here's to you."

"Come live with me and be my love,
And we will all the pleasures prove,
That valleys, groves, or hills, or fields,
Or woods and steepy mountains yield."
(Christopher Marlowe)

"I have known many,
Liked a few,
Loved one,
Here's to you."

"Let's drink to love,
Which is nothing,
Unless divided by two."

"To her whose beauty doth excel
Story, we toss these caps and sell
Sobriety a sacrifice
To the bright luster of her eyes.
Each soul that sips here is divine;
Her beauty defies the wine."
(Thomas Carew)

I am not sure what Mr. Carew had in mind when he wrote this poem but if you can memorize it and deliver it as the last toast of the day, it will be very impressive.

"The ocean is wide;
The sea is level,
Come to my arms
You little devil."

CHAPTER 9

The Family of Toasts

Toasts for Dad

As we have mentioned many times in this book, the best toasts are the ones that are given for normal everyday occasions and are used to celebrate everything about life itself. Very often we tend to neglect the people closest to us because we just take for granted the fact that they will always be there. As we all know, a time will come when our loved ones will be in a place far away from us. For me it was San Quentin, but that is a story for another time. What we need to do is to toast those around us in any place and at any time. Whether it be at a dinner, a party, or a family outing, take time to tell your loved ones how much you care about them.

> *"Raise a glass to the ones who raised us.*
> *Let's start with dear old dad. Here is a general yet sentimental toast to dad;*
> *Here's to my father. If I can become but half the man he is,*
> *I will have achieved greatness."*

Here is the same toast with a more comical twist:

> *"Here's to my Father. If I can become but half the man he is*
> *I will be very very short."*

And let's add another twist for the father who is a statistician or mathematician:

> *"Here's to my Father. If I can become 50 percent of the man he is, and he is 50 percent of the man his father was, that would make me only 25 percent of the man my grandfather was and 6.25 percent of my great, great grandfather. Thank goodness I will be twice the man that my son is."*

To thank dad for all he has done for you, you may find this toast useful.

> *"Dad, you paid for my schooling,*
> *And bought my first car,*
> *Now I'm moving to France,*
> *So I say au revoir."*

Here's one for the caring, sharing new age father.

> "*To the man who changed my diapers and read to me*
> *from Voltaire,*
> *I'd like to grow to be like you, but I hope to keep all of*
> *my hair.*"

And this one, given by his daughter, will melt the toughest man,

> "*In the words of Cole Porter, 'My heart belongs to daddy.'*"

And one that my dad would have really appreciated:

> "*Here's to my dad who always taught me not to let the truth get in the way of a good story.*"

To sum up the toasts for dad, I turn to the following words of wisdom.

> "*A father is someone you look up to no matter how tall you grow.*"

I remember my mom quoting part of this poem whenever she wanted my father to stop toasting and come home. It would make a good toast for the end of the evening when you have been honoring dad.

> "*Father, dear father, come home with me now,*
> *The clock in the belfry strikes one;*
> *You said you were coming right home from the shop*
> *As soon as your day's work was done.*"
> *(Henry Clay Work)*

Many famous people have had many things to say about their fathers. You can use some of these thoughts in your own toast to dear old dad.

> *"To father—*
> *Directly after God in heaven comes Papa."*
> (Wolfgang Amadeus Mozart)

> *"Dad, you couldn't have done it better. You are actually pretty amazing especially because I'm fully aware of the demanding brat I was."*
> (John Travolta)

> *"My father told me the key to financial success was to have only one credit card."*
> (Bruce Currie)

> *"My father has given me the greatest treasure a father can give—a piece of himself."*
> (Suzanne Chazin)

> *"Dear Dad,*
> *It is hard sometimes for a man to say this to another man; but I love you very much—always have, always will."*
> (George Bush)

I think every child in history has shared these thoughts of Mark Twain. I did when I was a teenager and I am sure that my daughter does today. Live and learn.

> *"When I was a boy of fourteen, my father was so ignorant I could hardly stand to have the old man around. But when I got to be twenty-one, I was astonished at how much he had learned in seven years."*
> (Mark Twain)

Toasts for Mom

Mothers, unlike fathers, love all of that sentimental junk. They want to be toasted with flowery words and poems that bring a tear to the eye. One of the most famous toasts to moms everywhere is the old song entitled "Mother." I am sure that you still remember the lyrics. I remember some of them and I believe they went something like this:

> "*M is for the million things you gave me,*
> *O is for the orange Jell-O she made with shredded carrots in it*
> *T is for the thermometer she brought out every time I said I was too sick to go to school.*
> *H is for her hair which she pulled out by the roots when I thought it would be a good idea to shave the cat.*
> *E is everything else that isn't included in the previous four lines.*
> *R is for the rules that I had to live by as long as I was living in her house.*
> *Put them all together, they spell MOTHER, a word that means the world to me.*"

If you are looking for something even more sentimental for mom, try one of these classic toasts.

> "*To the mother who bore me,*
> *There's no one more bold,*
> *She's dearer by far*
> *Than all the earth's gold.*"

One of my favorites has a nice little plot twist of which even O. Henry would approve.

> "*Here's to the happiest hours of my life;*
> *Spent in the arms of another man's wife,*
> *My mother!*"

For a very nice toast that will make everyone in attendance collectively say, "Awwwwwwww," try this one on for size.

> "*We have toasted our futures,*
> *Our friends and our wives,*
> *We have toasted each other*
> *Wishing all happy lives:*
> *But I tell you my friends,*
> *This toast beats all others,*
> *So raise your glasses once more*
> *In a toast to—our mothers.*"

Perhaps you can find the perfect toast for you mom from among the following.

> "*To mom, who was like a comfortable quilt,*
> *She kept us kids warm but never smothered us.*"

> "*To mom, who always wanted a few moments to herself,*
> *Let's all leave her alone while she does the dishes.*"

> "*To a mother who is the envy of everyone she knows,*
> *She has perfect children.*"

> "*To my mother, who always hoped that her daughters would get a husband as good as she did but knew her sons would never get as good a wife as their father did.*"

> "*The sweetest sounds to mortals given*
> *Are heard in Mother, Home, and Heaven.*"
> (W.G. Brown)

> "*Whatever else is unsure in this stinking dunghill of a world a mother's love is not.*"
> (James Joyce)

"Here's to my mom who spent half her time worrying how I'd turn out and the other half worrying when I'd turn in."

"All that I am or hope to be,
I owe to my angel mother."
(Abraham Lincoln)

"A mother is a mother still,
The holiest thing alive."
(Samuel Taylor Coleridge)

"Oh, the love of a mother, love which none can forget."
(Victor Hugo)

Here are some prose selections, which are not technically toasts, that could be incorporated into your toast/tribute for your mom. Somehow, when it comes to honoring mom, we never seem to run short of words.

"The love of a good mother for her children, is in a class by itself. In other words, it is unique, especially unique in fact. Unique because there is nothing else like it in this big world in which we all live and have our being. Especially unique because it is ever-trusted, ever-unchanging, and ever-enduring."
(Samuel Johnson)

"Most all of the other beautiful things in life come by twos and threes, by dozens and hundreds. Plenty of roses, stars, sunsets, rainbows, brothers and sisters, aunts and cousins, but only one mother in the whole world."
(Kate Douglas Wiggin)

"A mother is the truest friend we have. When trials, heavy and sudden fall upon us; when adversity takes the place of prosperity; when friends who rejoice with us in our sunshine desert us; when trouble thickens around us, still will she cling to us, and endeavor by her kind percepts and counsels to dissipate the clouds of darkness, and cause peace to return to our hearts."
(Washington Irving)

"Who ran to help me when I fell,
And would some pretty story tell,
Or kiss the place and make it well?
My mother."
(Ann Taylor)

Finally, I turn to an old proverb which serves as the basis for a perfect toast for mothers everywhere.

"God could not be everywhere, so he made mothers."

Toasts for Sons

Send your son to the marketplace and you shall find out with whom he will associate.

—LEBANESE PROVERB

Sometimes a toast is all that a son needs to really know how much his parents love him. In that instance, give a toast like this.

"To our son:
We gave you life,
We gave you clothes,
We gave you milk and honey.
Now you're on your own
We can't give any more
'Cause mom and I spent all the money."

This quote from Sigmund Freud says a lot about a son's relationship with his mother and would serve well as the foundation for a toast.

“If a man has been his mother’s undisputed darling he retains throughout life the triumphant feeling, the confidence in success, which not seldom brings actual success with it.”
(Sigmund Freud)

“Children begin by loving their parents; as they grow older they judge them; sometimes they forgive them.”
(Oscar Wilde)

Toasts for Daughters

Watching your daughter being collected by her date feels like handing over a million dollar Stradivarius to a gorilla.

—Jim Bishop

As part owner of a daughter, I know that you worry about them constantly. You worry that they will be beautiful, smart, talented, thoughtful, and independent, but you also worry that they will have the good taste and common sense to refrain from getting a tattoo of a snake on their breast. Daughters, unlike sons, are a constant source of worry, and because of that should be toasted often. In an informal family environment you can toast your daughter every day, and, at the same time, subliminally instill your hopes and desires in her mind. For example:

“To our daughter,
We’ve watched you grow from a little girl,
To a beautiful woman of style.
We’d tell you this more often if
You came home once in awhile.”

I have prepared this toast to be delivered at my daughter’s wedding, which, since she is only sixteen, I hope is many years away.

“To give you everything you asked
I busted my tail at work.
Now all I ask you in return,
Please don’t marry this jerk.”

Daughters should be toasted for every accomplishment. Do not hesitate to toast your daughter's first dance recital, a good report card, or a successful band concert.

The following toast is designed for fathers to toast their daughters on all occasions and will get you major points with your wife.

> *"I toast my daughter who is surpassed in beauty, charm, and grace only by her mother."*

Toasts for Grandparents

At my age flowers scare me.

—George Burns

Grandparents are very special people. They are old, they are cranky, and they are the only people who can yell at your parents and get away with it. It is always good to toast your grandparents, especially in family situations. When you toast your grandparents at a family function you accomplish several things.

First, you establish the fact that grandparents are elders to be respected and honored. We tend to forget this in our western culture that worships youth. Grandparents are your genetic link to the past and much can be learned from them.

Second, if you don't toast your grandparents at a family function but toast anybody else, they will remind you that they went through the Great Depression by uttering a phrase like, "In my day we couldn't afford toasts, but this family dishes them out like they're free."

Thirdly, toasting your grandparents reminds them how much you love them and that maybe they should adjust the will to leave you a little something extra.

This delightful all-purpose toast for grandparents is certain to make them smile.

> *"Let us raise our glasses*
> *And then imbibe*
> *To the wonderful couple*
> *Who started this tribe."*

Here's another grandparent toast that not only works at all occasions but is also the absolute truth.

> "*Here's to our grandparents, the cheapest babysitters in the world.*"

If you are reading this book and just happen to be a grandparent, you should be prepared to return a toast that is offered to you. When your grandchildren propose a toast to you, it is both acceptable and proper to offer a toast in return. Perhaps you would consider something along these lines.

> "*To our grandchildren—our revenge on our children.*"

Of course, if you are one of those "serious" grandparents, you may wish to give a toast without any levity. In that case, you could use this one.

> "*Here's to our grandchildren, may they always do our family proud.*"

Or, you can combine levity with seriousness and deliver a toast that will bring a smile to the faces of everyone involved.

> "*Here's to our grandchildren, God's way of compensating us for growing old.*"

Toasts for Brothers

Am I my brother's keeper?

—GENESIS 6:9

Am I my brother's inn keeper?

—CONRAD HILTON

Brothers come in two varieties, older brothers and younger brothers. Older or big brothers will generally protect you if you are a girl and will give you noogies and wedgies if you are a boy. Big brothers are role models and teachers. If you belong to a family of royalty, the older brother is the one who will eventually be king, so you should always be nice to him.

Etiquette Tip: Companions and Friends

An elderly or infirm relative who brings a companion, or a dating relative who brings a special friend to a family gathering is asking the rest of the family to welcome that person into the fold.

Paid companions or nurses should be accorded the respect shown any friend. They should be included in place settings and given relief from duties while the rest of the family takes over for a while.

Friends and dates may be enfranchised more warmly. It is a nice gesture to have one or two generic, gender-neutral gifts on hand at holiday time to be able to provide a visitor with something to unwrap.

Younger brothers are usually more sensitive than their older counterparts. They are sensitive because they were always forced to wear hand me down clothing. While older brothers are more likely to tease you in front of your friends, younger brothers are more likely to kill you in your sleep.

Here's to our brothers.

"*Here's to my brother, who is just an 'R' away from being a real bother.*"

"*When God created brothers*
He made them thoughtful and kind.
When God created brothers,
He must have had you in mind."

"*To my brother—I think you are terrific, but then with me, everything is relative.*"

Toasts for Sisters

"*Here's a toast to a terrific sister . . . I'm sure somebody has one.*"

"*To my sister, a person with whom I share my parents, nothing else, just parents.*"

"*We've toasted the mother and daughter*
We've toasted the sweetheart and wife;
But somehow we missed her,
Our dear little sister,
The joy of another man's life."

Toasts by Sisters

"To my sister and all of the secrets we share."

"Here's to my sister
Who listens to my woes,
When you're not looking,
I wear all your clothes."

"For there is no friend like a sister
In calm or stormy weather;
To cheer one on the tedious way,
To fetch one if one goes astray,
To lift one if one totters down,
To strengthen whilst one stands."
(Christina Rossetti)

If your sister is getting married, you will want to check the wedding section of this book, but I thought this one was perfect from one sister to another on her wedding day:

"Through the years, I've dried away tears
And listened to troubles with men.
Here's a toast that starting today
I never need hear it again!"

Toasts for Aunts and Uncles

There are not a lot of toasts written especially for aunts and uncles, but that doesn't mean they shouldn't be toasted. Sometimes you can use an existing toast and simply customize it to fit your uncle or aunt. For instance:

"Here's health to you
And wealth to you
And the best that life can give to you.
May fortune still be kind to you
And Life be long and good to you
Is the toast of your nieces and nephews to you."

If you think that a more personalized toast is needed for your aunt or uncle, you may have to write one on your own. The only problem with writing a rhyming toast for these relatives is that it is difficult to find words that rhyme with uncle. Aunt is an easier word to rhyme (remember it is pronounced "awnt" and not "ant"). Here's a sample.

> "*Here is a toast to my favorite aunt.*
> *I tried to rhyme it but I just cahn't.*"

Perhaps we should try to customize an existing toast one more time for your favorite uncle or aunt.

> "*Along the way, some of us are fortunate to be blessed with a very special (uncle or aunt). I don't want to be remiss in saying 'Thank you for being so special.'*"

Toasts for Cousins

If you want to create a toast for your cousin, I would suggest that you begin by finding all of the words that rhyme with cousin. These words would include moccasin, adrenaline, and Mickey Finn. Once you have developed this list, throw it away, because none of these words will be useful in a toast. So rather than being bogged down by the use of the word cousin, take an alternative approach like this.

> "*To our cousins and friends,*
> *They know the most about us,*
> *but refuse to believe it.*"

Or possibly:

> "*Here's to my many cousins, to whom everything always seems relative.*"

CHAPTER 10

High-Level Toastage

While most toasts are given in informal settings like taverns or dinner tables, there is a formal protocol that is usually followed when proposing a formal toast. Formal toasts take place at fancy events like presidential inaugurations, royal coronations, and top-level business meetings. At these events, the person proposing the toast would be well advised to stick to the rules for a successful toast.

First of all, at formal affairs the toast is offered after dinner and before the speaker—if the event calls for one—rises to speak. It is the duty of the official toastmaster to propose the toast to the parties or event being celebrated. At the conclusion of the toast, the toasters raise their glasses and drink the contents completely in the "bottoms up" tradition. The person being toasted, however, neither stands nor drinks during the toast but simply sits there to accept the honor.

After the designated toastmaster has made his toast, he may call on others who would also like to make a toast, and the whole procedure starts again. If you want to stick to the letter of the law—even though there currently are no laws governing toasting, so if you screw up you will not get tossed into toaster's prison—as the toast giver, you should do the following:

1. Stand and propose a toast to the guest of honor.
2. Look that person (the guest of honor) right in the eye, but avoid starring or giving one of those creepy looks like you see in horror movies just before the person turns into a werewolf.
3. Nod your head to the person of honor like you would nod your head to the stranger at the end of the bar who just bought you a beer.
4. Raise your glass and invite the other guests to rise and join you in a toast.
5. If the guest of honor stands up, he obviously hasn't read this book. Tell him to sit down and not to touch his glass until you say so. If he makes a move for the glass, rap him across the knuckles with the blunt end of a dinner knife.
6. Recite your toast in a loud voice. Assuming that you have practiced this toast many times, say it in a clear loud voice. If you did not practice this toast and commit it to memory, you are going to look like a dork. It is better to read the

prepared toast than it is to make something up on the fly. Unless you are Robin Williams you should not plan on making something up when you get there. Your toast should be well thought out, planned out, and written out. Practice it until you can recite it verbatim. Practice your toast at home, in the car, and in the shower. Get to the point where you could deliver that toast at any time or any place and you will be ready to give it in public.

7. If you, like many people, dread the thought of speaking in public, imagine that the rest of the people are not there and deliver your toast directly to the guest of honor. Block out the other people in your mind and look only at the person to whom you are delivering it. Focusing in on one person should make you less nervous by getting you to forget that there are dozens of people around you who are waiting for you to screw up. It also helps you to forget that you are not 100 percent positive that your zipper is up at this particular point in time.
8. After giving the toast, take a drink from your glass. If yours is the only scheduled toast of the evening, you may safely drain your glass; you deserve it after what you have been through. If, however, more toasts will be given throughout the evening, it would be more prudent to sip from your glass instead of gulping it. You do not want to get too gooney too early in the evening.

Toasts for Business Accomplishments

Toasts may be appropriate at a variety of business occasions including retirement parties, promotions, transfers, new hirings, etc. Each one should be customized for the individual being honored, but you can begin with the core of a more generic business toast. Here are several you can use for the basic outline for your toast.

“*To a job well done.*”

“*Napoleon, when asked which of his many armies and troops he considered best, answered: ‘Those which are victorious.’ Here’s to the victors.*”

Tips for Improving Your Speaking Voice

- Avoid hot or cold liquids just before speaking. If necessary, sip cool (not iced) water as you speak.
- Avoid dairy products before speaking. They can make your throat feel thick.
- Learn how to relax the muscles in your throat and neck.
- Stand up straight. Balance your weight evenly on both feet.
- Breathe normally. Don’t hyperventilate.
- Avoid wearing shirts, blouses, ties, or jewelry that are too tight around the neck.
- Don’t clear your throat repeatedly. It can cause hoarseness.

> *To goodwill, which Marshall Field described as, 'the one and only asset that competition cannot undersell or destroy.'*

From here, you can customize your toast for the particular person or event being honored. For instance, if you are toasting Lou, who is being honored as salesman of the year, you could begin with a nonspecific business toast such as:

> *Calvin Coolidge once said 'The business of America is business.'*

From here you could cite Lou's accomplishments like this:

> *. . . and nobody has done more business this year than Lou Boobedoo. Lou has once again led the company in sales. Here's to a job well done Lou.*

See, it's easy to make up your own toast. And the more you practice, the better you will get. You can also search quotation books and business books to find a quotation that will set up your toast. From there, you can combine your thoughts and feelings with some of the other toasts in this book to create a one-of-a-kind presentation.

Here are some other idea starters to give you an edge in writing your business toast.

> *Novelist Joseph Heller said, 'I think that maybe in every company today there is always at least one person who is going crazy slowly.' I leave it up to your decision if that one person is the man we honor tonight.*

> *Business has only two basic functions—marketing and innovation.*
>
> (Peter Drucker)

> *To be a success in business, be daring, be first, be different.*
>
> (Marchant)

"There are two times in a man's life when he should not speculate; when he can't afford it and when he can."
(Mark Twain)

"He's a businessman, I'll make him an offer he can't refuse."
(Mario Puzo, The Godfather*)*

"When you are skinning your customers you should leave some skin on to grow again so that you can skin them again."
(Nikita Khrushchev)

"The customer is always right."
(H. Gordon Selfridge)

"Here's the rule for bargains: 'Do other men for they would do you.' That's the true business precept."
(Charles Dickens)

One of the most oft quoted toasts when it comes to personal or business achievement was that given by Julius Caesar when he uttered,

"Veni, vidi, vici (I came, I saw, I conquered)"

Business accomplishments are also toasted when it is an occasion for the whole company to celebrate. This could include getting a new account, a merger or acquisition, or a rise in the stock price. Most of the time these toasts are held after hours or at a party where champagne can be used as the toasting conduit. But business accomplishment toasts can take place at other times with any beverage from water to coffee. Here are some ideas for toasts covering accomplishments by the entire organization.

"This accomplishment would not have been possible without the efforts of the entire team, and for that I salute you. Always remember that there is no 'I' in TEAM."

"When I think about being a team, I think of Babe Ruth who said, 'The way a team plays as a whole determines its success. You may have the greatest bunch of individual stars in the world, but if they don't play together, the club won't be worth a dime.' We are worth far more than a dime today as we toast the accomplishments of this terrific team."

When creating a toast for the successes of a team, it is always a good idea to include the words of a celebrity or an authority on the subject. Here are some teamwork related quotes that can be used as the basis for your creation.

"Margaret Carty once said, 'The nice thing about teamwork is that you always have others on your side.' And with all of you on one side, we will continue to carry this great success well into the future."

"Coming together is a beginning, staying together is progress, and working together is success."
(Henry Ford)

"A team is a team is a team. Shakespeare said that many times."
(Dan Devine)

"'The achievements of an organization are the results of the combined effort of each individual.' This is a quote by legendary football coach, Vince Lombardi, and I can safely say that each individual on our organizational team has contributed greatly to this success. For that I toast you all."

"Alone we can do so little; together we can do so much."
(Helen Keller)

"Douglas Murray Mcgregor is credited with saying, 'Most teams aren't teams at all but merely collections of individual relationships with the boss. Each individual vying with the others for power, prestige and position.' I don't know if that is what is happening here but it sure seems to work for us. So keep vying and our team will remain strong."

"No problem is insurmountable. With a little courage, teamwork and determination a person can overcome anything."
(B. Dodge)

"In the words of my mother (and I am sure many other mothers too) 'Many hands make light work.'"

"Individuals play the game, but teams win championships. I want to thank you and toast all of the individuals who played their part in this team game and helped us accomplish these incredible results."

"Teamwork is the ability to work together toward a common vision. The ability to direct individual accomplishments toward organizational objectives. It is the fuel that allows common people to attain uncommon results."

"There can only be one state of mind as you approach any profound test; total concentration, a spirit of togetherness, and strength."
(Pat Riley)

"A well-run restaurant is like a winning baseball team. It makes the most of every crew member's talent and takes advantage of every split-second opportunity to speed up service."
(David Ogilvy)

A Toast To Our Customers

Nothing will butter up a customer more than giving a special toast to him or her at a company function. A good example would be something along these lines.

"I propose a toast to the most important person in this room, our customer. Without you, we would have no one to create for, to produce for, and to deliver for. We appreciate your business and hope to work with you for many years to come."

Toasts for Personal Achievement

We have a great many personal achievements in our life. For some of us, just getting up in the morning is a personal achievement worthy of a toast. But in this chapter the personal achievement we are toasting is one of epic proportions. Perhaps it is to toast a large donation to charity, or maybe for special achievement as a civic leader. Maybe you are toasting someone who just climbed Mt. Everest, or a member of the military cited for honors.

Personal achievement toasts have much in common with business achievement toasts. Usually there are a large number of people present. One person has been designated as the toastmaster, and the toast is appropriate after dinner but before the guest of honor is asked to speak.

Personal achievement toasts are also like their business achievement counterparts in that the best ones are those that are customized just for the recipient. Start with a generic toast or a celebrity quote and build the toast to highlight the recipient's achievements.

As an example, let's say that you have been asked to give a toast at a dinner given in honor of Joe Gerr, who completed the Ironman Triathlon and raised thousands of dollars for a charity in the process. Joe's accomplishments are twofold. First, he completed a race involving a 2 ½-mile swim, a 112-mile bicycle race, and a 26-mile run. This is a major feat. But on his way to completing the triathlon, Joe achieved another honor by raising a large amount of money for charity. To toast a man with these accomplishments, I would begin my toast with a quote about persistence, perhaps this one from Winston Churchill:

> *“In toasting Joe Gerr, I am reminded of the words of*
> *Winston Churchill who said,*
> *'Sure I am of this, that you have only to endure to conquer.*
> *You have only to persevere to save yourselves.'*
> *Joe has indeed persevered in his most recent*
> *accomplishment . . . ”*

From here, I would look for a piece on generosity to reflect his contribution to charity. If I couldn't find the right words about charity, I could make them up like this:

"... he showed us that not only does he compete with heart, but that he can open his heart to help others who cannot compete."

Or how about,

"... he believes that unless a man is a recipient of charity that he should be a contributor to it."

Not bad, huh? Now for the big finish I would select a toast of good wishes for the recipient.

"Joe, just as you have lifted the clouds from the lives of many children, we wish you the best and that the clouds in your life form only a background for a lovely sunset."

And there you have it, a customized toast in seconds. It's the Toast-O-Matic: it dices, it slices, it makes buckets of julienne fries, and it really, really works. And if you order right now you will get the Toast-O-Matic and the Miracle Machiavellian juice extractor. Operators are standing by to take your order. And while you are waiting for delivery, here are some toast segments that will come in handy as you construct yours.

"To a person so generous that it makes me want to say, 'Yes, Virginia, there is a Santa Claus.'"

"To quote Jonathan Brown, 'Whenever the occasion arose, he arose to the occasion.'"

"______ came forward when we really needed him and in doing so he proved that old adage, 'When it gets dark enough, you will see the stars.'"

"May the saints protect you, and sorrow neglect you, and bad luck to the one that doesn't respect you."

"May you live respected and die regretted."

The words of Henry David Thoreau make for a beautiful salute or prelude to a toast for a person who has achieved the dream they envisioned for themselves.

> *"Go confidently in the direction of your dreams!*
> *Live the life you've imagined! As you simplify your life,*
> *the laws of the universe will be simpler;*
> *solitude will not be solitude, poverty will not be poverty,*
> *nor weakness weakness."*

Testimonial Dinner Toasts

Testimonial dinners are given when employees retire, get promoted, leave the company, or celebrate a milestone anniversary with the organization. They sometimes take the form of a roast where the guest of honor is teased and kidded about his career. Toasts are indeed part of a roast and snappy roast lines can also serve as the foundation for a toast.

Here are some toasts and roasts for your next testimonial dinner.

> *"To my fellow workers:*
> *We've made some profit,*
> *We've made some loss,*
> *We've made them both,*
> *Despite the boss."*

> *"To those who toil hard in the workplace*
> *I raise my glass on high.*
> *To those who gave their all for the company,*
> *Here's a toast to me and one other guy."*

> *"We work in the trenches*
> *Day after day.*
> *Your friendship makes it worthwhile,*
> *It's certainly not the pay."*

> *"I toast a person who is always good for a laugh, even though it usually comes behind his back."*

"I toast a self-made man, which certainly relieves the lord of a lot of responsibility."

"To a man who always has his foot to the pedal, his shoulder to the wheel, and his nose to the grindstone. How he got any work done in that position I'll never know."

"When I think of the responsibility this man has to shoulder, I am reminded of the words of Will Rogers who said, 'The man with the best job in the country is the vice president. All he has to do is get up every morning and say, "How's the President?"'"

"Hard work never killed anybody, but our guest of honor always thought, 'why take a chance?'"

"To our guest of honor who believes that all work and no play makes Jack a dull boy. So now he hangs out with Jack."

Toasts for Campaign Fund Raising Dinners

I have attended several of those $100 a plate fund raising dinners, and in total honesty, I have to tell you that the food was no better than a $4 a plate dinner. I guess the other $96 is where the fund raising part comes in. The people who should be toasted at a fund raising dinner are the people who organized the party and the people who are the "draw" for getting people to attend the dinner. For instance, if the president were the main guest at a fund raising dinner, he, along with the organizers of the event, are the ones to be toasted.

The toast should wish the recipient success in the next election and continued success in the political arena. Quotes from politicians and statesmen are good launching points for a toast, but I would suggest sticking to quotes of people from the same political party as the recipient.

One Toast = x(x-1) (2)

The generally accepted action following a toast is for the participants to gently clink glasses with each other. The problem is that in a large group of people you may have to clink literally hundreds of time. You have to clink with everybody else, and they in turn have to clink with everybody else, and before you know it the entire room is a cacophony of clinks.

If you want to know how many clinks will take place following your toast you can follow the simple formula above. X equals the total number of participants in the toast. If, for example, there were fifteen people present for the toast, x would equal 15. Multiply 15 by 14 (x-1) and you get 210. Divide this number by 2 and you will soon discover that your toast will produce 105 clinks of the glass.

The quotes you use for a toast could include those about politics, elections, or any issues that are near and dear to the candidate. Here are some examples:

"Man is by nature a political animal."
(Aristotle)

"Politics are almost as exciting as war, and quite dangerous. In war, you can only be killed once, but in politics many times."
(Winston Churchill)

"Political action is the highest responsibility of a citizen."
(John F. Kennedy)

"There are times in politics when you must be on the right side and lose."
(John Kenneth Galbraith)

"When you're abroad you're a statesman;
when you're at home you're just a politician."
(Harold Macmillan)

"If you do not tell the truth about yourself you cannot tell it about other people."
(Virginia Woolf)

"No legacy is so rich as honesty."
(Shakespeare)

"My country, great and free!
Heart of the world, I drink to thee!"

Toasts for Winning the Election

Toasts given on the winning side are among the easiest to make. After all, you won, what's not to be happy about? You could give a toast to victory, hard work, or the gullibility of the voters. In fact, it would be hard to make a bad toast in the celebration of winning an election. The only topic I would avoid would be anything derogatory about the losing opponent. For instance, this toast would not be considered to be in the best of taste.

> *"Here's to victory over the lying scum weasel."*

Neither would this one:

> *"Two, four, six, eight,*
> *My opponent will have to wait.*
> *He won't get this office today,*
> *'Cause I whupped his butt and now he'll pay.*
> *Nyah, nyah, nyah, boo boo."*

When you make a toast for winning an election, keep it simple and upbeat. Since you probably won't know if you are on the winning side or the losing side until election night, you won't have as much time to practice a toast as you would in a different business environment. For this reason it is wiser to memorize a simple toast that will fit the occasion. As we said before, no matter what you say to the winning side, they are going to love it. You can't go wrong if you stick to topics like integrity, hard work, ambition, truth, justice, and the American way.

> *"To the desire to triumph. In the words of Vince Lombardi, 'Winning isn't everything—it's the only thing.'"*

> *"Here's to living in America. Let us always remember that the last two syllables of American are I CAN."*

Drinks

El Presidenté

1 1/2 oz light rum
1 oz. lime juice or
juice of 1/2 lime
1/2 oz. pineapple juice
1 tsp. grenadine

Combine ingredients in a shaker nearly filled with ice. Strain into a cocktail glass.

Vice Presidenté

(Non-alcoholic)
2 oz. pineapple juice
1 oz. lime juice or
juice of 1/2 lime
1/2 oz. grenadine
1 tsp. fine sugar

Combine ingredients in a shaker nearly filled with ice. Strain into a cocktail glass.

Apple Pie

1 oz. rum
1/2 oz. sweet vermouth
1 tsp. apple brandy
1 oz. lemon juice or
juice of 1/2 lemon
1/2 tsp. grenadine

Combine all ingredients in a shaker half filled with ice. Shake well. Strain into a cocktail glass.

"We toast the power of the human spirit by recalling the words of William Faulkner who said, 'I believe that man will not merely endure, he will prevail . . . because he has a soul, a spirit capable of compassion and sacrifice and endurance.'"

Toasts for Losing the Election

Nobody likes to lose, but in an election there is always going to be at least one loser and sometimes more. In fact, I think it is safe to say that in any given election there are more losers than winners. Following that logic, there should be more losing toasts than winning toasts. Unfortunately, that logic doesn't apply. It is difficult to toast to a losing cause, but you do it to recognize the dedication and hard work of the candidate and everybody who worked for his or her election.

Here are some toast ingredients that you can combine with your own thoughts and feelings to construct a toast to a fight well fought.

"In the immortal words of John Paul Jones, 'We have not yet begun to fight.'"

"To quote Victor Hugo, 'If we must suffer, let us suffer nobly.'"

"To our enemies—we will forgive, but we will never forget."

"In the words of John F. Kennedy, 'Forgive your enemies, but don't forget their names.'"

"Here's to health, peace, and prosperity—may the flower of love never be nipped by the frost of disappointment, nor the shadow of grief fall among a member of your circle."

Cheers!

References

Irish Toasts, Chronicle Books, 1987

Complete Book of Roasts, Boasts, and Toasts, Elmer Pasta, Parker Publishing Co, Inc. 1982, West Nyack, NY

Scottish Toasts and Graces, Charles MacLean, The Appletree Press Ltd., 1993, Belfast, Northern Ireland

Crisp Toasts (Wonderful Words That Add Wit And Class Every Time You Raise Your Glass), William R. Evans III and Andrew Frothingham, St. Martin's Press, 1992

Toasts, Paul Dickson, Delacorte Press, 1981

Toasts, Paul Dickson, Crown Publishers, 1991

An Almanac of Words at Play, Willard R. Espy, Clarkson N. Potter, Inc., 1975

Listening To America, Stuart Berg Flexner, Simon & Schuster, 1982

Laughter Doesn't Hurt, Dale Irvin, Kleenan Press, 1997, Downers Grove, IL

Funny Business Newsletter, Dale Irvin, Just Imagine

The Lawyer Joke Book, Sid Behrman, Barnes & Noble Books, 1993

Famous Lines, Robert Andrews, Columbia University Press, 1997

The Wit & Wisdom of Winston Churchill, James C. Humes, HarperPerennial, 1995

The Internet Movie Database, 1990–1998

Peter's Quotations, Laurence J. Peter, William Morrow and Co., 1977

Chase's 1997 Calendar of Events, Contemporary Publishing Co., Chicago, IL

Laughlin's Fact Finder, William H. Laughlin, Parker Publishing Co., 1969, West Nyack, NY

Bartlett's Book of Love Quotations, Compiled by Barbara Ann Kipfer, Little, Brown and Co., 1994

Roasts & Toasts, Gene Perret, Sterling Publishing Co., 1997

Playboy's Host & Bar Book, Thomas Mario, Playboy Press, 1971

The Pocket Book Of Quotations, Edited by Henry Davidoff, Pocket Books, 1952

21st Century Dictionary of Quotations, Edited by The Princeton Language Institute, Dell Publishing, 1993

Cocktail Hour, Jess M. Brallier and Sally Chabert, Contemporary Books, 1996, Chicago, IL

Wedding Toasts & Speeches, Jo Packham, Sterling Publishing Co.

The New York Times Almanac 1998, Edited by John W. Wright, Penguin Putnam Inc.

Veni, Vidi, Vici, Eugene Ehrlich, Harper Perennial, 1995

In an Average Lifetime, Tom Heyman, Ballantine Books, 1991

Practical Proverbs & Wacky Wit, Vern McLellan, Tyndale House Publishers, 1996, Wheaton, IL

The Guinness Book of World Records, Bantam Books, 1998

Illuminating Wit, Inspiring Wisdom, Wolfgang Mieder, Prentice Hall Press, 1998

The Ultimate Birthday Book, Clare Gibson, Barnes & Noble Books, 1998

Index

S

T

U

V

W

Y

Z

EVERYTHING

Trade paperback, 272 pages
1-55850-807-4, $12.95

The Everything Etiquette Book

by Nat Segaloff

The Everything Etiquette Book is the most comprehensive resource you need to deal with every conceivable situation you might encounter. This information-packed book distills hundreds of years of proper behavior into streamlined rules you can apply to today's world. It features quick tips and helpful hints that you can apply from cradle-to-grave.

The Everything Wedding Book, 2nd Edition

Janet Anastasio, Michelle Bevilacqua, and Stephanie Peters

This completely revised edition is packed with information, checklists, calendars, budgeting ideas, and advice and insights on

- Handling the stickiest situations
- Ceremony and reception ideas the bride and groom can use that will make everyone happy without losing their cool or their shirt
- The steps to follow to find the right attire, caterer, reception site, flowers, musician, photographer, and anything else they need.
- Advice on how to make it through alive when dealing with scheduling, budgeting, and other nitty-gritty tasks
- And everything else anyone needs to know to plan the perfect wedding!

Trade paperback, 304 pages
1-58062-190-2, $12.95

Available Wherever Books Are Sold

If you cannot find these titles at your favorite retail outlet, you may order them directly from the publisher. BY PHONE: Call 1-800-872-5627. We accept Visa, MasterCard, and American Express. $4.95 will be added to your total order for shipping and handling. BY MAIL: Write out the full titles of the books you'd like to order and send payment, including $4.95 for shipping and handling, to: Adams Media Corporation, 260 Center Street, Holbrook, MA 02343. 30-day money-back guarantee.